USES AND ABUSES OF THE CLASSICS

Uses and Abuses of the Classics
Western Interpretations of Greek Philosophy

Edited by

JORGE J.E. GRACIA and JIYUAN YU
State University of New York – Buffalo, USA

First published 2004 by Ashgate Publishing

Reissued 2018 by Routledge
2 Park Square, Milton Park, Abingdon, Oxon OX14 4RN
605 Third Avenue, New York, NY 10017

First issued in paperback 2021

Routledge is an imprint of the Taylor & Francis Group, an informa business

© The contributors 2004

The editors have asserted their moral right under the Copyright, Designs and Patents Act, 1988, to be identified as the editors of this work.

Typeset by IML Typographers, Birkenhead, Merseyside

All rights reserved. No part of this book may be reprinted or reproduced or utilised in any form or by any electronic, mechanical, or other means, now known or hereafter invented, including photocopying and recording, or in any information storage or retrieval system, without permission in writing from the publishers.

A Library of Congress record exists under LC control number: 2004002018

Notice:
Product or corporate names may be trademarks or registered trademarks, and are used only for identification and explanation without intent to infringe.

Publisher's Note
The publisher has gone to great lengths to ensure the quality of this reprint but points out that some imperfections in the original copies may be apparent.

Disclaimer
The publisher has made every effort to trace copyright holders and welcomes correspondence from those they have been unable to contact.

ISBN-13: 978-0-815-39885-1 (hbk)
ISBN-13: 978-1-351-14348-6 (ebk)
ISBN 13: 978-1-138-35790-7 (pbk)

DOI: 10.4324/9781351143486

Contents

List of Contributors vii
Preface ix

1 Interpretation of the Philosophical Classics: Clarification and Issues 1
   Jorge J.E. Gracia

2 Plato on the Pre-Socratics 11
   Livio Rossetti

3 Aristotle and the Pre-Socratics 37
   Thomas M. Robinson

4 Nietzsche on the Beginnings of Western Philosophy 47
   Gareth B. Matthews

5 Aristotle's Reading of Plato 61
   Daniel W. Graham

6 Augustine and Platonism: The Rejection of Divided-Soul Accounts
   of Akrasia 75
   Scott MacDonald

7 Heidegger's Hermeneutic Reading of Plato 89
   Kah Kyung Cho

8 Maimonides on Aristotle: Judaism and Science Reconsidered 109
   Tamar M. Rudavsky

9 Averroës on Aristotle 125
   Alfred Ivry

10 Thomas Aquinas' Commentary on Aristotle's *Metaphysics* 137
   John F. Wippel

11 MacIntyre's Interpretation of Aristotle's Ethics 165
   Jiyuan Yu

Bibliography 183
Name Index 193
Subject Index 198

List of Contributors

Kah Kyung Cho is State University of New York Distinguished Teaching Professor of Philosophy at the University at Buffalo. He is the author of *Philosophy of Existence* (in Korean, 1961; 13th edition 1995) and *Bewusstsein und Natursein* (1987) and numerous articles. He is editor or co-editor of *Philosophy and Science in Phenomenological Perspective* (1984), *Phänomenologie der Natur* (1999) and *Phänomenologie in Korea* (2001).

Jorge J.E. Gracia holds the Samuel P. Capen Chair in Philosophy and is State University of New York Distinguished Professor at the University at Buffalo. He is the author of 16 books, including *Old Wine in New Skins* (2003), *How Can We Know What God Means?* (2001), *Texts* (1996), *A Theory of Textuality* (1995), *Philosophy and Its History* (1992) and *Introduction to the Problem of Individuation in the Early Middle Ages* (1984, 1986) and of numerous articles. He has edited 18 books, including *Literary Philosophers* (2002) and *The Classics of Western Philosophy* (2003).

Daniel W. Graham is A.O. Smoot Professor of Philosophy at Brigham Young University. He is the author of *Aristotle's Two Systems* (1987), editor of the collected papers on ancient philosophy of Gregory Vlastos, *Studies in Greek Philosophy* (1995), translator–commentator of *Aristotle: Physics, Book VIII* (1999), and co-editor with Victor Caston of a *Festschrift*: *Presocratic Philosophy: Essays in Honour of Alexander Mourelatos* (2002). He has published numerous scholarly articles on Aristotle, Plato, Socrates and the Presocratic philosophers and is a member of the editorial board of *Apeiron*.

Alfred Ivry is the Skirball Professor of Jewish Philosophy and Professor of Middle East Studies at New York University. Author and editor of many articles and books, Ivry has recently edited and translated Averroës' *Middle Commentary on Aristotle's De anima*.

Scott MacDonald is Professor of Philosophy and Norman K. Regan Professor in Christian Studies at Cornell University. He has published widely in medieval philosophy. He is the editor of *Being and Goodness* (1991).

Gareth B. Matthews is Professor of Philosophy at the University of Massachusetts/Amherst. He is the author of *Thought's Ego in Augustine and Descartes* (1992), *The Philosophy of Childhood* (1994) and *Socratic Perplexity and* the Nature of Philosophy (1999), and editor of *The Augustinian Tradition* (1999) and *Augustine 'On the Trinity' 8–15* (2002).

Thomas M. Robinson is Professor of Philosophy at the University of Toronto, specializing in Platonism and Presocratic Philosophy. He is the author of several books, including *Plato's Psychology* (1970, 1995); *Contrasting Arguments: An Edition of the Dissoi Logoi* (1979); *The Greek Legacy* (1979); *Heraclitus: Fragments. A Text and Translation with Commentary* (1987); (Laura Westra co-editor) *The Greeks and the Environment* (1997); and *Cosmos as Art Object. Studies in Plato's Timaeus and Other Dialogues* (2002).

Livio Rossetti is Professor of Philosophy at the University of Perugia, Italy. He is the founder and past president of the International Society for Platonic Studies, and has published numerous volumes on the Pre-socratics, Socrates and Plato. His recent books include *Understanding the Phaedrus* (1992, ed.); *Plato Euthyphro* (1995) and *Introduzione alla Filosofia Antica* (1999).

Tamar M. Rudavsky is Professor of Philosophy and Director of the Melton Center for Jewish Studies at The Ohio State University. She is the editor of *Divine Omniscience and Omnipotence in Medieval Philosophy: Islamic, Jewish and Christian Perspectives* (1984) and *Gender and Judaism: Tradition and Transformation* (1995), and author of *Time Matters: Time and Cosmology in Medieval Jewish Philosophy* (2000). Recent articles include: 'Medieval Jewish Neoplatonism', in *Routledge History of World Philosophies*, vol II: *History of Jewish Philosophy* (1997); 'The Hermeneutics of Interpretation: The Case of Spinoza and Galileo', *Journal of the History of Ideas* (2001); and 'Christian Scholasticism and Jewish Philosophy in the Fourteenth and Fifteenth Centuries', in *The Cambridge Companion to Medieval Jewish Thought* (2003).

John F. Wippel is Theodore Basselin Professor of Philosophy at The Catholic University of America. He is author of *The Metaphysical Thought of Godfrey of Fontaines* (1981); *Metaphysical Themes in Thomas Aquinas* (1984); *Boethius of Dacia: 'On the Supreme Good', 'On the Eternity of the World', 'On Dreams'* (1987); *Mediaeval Reactions to the Encounter between Faith and Reason* (1995); *The Metaphysical Thought of Thomas Aquinas* (2000); co-author and co-editor (with Allan B. Wolter) of *Medieval Philosophy: From St. Augustine to Nicholas of Cusa* (1969); co-author (with B.C. Bazán, G. Fransen and D. Jacquart) of *Les questions disputées et les questions quodlibétiques dans les facultés de théologie, de droit et de médicine* (1985); and editor of *Studies in Medieval Philosophy* (1987).

Jiyuan Yu is Associate Professor of Philosophy at the State University at Buffalo and a Fellow at the National Humanities Center (2003–4). He is the author of *The Structure of Being in Aristotle: A Study in the Metaphysics* (2003), the co-compiler (with Nicholas Bunnin) of *The Blackwell Dictionary of Western Philosophy* (2004), and the co-editor (with Jorge Gracia) of *Rationality and Happiness: From the Ancients to the Early Medievals* (2003).

Preface

From very early on, Western philosophers have been obsessed with the understanding of a relatively few works of philosophy. Everyone knows Whitehead's claim that Western philosophy is nothing but a series of footnotes on Plato. This is an exaggeration, no doubt, for there is more to Western philosophy than commentary, and certainly Plato has not been the only source of inspiration for, and debate in, it. But it is certainly true that a few works from Greek philosophy have played a disproportionately large and fundamental role in the development of Western philosophy. They have dominated the curriculum in the past, they do in the present, and there is no indication that they will not do so in the future. Which introductory course in philosophy does not include some Dialogues from Plato? Are there respectable courses in ethics in which Aristotle's *Nicomachean Ethics* is not discussed? And is not a course in ancient philosophy part of the curriculum of every university in the West?

These texts also capture an extraordinarily large part of the attention of historians of philosophy. Although there is much interest in, and activity with respect to, other periods of the history of philosophy, the attention that ancient Greek philosophers have received, and continue to receive, is disproportionate by comparison. The number of books, articles, conferences and discussions of their works take up a good portion of the effort by Western historians. Perhaps more significant still, this attention cuts across all philosophical traditions and perspectives. Whereas certain periods of the history of philosophy are generally the province of particular groups, ancient Greek philosophy is the subject of every philosopher's attention.

The interest in a few works of Greek philosophy is not just a matter of curriculum or of historical scholarship. Much philosophical work in the West has been, and is still, done in the context of the discussion of them. Indeed, some of the greatest periods of Western philosophical development have been prompted by work on these texts, and some of the greatest philosophers of all times have been heavily influenced by them. What sense could one make of the thirteenth and nineteenth centuries, for example, without reference to these works? And what would Augustine have been without Plato, Aquinas without Aristotle, and Nietzsche without the Pre-Socratics? Can we make sense of Averroes, Maimonides, Hobbes, Leibniz, Hegel, Popper, Heidegger and MacIntyre without mention of the Greeks?

Equally important for Western philosophy has been the reflection on the pointed issue concerned with the interpretation of texts. From the very beginning, questions about the role of textual interpretation in the development of a philosophical conceptual framework, and the proper procedures to be followed, were raised and controversies ensued. These questions surfaced among the Greeks in the context of the interpretation of their literary classics, such as the *Iliad* and the *Odyssey*. Among the Hebrews, they were posed in the context of what they considered to be God's revelation. Both currents affected the thought of early Christians and Muslims and became part of the mediaeval European tradition. The interest in these issues increased with time. Explicit controversies surrounding them were common throughout the Middle Ages, became particularly intense in the Renaissance, and survived the unhistorical bias of early modern philosophy, to flourish with renewed vigour in the last two centuries.

The interpretation of the Greek classics, then, occupies a unique and central place in Western philosophy, not only because the classics do, but also because the very issue of their interpretation has been a philosophical problem central to Western philosophy. Yet, in spite of its importance, so far there has been no substantial attempt at examining the various ways in which the different periods of the history of philosophy have approached these texts. This volume aims to be a first step in this direction.

The number of interpretations of the Greek classics that have been given in the past two thousand years is very large, and to examine even the most important of them would be a formidable task well beyond what is possible in a volume of this size. Instead of attempting the impossible, then, we have picked some major philosophers from periods of the history of philosophy in which the interpretation of the classics has been particularly significant. Moreover, for the sake of breadth, we have chosen authors who come from different traditions and periods, for this should serve to show how their perspectives affect their interpretation. At the same time, we have reduced the number of texts to those from the Pre-Socratics, Plato and Aristotle for the sake of economy. The last two require no justification insofar as they constitute the core of what we call the Greek classics in Western philosophy today. The case of the Pre-Socratics is not so clear; nonetheless, they set the basis for what came after them, have been the source of philosophical interest throughout the history of Western philosophy and were the object of interpretations by both Plato and Aristotle. Indeed, it is particularly intriguing to see how Plato and Aristotle, with whom so much Western philosophy has been concerned, themselves interpret their predecessors.

This volume does not include papers whose topic is primarily historiographical. Instead, we have chosen those that discuss particular authors' interpretations of ancient Greek texts and philosophers. The idea is to reveal by example. Often, what philosophers tell us they, or others do, with the classics is different from what they actually do. The reason is not difficult to surmise: their theories get in the way of their description. But it is in what they in fact do when they interpret the classics that reveals more clearly how these texts are handled. This does not mean, of course, that the papers do not speak to the pertinent historiographical issues, or that their authors do not make claims about them. They certainly do both. Rather, it means that their primary focus is to present interpretations by other philosophers of the Greek classics, through which readers will be able to draw their own conclusions concerning historiographical procedures. Much, then, is left for readers to do. This volume is meant as a starting point of philosophical reflection, not as the presentation of finished historiographical theories.

The papers contained in the volume were originally presented at the IV Samuel P. Capen Symposium in Philosophy organized by the editors and sponsored by the Samuel P. Capen Chair in Philosophy, the Department of Philosophy and the State University of New York Conversations in the Disciplines. We are grateful to these sponsors for their generous support. We would also like to thank Sandro D'Onofrio for compiling the index. Most of all, however, we are grateful to the authors of the articles for their participation in the symposium, their permission to include the articles in this volume, and their willingness to accommodate editorial suggestions and changes. Without their support and good will, this volume would have been impossible.

The Editors

Chapter 1

Interpretation of the Philosophical Classics: Clarification and Issues

Jorge J.E. Gracia

The interpretation of philosophical classics poses two initial questions: what is a philosophical classic and what is an interpretation? Without answers to these questions, we cannot really claim to have understood all that is involved in interpreting the philosophical classics. Unfortunately, the answers to both questions are highly contested. The degree of disagreement concerning the first can easily be gauged from the fact that Italo Calvino lists more than ten different ways in which the classics can be taken in his well-known article, 'Why read the Classics?'[1] And the number of views concerning interpretation is not smaller by any means. Indeed, the philosophical literature, let alone that in other disciplines, is full of different and conflicting views about interpretation.[2] Here, it is not possible to examine even a small number of the views that have been proposed about the notion either of a classic or of interpretation. Rather, I shall have to make do by proposing a view of a philosophical classic and two different conceptions of interpretation that it is hoped will help readers to think about the chapters of this volume.

The Philosophical Classics

A convenient and useful way to conceive a philosophical classic is to think of it as a text of philosophy that has become established in the canon of texts that are read and reread because of their philosophical value. It is important to emphasize that the value is philosophical rather than historical. There are many texts of philosophy that had enormous influence shortly after they were composed and even in later periods of the history of philosophy, but which have subsequently ceased to be read or consulted for philosophical reasons. These texts have historical significance in that they make us understand certain periods of the history of philosophy, including the one in which they were produced. But, because they have ceased to be regarded as philosophically relevant, they cannot be considered classics in the way I have proposed here. Christian Wolff's famous *Ontology* was one such book for, although it was widely read for a period of time after its publication, it eventually disappeared from the philosophical canon. Indeed, I am quite sure that many Western philosophers today have never heard of it and, of those who have, only a handful have ever held the book in their hands, let alone read any part of it.

For our present purposes, even the narrow understanding of a classic that I have provided is still too broad insofar as it can include works of rather recent origin. Indeed, we often speak of the classics of modern philosophy or even of the classics of twentieth-century philosophy.[3] Descartes' *Discourse on Method* has clearly become a classic and so has Austin's *How To Do Things with Words*. These texts are read and reread not only for their historical interest, but also and perhaps primarily, because of their philosophical value. Indeed, they are not just read, they are a constant source of written philosophical commentary and discussion, and have become almost indispensable tools in the analysis of certain problems of perennial interest to philosophers.

The texts with which this volume is concerned, however, comprise a much narrower category. We might say that they are the classics *par excellence*: they are the classic philosophical texts from Western antiquity. Normally, this category also includes works from Latin authors, but it is a fact that very few philosophical works of Roman origin are seriously discussed by philosophers today. Even such important works as Marcus Aurelius' *Meditations*, or some of Seneca's *Letters*, are read more for the historical insight they offer than for their philosophical pertinence. Perhaps this will change, and at a later time they will join the list of classics in the narrow sense I have proposed, but they are not classics now.

This last point is important because it indicates that the canon of classics, even of those belonging to ancient Greece and Rome, is not permanent. It is altogether possible that some texts will be dropped from it and some added. Canons are the product of history and as such are as open to future change as all future history is. But this, of course, is of no concern to us here, for our interest is in the Greek classics as we think of them today. For our present purposes, then, a classic is a text from ancient Greece, considered to be of perennial philosophical interest, which continues to be read and discussed today.

Interpretation

The notion of interpretation is even more contested than the notion of a classic. There are two particularly important conceptions of it that are in use, even if seldom explicitly acknowledged. According to one, an interpretation is a certain understanding that someone has of a text. Thus we speak of your or my interpretation of the first line of Aristotle's *Metaphysics*, 'All men by nature desire to know.' In this sense, an interpretation consists of the acts of understanding that persons entertain when they think about this line.

Another way to conceive an interpretation is as a text (call it *interpretans*) through which the interpreter aims to cause an understanding of another text which is under interpretation (call this *interpretandum*) in an audience. In this sense, Aquinas' *Commentary on Aristotle's 'Metaphysics'* is an interpretation of Aristotle's *Metaphysics*. Obviously, this is not an understanding but a text that presupposes an interpretation in the first sense, that is, an understanding on the part of the interpreter. For our purposes, both senses are important. The first is so because we need a notion of the understanding that the interpreters of the classics had and tried to express through the texts they composed about the classics. We need to be able to talk about Aquinas' interpretation of Aristotle's *Metaphysics* as his understanding of it. But, of course, we have access to Aquinas' understanding of Aristotle's *Metaphysics* only through what he wrote about it, that is, through the text of his *Commentary*, and this requires that we also use the notion of interpretation as a text. In this sense the *Commentary* is the interpretation.

Aims of Interpretation

One of the greatest sources of misunderstanding concerning interpretation is the belief that all interpretations have, or should have, the same aim, and this belief extends both to those who judge the value of particular interpretations and to those who engage in the production of interpretations. Before we evaluate particular interpretations of the classics, then, we need to have some ideas as to some of the most common aims that are pursued in interpretations. But before I list these, I should warn readers that very seldom do interpreters pursue one and only one of the aims I am going to list, even when they explicitly state that they are doing so. There is often a gap between the theory and the practice of interpretation. Moreover, most interpreters are not even clear about the aims they pursue except in a very general and usually unhelpful way. With these warnings in mind, let me now list some of the most common aims pursued in the interpretation of texts.

They break down into two general categories: interpretations that seek an understanding of *the meaning* of the text under interpretation (call them I_m), and interpretations that seek an understanding of *the relation* of the text, or its meaning, to something else brought into the picture by the interpreter (call them I_r). The first aim can be broken down further, because the meaning of a text can be taken in at least four different ways: the meaning as (1) determined (that is, understood or intended) by the author(s), (2) determined (that is, understood) by a particular audience or audiences, (3) considered independently of what the author(s) or any particular audience(s) understood, and (4) including the implications of the meaning (taken in any one of the previous ways in which the meaning is understood).

In (1), the interpreter is after an understanding similar to the understanding the author(s) of the text had of, or intended for, it – say what Aristotle thought he meant, or intended to mean, when he wrote that 'All men by nature desire to know.' In (2), the interpreter pursues an understanding similar to that which a particular audience or audiences had of it – say, what Greeks contemporary with Aristotle understood by the mentioned sentence. In (3), the interpreter aims at an understanding of a text regardless of what its author(s) or any particular audience(s) understood it to mean – what 'All men by nature desire to know' means, independently of anyone's understanding of it, including the author(s). (Whether there is such a meaning is a matter of intense debate among philosophers, but the issue does not need to be settled here; indeed, some philosophers, such as Quine and Derrida appear to reject meanings altogether.) In (4), the interpreter wishes to achieve an understanding not just of the meaning of the text in any of the ways mentioned, but also of its implications; the issue is not to understand, say, just what Aristotle understood when he wrote the famous sentence, but also the implications of what he understood and of which he may or may not have been aware at the time.

So much for the aims of understanding the meaning of a text (I_m). The other aim mentioned involves understanding the relation of a text, or its meaning, to something else (I_r). Because this something else can be practically anything, the possibilities that open up are very large. Interpreters may seek to understand the relation between a text and many kinds of things: for example, a text and another text (Aristotle's *Metaphysics* and Aristotle's *Physics*); a text and a date (Aristotle's *Metaphysics* and the date of his birth); a view expressed by a text and the view expressed by some other text (Aristotle's view of forms put forth in the *Metaphysics* and Plato's view of them as presented in the *Parmenides*); the meaning of a text and one or more historical events (the meaning of Plato's *Apology* and Socrates' trial); a text and a person, whether the author or someone else (Plato's *Crito* and Socrates); a text and the morality of its author; and so on.

For historians of philosophy, many of these aims are pertinent, but usually the most commonly sought after involves the relation of various conceptual schemes to the views presented in a text. But what kinds of conceptual schemes are these? Here are some examples: feminist, Freudian, Marxist, Thomist, sociological, psychological, theological and literary. One may, for instance, attempt to understand Aristotle's 'All men by nature desire to know' in terms of a feminist scheme. Under these conditions, it becomes important to relate Aristotle's text and its meaning to feminist principles and to see how Aristotle's thinking as revealed by this sentence also reveals for us his view of women. The same can be applied in the other cases, so there is no need to extend the discussion further.

Naturally, in order to achieve these various ends, it is necessary to adopt particular approaches. So we need to turn next to the approaches frequently used in interpretation.

Approaches Used in Interpretation

The approach to be used in interpretation directly depends, quite naturally, on the aim pursued. But there are certain procedures or methods that seem to be conditions of all interpretations of texts, whereas there are others that are not. Whether they are or not depends in turn on the role played by various factors in interpretation. So I begin by distinguishing between general and specific factors that affect interpretation. Among the first, four stand out: linguistic, logical, historical and cultural. As groups of signs used to convey meaning, texts are linguistic entities.[4] Interpreters, then, need to deal with them as such and are, therefore, required to know the languages of the texts: they need to know the meaning of the words used and the rules according to which the words are put together in the texts. This kind of linguistic information is essential to the interpretation of any text. Without it, interpreters are powerless to understand, or cause an understanding of, texts.

Logic is also essential. Texts are intended to convey meaning and this is constituted by concepts and their interrelations. Philosophical texts in particular often contain claims and arguments to support those claims, and logical analysis is essential in the understanding of these, for it is in logic that we learn the rules that reveal the structures of both arguments and complex claims.

Historical facts are also indispensable for interpretation, although this is sometimes disputed. Certain current philosophers claim that an interpreter is not required to know anything historical about a text, particularly literary ones, for interpreters should only be interested in what a text tells them and not in anything surrounding its history, including the identity of the author or the historical audience of the text at the time of its composition. But can we really even know that something is a text if we do not have some historical information about it? Some texts from past cultures look like artistic or decorative designs (consider Mayan and Egyptian glyphs), and it is only through the historical facts that surround them that we are able to tell they are texts. Some of these facts, such as dates, places and the identity of authors, seem very important, even if not indispensable, for the interpretation of texts. Of course, in certain interpretations these factors play more important roles than in others, but in most they play at least some role.

The fourth and final set of factors that play a role in the interpretation of texts is culture. Language, of course, is part of culture, but I have already singled out language earlier, so here I am concerned with cultural factors other than language. Culture has to do with certain practices and views that groups of people have. Among other functions, these practices serve to give meaning and significance to what members of these groups do and make. And among the things they produce are texts which, for this reason, make sense only when considered in the context of the groups' practices and views. Again, to repeat a point made earlier, although in a slightly modified form: we cannot judge that something is a text when it is taken out of its cultural context, for it is the latter that provides us with the criteria to identify it as a text. Figures and lines arranged on a wall are a text only if they are used as signs to convey meaning, and this is possible only if there is an actual composer and one or more actual or potential recipients that have some practices and views in common. Otherwise, there could be no possible communication and therefore no text. In a Wittgensteinian twist, one could say that texts are the products of ways of living or forms of life, and so knowledge of those ways or forms is essential for their identification as texts and for their understanding. To play the textual game, one must know the rules, and the rules are supplied by culture.

The exclusive consideration of each of these factors yields a different approach to the interpretation of texts: linguistic, logical, historical and cultural. But none of the approaches is by itself methodologically sound, for all four of the factors need to be taken into account if interpretations are going to be accurate and sensible, and not fall into anachronism. Imagine for a moment that logic is emphasized to the detriment of the other factors mentioned. How could the interpreter avoid linguistic mistakes, anachronisms and cultural inaccuracies?

So much for the four general kinds of approaches that are required by all interpretation. Apart from these, there are also other, specific approaches that are required for particular kinds of interpretations, although not for all. Because the number of possible kinds of interpretations is infinite, there is no point in even attempting to give a list of these approaches. Mention of a couple of examples should suffice.

An obvious case is that of theology, in theological interpretations. If interpreters seek to provide a theological interpretation of a certain text, it is essential to presuppose the theology.[5] This supplies all kinds of principles, some of which will be hermeneutical. For example, a Roman Catholic interpretation of the Bible will presume that no interpretation of it can contradict established Roman Catholic doctrine. Texts that speak of Christ having brothers, then, must be understood to be referring to cousins. Something similar applies to Freudian interpretations. In this case, Freud's theories about the unconscious, the libido, and so on, are presupposed, for it is the task of the interpreter to understand the text in relation to these.

In short, the way one approaches a text and the method one uses to interpret it depend very much on the aim pursued. But there are certain general requirements that apply to all interpretations and make certain hermeneutical procedures indispensable.

Some Pertinent Questions

In view of the foregoing, what are the pertinent questions that the philosopher interested in past interpretations of the classics needs to ask? Five appear particularly appropriate: (1) what are the aims that interpreters have pursued in their interpretation of the classics, (2) how have interpreters pursued these aims, (3) how successful have they been, (4) what does this tell us about the interpreters themselves and about the period in which they lived, and (5) what does it reveal about the classics themselves, if anything? It is important to keep these questions separate in order to prevent confusions as to the import of the conclusions reached.

Answers to these questions require careful attention and exegesis of particular interpretations to yield hermeneutical information. The first two require historical answers. The third question, however, aims at a value judgement, which can take place on the basis of two different sets of criteria, depending on whether the criteria are those according to which the interpreters themselves would judge their interpretations or the criteria are brought into play by others who seek to judge the success of the interpretations.

The answers to the fourth and fifth questions are particularly important both historically and philosophically, for they are supposed to reveal not only important aspects of the philosophy of the interpreters, but even, it is hoped, something about the classics themselves that otherwise might not be noticed.

The tasks posed by the last three questions, however, involve a different approach from those of the first two. Whereas, in the former, attention to the interpretative text is paramount, the latter involve something different. The answer to the third question requires the application of evaluative criteria to conclusions concerning aims and procedures previously established. And the answers to the fourth and fifth entail drawing generalizations about the conclusions reached in answer to the first two questions, exploring relations between particular conclusions and the pertinent phenomena of the period, and comparing what these interpretations propose with the standard or prevalent understandings of the classics.

Answers to the fourth and fifth questions are facilitated and can potentially yield more rewarding results if interpretations of the same texts by interpreters from different philosophical traditions and historical periods are compared. Each person, each philosophical tradition and each age views the classics from a unique historical vantage point. This is to say that they see them through a set of presuppositions, biases and interests. Moreover, individual perspectives are affected by philosophical traditions embedded in the age of the interpreters, but the reverse also takes place.

Interpreters live in houses with different windows. Some houses have large windows, some small; some have windows only on one side, others have windows on more than one side; some have windows covered by blue glass, and some have windows covered by pink glass; some have square windows, others have rectangular, octagonal or circular ones; and some have windows located high up, near the ceiling, and others have them located way down, near the floor. What those who dwell in these houses see when they look out through the windows, then, can be very different. Some see more than others; some see a landscape tinted by a certain colour; the sight of some is framed by an octagonal shape, but that of others by a square one; and so on. All these perspectives yield information about what is outside the house, even if only fragmentary and affected by a vantage point.

The same is true of the interpretation of the philosophical classics. The understanding that interpreters get from these texts is always mediated by their own individual, philosophical and historical perspectives. When we examine these and compare them with ours, we discover something about the classics themselves. But, perhaps even more important, we discover something about ourselves. Perhaps the greatest benefit of the study of the history of philosophy is precisely that it makes us understand ourselves better through the understanding we have of others. This same benefit is found in the study of the various interpretations to which the classics have been subjected, except that the benefit is even greater in this case insofar as the focus on particular texts and their understanding by others throughout history reveal more clearly and easily the perspectives from which others, and consequently ourselves, view them.

In short, we can learn more about ourselves by looking at how we, and others, look at something else. Self-reflection is a difficult thing because of the obstacles we encounter in attempting to see ourselves objectively and directly. Indeed, we cannot; we always need a mirror to do so. But, even when we examine our interpretations of the classics and compare them with their interpretations by others, we can indirectly and objectively become the object of reflection; we understand ourselves through the understanding that others and we have of something else.

The study of the interpretation of the classics, then, has an important role to play in doing philosophy, for it opens the way to self-knowledge and this is, as Socrates knew only too well, the beginning of all wisdom.[6] Without self-knowledge, we are not very different from non-human animals. The morals to be learned from the hermeneutic analyses contained in this book, then, belong to philosophy and not just to history.

Uses and Abuses of the Classics

From this it should be clear that what constitutes the use or abuse of a classic depends very much on the kind of aim interpreters pursue and the hermeneutical assumptions they make.[7] Consider the traditional view that the aim of an interpretation is to discover or reveal what is often called 'the mind of the author'; that is, what the author thought the text meant or what he or she intended to convey through it. Obviously, if one adopts this kind of interpretation as paradigmatic, any other kind of interpretation will appear inadequate. An interpretation that provides an understanding of what an audience understood, makes explicit a meaning independent of the author's meaning or includes in it implications of which the author was unaware would all constitute interpretive abuses. Even more inadequate and illegitimate would be interpretations that seek to relate a text or its meaning to factors the interpreter brings into the picture. Indeed, these are the grounds on which many oppose feminist, Marxist or Freudian interpretations, for example.

On the other hand, if one adopts Foucault's view, according to which the author of a text is a mere fiction invented by an interpreter, then interpretations that seek to determine the mind of the author are illegitimate and spurious. Indeed, for this reason they should be considered abusive.

The legitimate uses of a text, that is, what is considered its legitimate understanding, depends on the aim pursued. There are no absolute criteria to judge the legitimate use or the illegitimate abuse of a text. Criteria of interpretation vary and depend on aim. The most frequent mistake of hermeneuticists is to assume the opposite, namely, that there are absolute standards of interpretation.

This does not mean, however, that when an interpretative aim is set, there are no criteria to determine the legitimacy of an interpretation. Indeed, often the end will clearly establish parameters of legitimacy. For example, if the aim is to discover the mind of the author, it is obvious that relational interpretations will not generally do. If the aim is to understand what Aristotle meant in the *Metaphysics*, any attempt to relate this text to Christian principles would appear to be abusive. Keeping this in mind, readers can look at the interpretations included in this volume and perhaps place them more easily within a historiographical perspective that will allow them to understand and judge the interpretations.

However, the issue becomes complicated because the chapters of this volume present interpretations of interpretations, rather than just interpretations: Rossetti's interpretation of Plato's interpretation of the Pre-Socratics, Matthews' interpretation of Nietzsche's interpretation of the Pre-Socratics, Ivry's interpretation of Averroes' interpretation of Aristotle, and so on. So we should pose two sets of questions for each chapter. One set applies to the interpretations provided by the authors of the chapters, and a second to the interpretations provided by the philosophers discussed in the chapters. For example, in relation to Matthews' piece we should ask the following questions. (1) What aim does he pursue in his interpretation of Nietzsche's interpretation? Does he seek a meaning interpretation and, if so, of what kind? Or does he aim at a relational interpretation and, if so, again, of what kind? (2) How does he proceed? Does he emphasize logic to the detriment of history, for example, or does he have an approach that balances logic and history? (3) How successful is he in achieving the aim he pursues? (4) Does what he accomplishes tell us something about Nietzsche that we did not know before? And (5) does his interpretation reveal something about the Pre-Socratics themselves?

But we should also pose a second set of questions, this time directed at Nietzsche and his own interpretation of the Pre-Socratics. (1) What is his aim in the interpretation? Does he seek a meaning interpretation and, if so, of what sort? Or does he aim to develop a relational interpretation and, if so, again, of what sort? (2) How does he proceed? Is his emphasis historical rather than logical? (3) Does he succeed in achieving his aim? And (4) does his interpretation give us some new information about the Pre-Socratics?

Asking these questions of every chapter in this volume should yield interesting, even if perhaps different, results. Moreover, the effort to answer the questions should help clarify the issues involved in, and deepen the understanding of, philosophical historiography in general and the historiography of the Greek philosophical classics in particular.

Notes

1 Italo Calvino, 'Why read the classics?', in *Why Read the Classics?*, trans. Martin McLaughlin (New York: Pantheon Books, 1999), pp.3–9. See also D.J. O'Meara, 'Plotinus *Enneads* (250–270): A Philosophy for Crossing Borders', in Jorge J.E. Gracia, Gregory Reichberg and Bernard Shumacher (eds), *The Classics of Western Philosophy* (Oxford: Blackwell, 2003), pp.76–7.
2 I discuss interpretation in more detail in Gracia, *A Theory of Textuality: The Logic and Epistemology* (Albany, NY: State University of New York Press, 1995), pp.147–79. For other conceptions of interpretation, see Paul Ricoeur, 'Creativity in language: word, polysemy, metaphor', in Charles E. Reagan and David Stewart (eds), *The Philosophy of Paul Ricoeur: An Anthology of His Work* (Boston: Beacon Press, 1978), p.128; J.W. Meiland, 'Interpretation as a cognitive discipline', *Philosophy and Literature* 2 (1978): 25; Morris Weitz, *Hamlet and the Philosophy of Literary Criticism* (Chicago: University of Chicago Press, 1964), ch.15; and C.L. Stevenson, 'On the reasons that can be given for the interpretation of a poem', in Joseph Margolis (ed.), *Philosophy Looks at the Arts* (New York: Scribner, 1962), p.127.
3 Indeed, Blackwell recently published the volume mentioned earlier, *The Classics of Western Philosophy*, which contains essays on representative works from the entire history of Western philosophy.
4 I give a more complete definition of texts in *A Theory of Textuality*, p.4.
5 I have discussed the interpretation of texts regarded as revealed in Gracia, *How Can We Know What God Means? The Interpretation of Revelation* (New York: Palgrave, 2001).

6   For a collection devoted to the exploration of how the study of the history of philosophy is related to doing philosophy, see Peter Hare (ed.), *Doing Philosophy Historically* (Buffalo, NY: Prometheus Books, 1988). See also Gracia, *Philosophy and Its History: Issues in Philosophical Historiography* (Albany, NY: State University of New York Press, 1992), particularly chapter 3, where I present and examine various justifications of the study of the history of philosophy.
7   I discuss this issue in detail in *Philosophy and Its History*, chapter 5.

Chapter 2

Plato on the Pre-Socratics[*]

Livio Rossetti

1 The Iceberg Argument

During the twentieth century, scholars who interpreted what Plato's dialogues have to say about the Pre-Socratics commonly held that Plato was well-acquainted with the philosophers of the past and therefore is an important source of information concerning several Pre-Socratics. He 'did not think in an intellectual vacuum. Some of his profoundest and most original ideas resulted from the attempt to solve problems bequeathed by his predecessors, in whom he took the liveliest interest'.[1] Indeed, in Plato's dialogues, we find many passages that explicitly, and rather extensively, deal with Heraclitus,[2] Parmenides,[3] Zeno,[4] Empedocles,[5] Anaxagoras,[6] Protagoras,[7] Prodicus[8] and Hippias.[9] References to other authors are less frequent; Hippocrates is mentioned once,[10] Democritus never.[11] Usually, scholars concentrate on explicit references and carefully distinguish them from mere character portrayals, since the interchanges of individual philosophers with Socrates or other interlocutors often prove scarcely helpful in expanding or correcting our knowledge of their personality or doctrines.[12] Moreover, it is customary to pay little attention to the relationship between Plato and those Pre-Socratics whom he rarely mentions, with the notable exception of Pythagoras, whose influence upon Plato may well have been remarkable in spite of the few explicit references made in the dialogues.[13]

This is, broadly speaking, the standard approach to the matter. This approach, however, is likely to conceal some important features of the relationship between Plato and the Pre-Socratics and therefore to open the way for a biased perception of what all these passages could mean. Four arguments open the way to a more sensible treatment of the matter. First, focusing merely on explicit references is tantamount to concentrating only upon the visible part of an iceberg, much as if no 'invisible' part remained to be accounted for. Second, since Plato treats some authors as great philosophers, or at least as genuine ones, whereas he considers others to be minor ones or even not true philosophers, we should account not only for what he actually writes about individual philosophers, but also for the kind of preconception which seemingly affects his attitude toward them.

Third, Plato wrote his dialogues at a time when the criteria for being a philosopher were still rather tentative and unstable, though with one exception: Parmenides and those who discussed his theories in writing.[14] For this reason, in his reference to past masters, Plato contributed much, not only to the determination of the canon of presocratic Greek philosophers, but also to the future perception of the degree of importance of each philosopher within such a canon. As a matter of fact, something like a graded list of the philosophers of the past, with Parmenides at the top and the Sophists at the bottom, emerges from the dialogues, and Aristotle's own canon (plus graded list) is far from being unaffected by Plato's view. So Plato's decision to treat (or not to treat) some ancient intellectual as a philosopher is important historically.

A further reason to avoid concentrating only upon the philosophers ranked higher in Plato's list is the marked discontinuities, among different dialogues, in the attention he pays to different philosophers. Broadly speaking, in the aporetic dialogues only the Sophists occupy the space, whereas, in the later ones, a selected group of earlier philosophers largely replaces them. Moreover, whereas the Sophists portrayed or mentioned in these dialogues are often treated as mere butts of severe attacks, most philosophers dealt with in non-aporetic dialogues are treated with much greater respect and seriousness. Discontinuity, insofar as it cannot be explained as a matter of pure chance, is a clue to a change of attitude and is helpful with regard to a better assessment of the evolution of Plato's thought. Such a change of attitude, in turn, deserves careful scrutiny.

Collectively taken, these remarks should alert us to the invisible parts of the iceberg (whence my tentative label) and prepare the way for a different approach, aimed at explaining not only what Plato says, but also what sometimes he fails to say. In other words, we should account not only for all those glaring passages devoted to individual philosophers (such as Zeno), but also for those passages which easily go unnoticed because they offer only negative pieces of information. This chapter will therefore focus less on what Plato has to say about the greatest philosophers of the past and more on certain secondary topics such as how Plato conceives of the whole, authors upon whom he passes an unfavourable judgement or even has nothing to say, and above all the hints of a change in attitude.

2 The Past of Philosophy in Greece up to Plato's Times according to the *Hippias Major*

Plato does not merely deal with individual philosophers and points of doctrine. In addition to passages of this kind, his dialogues contain passages in which something like a historiographic framework is outlined, and he deals with periods and groups or subgroups of Greek philosophers rather than with individuals.

In this regard, the opening pages of the *Hippias Major* (the section 281c–283b of the dialogue) surely deserve a place of honour.[15] It is a passage where Plato's Socrates begins by frankly acknowledging that, in comparison with the Sophists, the philosophers of the past, and especially the so-called *physiologoi*, declined to be involved in public life and affairs, and at least from this point of view they are, by now, largely outdated despite the celebrity they enjoyed in the past. At the beginning of this text, Socrates devotes some words to Pittacus, Bias, *hoi amphi ton Milesion Thalen* and, with an elegant periphrasis, to some more recent thinkers of the same sort, up to and including Anaxagoras (281c). He then introduces the notion of progress and asks whether it would be appropriate to establish an analogy between progress in the arts and progress in *sophia* (281d). One of the Seven Wisemen, Bias, is mentioned as a glaring example of how great, in comparison with the Sophists, has become the obsolescence of the wise men of the past (281d–282a). Some further comments upon Gorgias, Prodicus and Protagoras as champions of the new wave follow.

More is said in the *Hippias Major* passage, but the other parts deal with evaluation rather than with the identification of some qualifying features of the already rich Greek philosophical tradition. Let me discuss the identifying parts of this passage in some detail. Plato, who here as well as elsewhere in the *Hippias Major*, speaks many times of *sophia* and *sophoi* but never uses the words *philosophia* and *philosophoi*, draws in this passage a distinction between the *palaiai* and the *sophistai* on the grounds of the systematic involvement of the latter in public life and affairs, and the lack of interest, or rather refusal of all that, on the part of the former. By contrasting 'those up to Anaxagoras' and those like Hippias, that is, the Sophists, he is recalling a distinction among two main groups of *sophoi*, or rather of *philosophoi*, and treats it as an idea already available and almost generally accepted, and which he also accepts in principle. Plato's way of discussing the matter in this passage is therefore such as to suggest that he is acknowledging an already established way of representing past Greek philosophy, notably a way articulated in two major periods and currents, or modalities of doing philosophy and being philosophers. As a matter of fact, Plato's Socrates assumes nothing that is neither new nor particularly controversial, although his comments are ostensibly affected by a wish to gratify Hippias and, at the same time, to alert the readers to the fact that (a) he is nevertheless rather cold about the Sophists, and (b) Hippias does not suspect the least lack of enthusiasm on his part. Moreover, Plato clearly suggests that the Sophists too deserve to be called *philosophoi* (no matter whether they are good or bad ones) and that they gave a substantial new beginning to Greek philosophy.

Let us assume that most of these ideas were already in circulation in the Athenian cultivated milieu well before the *Hippias Major*. If this is so, what may have been the role played by Plato? Did he just put these ideas in writing? In order to assess this point we have to take into account the proto-history of ancient Greek philosophy outlined by Hippias of Elis in one of his prose books. Thanks to two German scholars, Bruno Snell and Andreas Patzer,[16] we are now able, through the scant evidence available, to detect some aspects of this book by Hippias. In it, Hippias outlined a history of ancient Greek *Sophia*, and probably began by pointing out a shared idea among such old poets as Orpheus, Musaeus, Homer and Hesiod, namely that Oceanus and Thetys are the source of all things, and two points of doctrine about water ('All things are made out of water', 'The earth rests on water') credited to Thales. On these grounds, a famous passage of Aristotle's *Metaphysics* (I.3, 983^{b}29–984^{a}4), where it is said that, according to certain authors, those who made Ocean and Thetys the parents of creation had a view of nature similar to the theories held by Thales, is now reinterpreted as a mere summary of a passage from Hippias' proto-history of ancient Greek philosophy. In all likelihood, Hippias' outline then proceeded to deal with the theories held by several authors, from Thales to Empedocles (or even beyond), whom we are accustomed to treat as philosophers as well, and Plato's excursus in the *Sophist* (242c8–243a4, where the Stranger draws a comparison among those who maintained that being is threefold, twofold, unique or marked by a *concordia discors*) is likely to be based upon Hippias' treatment of the same topic. Some passages from other dialogues (notably from *Cratylus*, 402a–c) may present a similar situation. However, Hippias' outline may well have dealt only with the *physiologoi* while leaving the Sophistic movement out completely, for no reference to Gorgias and, more generally, to the Sophists occurs in the mentioned passage of the *Sophist*, although a reference to Protagoras occurs in a comparable passage of the *Theaetetus*.[17]

On these assumptions, it is likely that the *Hippias Major* passage supplemented Hippias' outline with a crucial new element, namely the integration of the Sophistic movement within the history of ancient Greek *sophia* (or philosophy) as a remarkably new (and, in a sense, disputable) way of doing philosophy as well as of being philosophers. This is, in any case, the first known attempt to set up a proper background for two remarkably different subgroups of ancient Greek philosophers, and the kind of history outlined in the *Hippias Major* quickly became a standard so widely accepted that, even among modern historians, it has been usual to speak of a 'naturalistic period', carefully distinguished from the partly subsequent and partly contemporary 'anthropological' one, to which the Sophists and Socrates belonged. Indeed, the picture has remained basically the same so far, with only some secondary discrepancies.[18]

In the same passage, Plato's Socrates has something more to suggest, if not to say, about the kind of evolution that affected the Greek philosophical tradition down to his own times. In 282b he begins by putting aside his previous references to *sophia* and talking rather of *humon ... techne*, 'your art', the professional abilities boasted by the members of the new wave in philosophy. Then he openly characterizes Gorgias as a Sophist. This is tantamount to insinuating a doubt about the possibility of taking the Sophists as *sophoi* or *philosophoi*. Behind this doubt, it is easy to detect, as a hint meant to escape the attention of the interlocutor, but not that of most readers, a reservation about the legitimacy of the Sophists' claim to be true philosophers. To suggest (not openly raise) a doubt about the legitimacy of this is something that squares perfectly with the attitude Plato's Socrates adopts towards Hippias as well as the Sophists in general within the aporetic dialogues. It therefore helps to understand why the word *philosophia* never occurs in this passage, although the historical excursus unmistakably deals with intellectuals that, at the time of Plato, were probably acknowledged as philosophers.

That said, Plato's Socrates offers a rather long excursus on the role played by 'those like Hippias' in the city and the considerable amounts of money earned by Gorgias, Prodicus, Protagoras and others (282b–d). When talking about these matters, he quietly reminds Hippias of the very different attitude shown by the *sophoi* of the past towards money for, he says, 'none of those men of old ever thought it right to be remunerated' (282c6–7, trans. R. Waterfield), nor were they disposed to lecture and display their own *sophia* for a fee, because they were 'so simple' (282d1-2) and did not realize the great value of money. Then, after some comments by Hippias, he resumes this comparison by insisting that the philosophers of the first group, including the last of them, Anaxagoras, found it normal to have no concern with money and for this reason deserve to be taken as 'so thoughtless in their speculations' (283a6) and, in the last resort, 'affected by *polle amathia*' (283a3), that is, as pretty ignorant or stupid.

In this case, too, it would not be appropriate to take Socrates' evaluations at their face value, without suspecting something behind the explicit judgements. However, the reader is expected to detect unambiguously the existence of one hidden message – or rather two, for, in addition to the idea (easily foreseeable for most readers from any time, I would say) that the old attitude towards money was much more appropriate for a *sophos* than the new one (and therefore that the Sophists' attitude is marked by a measure of disgraceful shamelessness), Plato may want to indicate Socrates' systematic refusal to get money from his pupils, to the point of disguising the teacher–pupil relationship under a personal friendship and the mere pleasure/will to spend time with somebody of whom one thinks highly.[19] A step further, and Plato could have questioned the legitimacy of their claim to be genuine philosophers, something he never does openly, despite the severity of his censure in this as well as in other dialogues.

Taken as a whole, the *Hippias Major* passage shows a surprisingly definite idea of past Greek philosophy as articulated in two main traditions, and quite an unfavourable attitude, based on moral grounds, toward the last one; however, Plato does not dare to leave the Sophists out of the realm of philosophy. The function of this passage as a guideline for future historians of Greek philosophy has been of the utmost importance.[20]

3 The Past of Philosophy in Greece up to Plato's Times According to Other Aporetic Dialogues: Does Shortage of References mean Disregard?

Elsewhere in the same *Hippias Major*, Anaxagoras happens to be mentioned (283a) because of a biographical detail, and later (289ab) we find a passing reference to Heraclitus, stemming from the parodistic example of the fine pot, where a couple of sentences of his (fragments 82–83 D.-K.) are quoted, though as witty remarks more than as philosophemes. Moreover, the dialogue includes (at 301b–c and d–e, unfortunately not in Diels-Kranz) an important reference to Hippias' own philosophical doctrines, something that suggests that Hippias developed a *sui generis* version of Eleaticism.[21]

Something more is to be found in a passage of the *Protagoras* (342e–343b), where Socrates reacts against poor imitators of the Laconic way of life in contemporary Athens and claims that the Seven Wisemen were true admirers, lovers and imitators of Sparta in their deeds, with the impressive brevity of most of their famous sayings as proof. But once we put aside the criticism against certain Athenian manifestations of Laconism, the reference made here to the Seven Wisemen remains empty (short sentences taken as supposed evidence of their genuine sympathy for Sparta). And it may not be by chance that the verses of Simonides chosen shortly after for discussion are far from being eminently Laconic in character.

This is all. If we insist on adding something more to so meagre a list, we could mention another well-known reference, that of *Apology* 26de on the availability of the book of Anaxagoras at a very low price in the agora. But, once more, this is all the aporetic dialogues have to say about the Pre-Sophists, and if they, particularly the *Protagoras*, show a certain interest in the theories held by some Sophists despite Plato's prejudices, the lack of interest in the philosophies originated in Miletus and Velia could hardly be greater.

So, the main message stemming from this subset of Platonic dialogues seems to be that there is not much to learn either from the Pre-Sophists or from the Sophists. The Pre-Sophists seem to deserve only a measure of admiration for their high morality (their sayings happen to be ignored), whereas the Sophists seem to be thought to be overrated, worthy of several warnings, and, in any case, lacking a future. For here Plato speaks of the Pre-Sophists only in terms of lack of expectations and interest for all of them and their theories, and treats them as dramatically old-fashioned. As to the Sophists, the *Hippias Major* passage certainly suggests, on the surface, that they display an undeniable progress over their predecessors, but it hardly conceals a second thought, namely, that by now they too, in turn, have been largely outclassed by Socrates – or, better, by the 'nouveaux philosophes' of the time: the Socratics, the group of new intellectuals and writers to which Plato himself belongs. Besides, even elsewhere in the aporetic dialogues, whenever a Sophist is involved in a talk with Socrates, the idea most often suggested is that he claims to be (and to make statements which are) much wiser and much more valuable than he actually proves to be when put to the test with 'the philosopher', Socrates, as his main interlocutor.

All things considered, the kind of evaluation Plato's Socrates suggests in the aporetic dialogues is that we have little to learn either from the Sophists or from earlier ancestors, both being champions of ways of doing philosophy that by his time had lost much of their actuality, value and interest. If one has to judge Plato's view from these dialogues, the past of Greek philosophy seems to have been brushed aside in its totality (or almost in its totality) as something lacking any actuality.

This is most surprising and it is scarcely helpful to suggest that this is because the aporetic dialogues focus on the present much more than on the past, or because they are marked by the pleasure of improvisation and a great penury of well-stated theories, or because the search for universal definitions is a new methodology that lacks important antecedents, and it is not among those philosophers of the past that the Socrates in Plato's aporetic dialogues expects to find something of value. These considerations might possibly account for the lack of interest in some particular theories, but Plato could equally have picked a number of maxims, paradoxes and other scattered sayings ascribed to different philosophers of the past, so as to make some use of their writings similar to the use he makes of Homer and other poets. As a consequence, we have to acknowledge that, at the time, references to the Pre-Socratics were probably taken to have no priority for Plato. Probably, a sense of basic disregard conditioned Plato's perception of them at the time of composing these dialogues. For a different interpretation could hardly account for the impressive shortage of references. It is therefore likely that, when in the *Hippias Major* passage the Pre-Socratics are said to be largely outdated in comparison to the Sophists, Plato indeed takes them as outdated, despite their high morality. The concern of Plato's reflection is the Sophists more than the older *sophoi* and involves a strong prejudice against them.

Nevertheless, the earlier Plato is a highly cultivated writer, in addition to a creative thinker. Hence his apparent lack of interest for the philosophers of the past until he was, say, 45, really begs for an explanation.

4 Changing Attitudes Towards the Pre-Socratics in Plato's Non-aporetic Dialogues

4.1

Before we offer a more convincing explanation, we should first explore the non-aporetic, doctrinal and, in all likelihood later, dialogues. In them, contrary to the 'philosophy' of the aporetic dialogues, Plato's Socrates began to behave as a theorist and developed a body of doctrines he treats as almost already available.[22] As a result, his new dialogues are full of theories and statements that are (often implicitly) claimed to be largely reliable, if not absolutely certain. And since it was also a common practice among the Pre-Socratics to make statements and arguments and to offer them as something endowed with a high level of reliability, it may well have been easy (or easier) for the non-aporetic Plato to pick up points of contact, enlightening comparisons and arguments against other arguments. Thus, given the new orientation of Plato's thought and writings, one could have expected to find in these dialogues the kind of attention to the best philosophers of the past that we look for in vain throughout the aporetic dialogues.

But things did not go exactly in this way. The *Phaedo*, for instance, has a passage where a well-known reference to Anaxagoras occurs. In it, however, Socrates is particularly emphatic in commenting on the dramatic inadequacy of Anaxagoras' theories and therefore reinforces the idea that he and his pupils, *the* modern philosophers of the period, have little to learn from the 'ancients'. Besides, the *Phaedo* contains nothing more that is relevant, save a passing allusion to Anaximenes and Empedocles (99b) which is marked by the same attitude.

The treatment given to the philosophers of the past by the largest dialogue of the same period, the *Republic,* is comparable. A prominent feature of this dialogue is the disproportion between the frequency of references to Homer and other poets (especially Hesiod, Pindar and the tragic poets) and the penury of references to early philosophers. Only in Book V do we detect the first implicit reference to some Pre-Socratics, when Socrates establishes the relations between knowledge, opinion and ignorance (477–8). This passage is therefore to be counted among the oldest sources of evidence of the influence that Parmenides' theories began to exert upon

Plato at the time. But this is still a superficial fascination on Plato's part, for he seems not yet to be aware of the serious problems of compatibility between Parmenides' ontology and his own theory of forms.

Apart from a passing reference to Heraclitus at V 498ab and a passing reference to the Pythagoreans at *Rep.* VII 530d6–10, we have to reach Book X in order to find further references to the Pre-Socratics. In Book X 599d–600d, we encounter a rather complex overview, partly comparable with that of the *Hippias Major*. In it Plato argues that Homer has been neither a legislator like Lycurgus, Charondas or Solon, nor an inventor like Thales and Anacharsis, nor an educator like Pythagoras, nor an advisor in political affairs as Protagoras, Prodicus and several others have been. This cannot be counted as a major reference to the Pre-Socratics, of course. Here Plato just qualifies the practical wisdom of certain wise men of the past: apart from the legislators, he identifies Thales as the author of several useful discoveries (without entering the least detail, but the context is laudatory), Pythagoras as a very special educator, and the Sophists as people who achieved remarkable success in public life. The leading idea of the paragraph is that all these people turned out to be more clearly useful to the *polis* than a poet like Homer. Implicitly, there remains a lack of real interest for all of them, something comparable to the general attitude adopted in the *Hippias Major* passage we have discussed above.

All in all, Plato's general attitude seems to have remained more or less the same so far, in spite of the immense differences which separate these two dialogues from the aporetic ones.

4.2

Let us consider now a rather homogeneous group of passages stemming from other 'mature dialogues'. In the *Symposium* (178b) one of Plato's speakers, Phaedrus, happens to recall an idea shared by Hesiod, Acusilaos and Parmenides; in the *Cratylus* (402ab) Socrates picks up a whole series of poetic statements found in Orpheus, Homer and Hesiod, all close to Heraclitus' conception of water; in the *Theaetetus* (152e), Socrates recalls an idea shared by Homer, Epicharmos, Heraclitus, Empedocles and Protagoras, but not Parmenides; and finally in the *Sophist* (242c–243a) the Stranger outlines the ontological theories of the past with explicit reference to Xenophanes and Parmenides, and a probable reference to Empedocles as well as to Pherecydes and Ion of Chios; then he elaborates a radicalized version of this history he calls 'gigantomachy'.

A remarkable similarity can be sensed in all four passages: richness and reliability of available information; an interest in the *doxai* held by different philosophers and poets of the past; an attitude of noticing a number of similarities between them; an attitude of not putting them aside as outdated and uninteresting although they may seem rather old-fashioned; and an attitude of not emphasizing the discontinuity between these theories of the past and the intellectual standards attained in the present. Clearly, we find here a new approach to these authors: now Plato is largely focused on the presophistic stage of Greek philosophy, while the Sophists are left out, with just one exception.

At least behind three of these passages the trace of Hippias' proto-history of philosophy surfaces.[23] Moreover, the fourth clearly has much in common with Isocrates' famous passage on the number of elements (infinite, four, three, two, one or none: *Antidosis* 268). However, for the sake of our present inquiry, the important thing is not to determine what Plato may have found in Hippias' book, but rather to note how he exploited, whatever the intermediate source, certain ideas known to have been supported by some wise men of the past.

In the passage more remotely related to Hippias, that of the *Symposium*, a reference to some Pre-Socratics takes place when one of the speakers, Phaedrus, looks for some quotations from selected authors in support of his own praise of love. He begins by quoting some hexameters by Hesiod, then makes a passing reference to Acusilaos, and finally quotes a hexameter by Parmenides, so as to conclude (178c1–2) that Eros is widely acknowledged as the most ancient of the Olympian gods. The cultivated speaker clearly attempts to reinforce, in this way, the reliability of his opening claims about Eros, and he does the same a little later when he makes further references to Homer (as well as to a couple of tragedies). This is a show of learning justified by the fact that Phaedrus was the first, among a crowded field of intellectuals, to make a speech in praise of Eros. Let me also note, in passing, that another valuable reference to ancient philosophers is found later, in the speech of Eryximachus, where the doctor, having developed some interesting ideas about the goal of medicine (to reinforce love or strife among different parts of the human body in order to keep the appropriate proportions among them), introduces a comparison with music and then a quotation from Heraclitus, together with some remarks about what Heraclitus could precisely have meant when talking of a discordant harmony (187a). In this way, a good quotation and the discussion of its proper meaning happen to be fully integrated into a rather sustained theoretical discussion of musical harmony.

A greater interest in what ancient authorities say affects the *Cratylus* passage mentioned above. Here Plato's Socrates first recalls a couple of statements of Heraclitus about water and then claims to find related notions in such authors as Homer, Hesiod and Orpheus.[24] Moreover, before making these references, Socrates announces that he has just sensed a sort of 'swarm of *sophia*' (401e6), which means that a number of pertinent learned references have just come to his mind and he consequently plans to use them. This is tantamount to acknowledging the value of some ideas launched by the *sophoi*, and it is not by chance that many references to Homer, as well as some to Hesiod, occur both before and after this passage.

Let us turn now to the *Theaetetus*, the dialogue where Plato shows the most marked attitude of acknowledging the great value of theories and theorists of the past. Here Socrates not only confesses a sense of intellectual inferiority (the word is 'shame') toward the great Parmenides (183e–4a), but also openly acknowledges the force of Protagoras' theoretical stance. He is clearly in search of arguments against the line of thought for which he credits Protagoras. However, there is no irony in his acknowledgment of how difficult it is to criticize him and to develop an alternative and more promising point of view: quite the contrary, readers are expected to acknowledge the difficulty of the task.

It is in this context that Plato mentions first several philosophers and poets of the past who, with the exception of Parmenides, have shared the idea of a universal flux, and then (153a–d) gives several stock arguments in favour of it. Therefore the philosophers mentioned here are taken as further authorities, as thinkers who, each in a different way, have contributed to the establishment of a longstanding theoretical stance. We note in passing that here Plato avoids drawing a difference between philosophers and poets, and also that he passes without the least hesitation over Protagoras as the initiator of a different way of doing philosophy in comparison with the other philosophers he mentions.

In the comparable passage of the *Sophist*, Plato is even more careful in calling attention to differences and formulating his judgements: Xenophanes is taken as the founder of the Eleatic 'family';[25] Pherecydes, Ion of Chios and Empedocles as weak thinkers; Heraclitus as the (or one of the) most subtle and intriguing one (that is, among the 'naturalistic' philosophers, for the outline given at 242c–3a leaves the Sophists out of concern); and Eleatic monism as an intriguing 'myth'. Moreover, he insists that a number of doctrines held by these philosophers are not to be taken at their face value, since otherwise a number of basic assumptions would remain concealed, and in a sense they were very skilled (even too skilled) at concealing them (243ab; cf. 242c). We discover then that what they have concealed is a group of serious paralogisms in which both dualists and monists are involved. In a sense this amounts to a lessening of the intellectual value of the group of philosophers who are taken into account here, but what Plato has in mind is that their theories and 'myths' are so well-structured and so well-protected that the most skilled competence of modern philosophers is needed in order to decode their thoughts and stand up to their arguments. In this way they (or at least some of them) are acknowledged as first-order thinkers, in no way obsolete, even if their theories will be rejected.

A few pages later, Plato establishes a different opposition between materialists and idealists, and treats their opposition as a superb 'gigantomachia' (246a4) while assuming that both subgroups use stock arguments meant to contrast the opposite view. Now it is up to Plato himself to make the attempt at reaching a higher level of analysis and overcoming a contraposition otherwise left without a solution: the theory of the five highest genres is in fact his own way out of it.

Let us, finally, have a look at the concluding remarks of the *dihairesis* that is meant to grasp the Sophist's true nature. A remarkable emphasis upon the intellectual value of the Sophist (because of a particular move of his) can be found in these passages. Especially at 236d–7a and 239b–d the Sophist (basically Gorgias because of his genial parody of Eleatic ontology in the *Peri tou me ontos*) is acknowledged as extremely subtle and well-casted. He is therefore almost unassailable despite the numerous and heavy criticisms which have just been addressed to him, to the point that Plato himself is needed in order to overcome the difficulty.

So, in the *Sophist*, the most representative among the Pre-Socratics and at least one of the Sophists are acknowledged as interlocutors worthy of the greatest respect despite the criticisms Plato levels against them. Therefore, if we consider the four doctrinal dialogues just discussed, we see that in these texts Plato pays greater attention to several Pre-Socratics and their theories, possibly with an eye to Hippias' proto-history, but not without introducing some of his own ideas and evaluations. It is enough to compare these passages with what Plato had to say about the Pre-Socratics in his aporetic dialogues for us to perceive a spectacular change in attitude towards the past of philosophy in Greece. What is most noticeable has to do with a change in status. The Pre-Socratics, who were straightforwardly dismissed in the aporetic dialogues (save for their high morality) as too old-fashioned and, therefore, as providing almost no help for the investigations at issue, are now treated with much greater interest and respect, to the point of acknowledging that it is difficult to oppose their way of assessing certain philosophical issues. Thus a reversal takes place, for although some of them are praised for the deep insight of their theories, no further mention is made of their moral qualities. Moreover, far from passing the same judgement on the whole group, the mature Plato is more careful in making distinctions, that is, distinctions of the stronger/weaker type, with Heraclitus – and to a greater extent Parmenides – at the top.

Another point worth noting is that, whereas the relatively recent philosophers are treated with greater respect, the Sophists are most often ignored, if not disregarded altogether, and are taken into account only rarely, or more precisely only twice: in the *Theaetetus* (where Protagoras is treated as a 'modern' Heraclitean) and the *Sophist*. At the same time, the status of the Sophists is changed. For they simply cease to be the primary interlocutors of the mature Plato, the only exception occurring in the *Sophist*. In short, rankings have been almost completely reversed.

Moreover, the same reversal appears in the *Parmenides*. Just consider the famous excursus on Zeno at the beginning (127e–8e)[26] and the supreme dialectical effort, led by Parmenides himself, that occupies the whole second part of the dialogue. This dialogue is unsurpassed in showing the degree of esteem Plato came to have for certain Pre-Socratics in the course of time.

4.3

From all this emerges that, at the time of the great metaphysical dialogues focusing on Parmenides, a very great esteem for some Pre-Socratics as true intellectuals replaced the previous, basically negative, attitude.[27] These ancient masters are now taken as bearers of an abundant *sophia* that deserves to be better known and should be duly studied. This, indeed, is what emerges especially from the *Cratylus* passage mentioned above (Socrates announcing that he has just sensed a sort of 'swarm of *sophia*') and the *Theaetetus* passage where Parmenides is treated as a philosopher worthy of the greatest attention and deserving to be studied more in depth before a definite judgement upon his teachings should be passed.

Based on this, one would expect a high level of attention to these masters in all subsequent dialogues, and that regardless of our ability to form a definite idea of the dialogues written in a later period. Yet this is unlikely to be the case, for Plato's interest in the Pre-Socratics again diminishes and references become rare and marginal, as, for example, in the *Philebus* (where Heraclitus happens to be quoted

(43a), Anaxagoras happens to be alluded to (28d), and a Gorgianic *topos* happens to be cited (58a–b) and the *Politicus* (just a non-explicit reference to the Pythagoreans and their conception of *metretike techne* at 285a). The same happens with the *Laws* where, aside from a few minor references, the only relevant passage is X 886c–e.[28] The *Timaeus* too, regardless of its time of composition, is marked by a reduced interest in the work done by the Pre-Socratics, despite the obvious analogy between Timaeus' monologue and a whole set of highly representative poems and treatises called *Peri physeos*.

Things being so, if we try to look at the whole picture we can speak of another unexpected change in attitude. For the aporetic dialogues paid enormous attention to the Sophists (though almost only as a recurrent target) and dismissed the Pre-Socratics as obsolete and uninteresting intellectuals (though worthy of admiration for their behaviour and practical wisdom). Then a period of increasing attention to some Pre-Socratics took place and opened the way for the 'metaphysical trilogy' (*Tht.*, *Parm.*, *Soph.*) which, in turn, largely put aside the Sophists (though treating Protagoras with respect in the *Theaetetus* and de facto Gorgias in the *Sophist*) and rediscovered the Pre-Socratics, to the point of treating some of them (especially Heraclitus and Parmenides) with the greatest respect, as true authorities in the field. But in a third, later period, Plato seems to have definitively put aside the Sophists and reduced his interest in the Pre-Socratics. A diachronic approach to the kind of judgements Plato passed upon the philosophers of the past therefore shows two main changes in attitude.

Whence a number of questions arise. Is it enough to acknowledge so prominent an instability in Plato's perception of the philosophical tradition of Greece prior to his own times and, consequently, in the attention he paid to it? Is it enough to acknowledge the reduced interest in this tradition that marks a good majority of his dialogues? Conversely, is it enough to acknowledge that, at least in a few of the dialogues, the Pre-Socratics were treated with the greatest respect, as true authorities in the field? What may lie behind these 'bare facts'?

5 The 'Velvet Revolution' of Plato's Times as a Possible Line of Explanation

5.1

Surely it is not enough to assume that the author of the aporetic dialogues is still rooted in Socrates' own attitude toward the Greek philosophical heritage, whereas the author of (some) later and doctrinal dialogues develops a personal and original interest in the theories of the past. The change did not take place when Plato expounded new theories of his own and supported them with arguments in dialogues such as the *Symposium* and the *Republic*. It occurs only in a later period, when Plato becomes aware of the fact that certain of his theories are open to objections deeply rooted in the theories other philosophers defended in a remote past. Besides, the 'conversion' is not a definitive one, for later on Plato seems once more to lose interest in the philosophers of the past.

Moreover, this line of explanation has almost nothing to say about the long period marked by a systematic disregard of the most ancient masters. Just consider that Aristophanes often draws the attention of Athenians towards a number of philosophers, and that Socrates certainly encouraged his pupils and other interlocutors to explore the ancient poets, if not the ancient philosophers as well.[29] By contrast, Plato is anomalous insofar as he always pays attention to the poets but for a remarkably long period of time is interested only in discrediting the Sophists and finds it normal to ignore the masters of the naturalistic period. And this despite the fact that, at least in his youth, the presophistic line of thought should still have been alive, although less successful than the Sophistic one.

Now it is all too easy to imagine why, at the beginning of his career, under the influence of Socrates, Plato may have been too severe with the Sophists. But why should he have been so cool toward the naturalistic philosophers? Would it be enough to assume that this particular lack of interest is also part of the Socratic heritage? Can Plato have been so conditioned by his master for almost three decades after his death? The problem lies, not with the period of appreciation, but with the long period of disregard on the part of so deep a mind and so subtle a writer. Should not we suspect something more behind his long, cold treatment of the Pre-Socratics?[30]

5.2

In what follows I outline a possible line of explanation that centres upon the connection between this particular *explicandum* and the probable collective force of the transformations that affected the philosophical scene in Athens soon after Socrates' trial and death. As will be apparent, what I have in mind is something largely neglected by historians: a 'velvet revolution' which may well have marked the crucial years when Plato's identity as a writer and thinker definitely took shape. This is because there is room to suspect that such a 'velvet revolution' lies behind Plato's anomalous treatment of the Pre-Socratics in so many dialogues. In order to present this thesis as concisely as I can,[31] I shall first point out some basic facts.

1. During the first half of the fourth century, the group of Socratics involved in the invention and exploitation of the so-called 'Socratic dialogue', twelve to fifteen people, authored more than two hundred works covering a larger number of books and encompassing ca. three hundred Socratic dialogues (including a number of short or very short dialogic units).
2. During the same period, while the Socratics flooded Athens (and therefore Greece) with their writings, and especially with their Socratic dialogues, almost no other book – let me repeat: almost no other book – was published which could be taken as philosophical in character but *un*affected by Socraticism. In other words, during this period, it became more and more unusual (if not difficult) to be a philosopher while remaining unaffected by Socraticism.
3. Whereas most pre-Socratic philosophers composed only treatises, most Socratics abandoned completely the treatise form in favour of the dialogue, at

least during the first period of their literary activity, and only few among them wrote treatises in a later period.
4. Whereas for most Pre-Socratic philosophers it was a common practice to make explicit claims in their books, and to argue for the tenability of these claims, in a number of Socratic dialogues there was no clearly stated *demonstrandum* that the author was ostensibly anxious to argue for.
5. As a consequence, at the time, philosophers as well as readers of philosophical books should have been well aware of how new this kind of communication strategy was, however short its life may have been (Plato himself seems to have shortly abandoned it in favour of dialogues where the main speaker had a doctrine of his to expound). Because of such a remarkable transformation, during the second decade of the fourth century the 'new age' of Greek philosophy should have become something quite obvious.

Now some detailed comments. In principle, the first of these points could well give rise to some surprise or incredulity, since we are not accustomed to give figures about the flux of Socratic dialogues in the first half of the fourth century. However, the following is well known: (a) Plato and Antisthenes wrote in total about one hundred titles covering a remarkably larger number of books; (b) Xenophon's *Memorabilia* encompass some sixty dialogues distributed in thirty-nine chapters and four books; and (c) each of several minor authors, such as Crito, Simias, Kebes, Glaucon, Simon and Aristippus, probably authored single works encompassing dozens of short Socratic dialogues. Once we are reminded of these, it is easy to conclude that the figures given above are at least not implausible. For the sake of the present inquiry, this may be enough.

My second point might also generate, at least at first glance, a measure of incredulity. But consider this: whereas during the first decades of the fourth century the Socratics were extremely prolific as writers, it is very difficult, if not impossible, to mention works written in the same period by other Greek philosophers.[32] For other periods, the fifth century included, it is easy to see that philosophers formed a largely diversified community; moreover, the Socratics lived, no doubt, in a pluralistic society; but for the period marked by their most intense activity as writers and philosophers almost no independent philosopher – and in any case no philosophical writing unaffected by Socraticism – happens to be known. If we look for contemporary philosophers who remained deaf to the new Siren of Socraticism, we could possibly mention the late Gorgias and the late Democritus, who may well have written most of their works before the beginning of the fourth century, and also Archytas of Tarentum, who was certainly a great mathematician, a gifted musician, a good writer and an enlightened politician (yet this man's contribution to philosophy remains a matter of mere inference[33]). Or we could mention Isocrates, a logographer and then professor of rhetoric who surely had some interests in philosophy, but devoted no work of his to philosophy and never seriously claimed to be a philosopher or to educate a new generation of philosophers. Or we could refer to the author of the Derveni Papyrus, who no doubt writes something of interest for philosophers, but without deserving (or claiming) to be a philosopher.

Who else was a Greek philosopher active at the beginning of the fourth century and was not a Socratic? No further name or title comes to my mind; on the other hand, historians of ancient philosophy and literature tacitly (possibly unwittingly) acknowledge so amazing a void by failing to mention additional names and/or titles.[34] Besides, the intellectuals mentioned above would eventually count as *the last representatives* of traditions that in any case were playing a remarkably decreasing role in the Greek philosophical community of the fourth century.[35]

Regarding my third point, it is well-known that for most Pre-Socratics and Sophists it has been usual to author treatises, didascalic poems and pamphlets, and no other kind of book, whereas, among the Socratics, if Antisthenes, Xenophon and perhaps Aristippus authored both Socratic dialogues and other prose writings unaffected by the adoption of the dialogue form, Aeschines of Sphettus, Phaedo, Simon, Crito, Simias, Kebes, Glaucon, Plato and (conjecturally) Euclides of Megara and Alexamenos of Teos, *abandoned once for all* the treatise form and authored only[36] Socratic dialogues. This too should be taken as a major and sudden event: for some time towards the beginning of the fourth century, new ideas in philosophy used to be launched in writing, not in the form of treatises, but almost exclusively by means of dialogues.

Fourth, until the end of the fifth century it had been normal practice among philosophers and scientists to write texts in which they enunciate one or more *demonstranda* and expound some theories, and then support them as best they could and claim to have been successful in doing so. It would be difficult to find exceptions to this rule among men of science in the fifth century. In comparison, the effort of most Socratic writers was impressively different. Plato's aporetic dialogues especially strive to represent people in the act of becoming perplexed when they face unexpected remarks and find it necessary to look for a more appropriate answer, or to represent Socrates in the act of preparing a new trap for his interlocutors according to how they have reacted to a previous counter-example. This is tantamount to saying that, for a while, Plato and some other (or most) Socratic writers tried to portray people in the act of thinking, and therefore in the act of adopting or modifying a theoretical stance *impromptu*.[37]

What is more, in Plato's aporetic dialogues (and possibly elsewhere) no positive conclusion stems from the exchange, and it is far from easy to single out a definite 'lesson' of the dialogue. In the aporetic dialogues, he has been especially careful (and especially able) to avoid offering notions and arguments suitable to be learnt as well as to remain basically unaltered. And sometimes – think, for instance, of the exegetical debate on the *Protagoras*, or the *Euthyphro*, or the *Laches* – Plato has actively tried to prevent his readers from forming a clear idea of the point(s) towards which he was imperceptibly leading his readers.[38] When something of the kind happens, it is the predicative content that vanishes, and it is the *demonstrandum* that disappears. Thanks to this new standard, one or more Socratics had the possibility of claiming to be philosophers *optimo jure* even if their books failed to offer definite teachings or claim to know that certain states of affairs are such and such. All this, I repeat, is contrary to what has been the rule for the whole tradition, from Thales to the Sophists.[39]

On these grounds should not we speak of a unique literary and philosophical season and a period of supreme creativity? This new way of doing philosophy may well have attained, at the time, a high degree of awareness (on the part of its protagonists, the Socratics) and visibility (to the eyes of contemporary readers). All these innovations could really have given the impression of the coming of a 'new age' for the otherwise already glorious philosophical tradition of Greece. The magic moment may have been a matter of a good decade about 395–385 BC, when the Socratics quickly became the 'nouveaux philosophes' of their own times and the intellectual creativity of some of them reached a marvellous climax. Then history continued, intellectuals moved in other directions, and Plato abandoned once and for all the aporetic typology of his dialogues in favour of a new standard where, broadly speaking, there is a teacher and there is a teaching.[40]

In the meanwhile a spectacular gap between old and new ways of doing philosophy, of being a philosopher, and especially of writing philosophical texts had possibly been established, a gap wide enough to leave the impression of an unbridgeable discontinuity with the past. Indeed, in few other periods in Western philosophy has an attitude of diluting if not dissolving the difference between philosophy and literature – plus a measure of anti-academicism, the wish to reach a wider and less specific readership, and a preference for intellectual challenges – reached a comparable level. In few other periods was the impression of living an irreversible evolution in the ways of doing philosophy so widely shared, if only for short periods.

This momentous 'velvet revolution' has unfortunately – and astonishingly – escaped the attention of most historians, who have been much more impressed by the following phase of development in Greek philosophy, when metaphysics newly occupied the stage and a rediscovery of the philosophical treatise form at the expense of the dialogue took place. As a matter of fact, since Eduard Zeller we have been told many times that the second first-order change affecting Greek philosophy after the Sophistic movement occurred only when Plato became the superb metaphysician we all admire. Clearly, this implies a denial of the importance of what happened just before, at the time of Plato's aporetic dialogues.[41] But now we can easily acknowledge that both phenomena occurred during a remarkably short period of time and assert that, when Plato suddenly became, among other things, a splendid metaphysician (possibly not later than ca. 380 BC), the flux of *Sokratikoi logoi* was still a matter of just ten to fifteen years and therefore was a relatively young event for the intellectual and philosophical community of Athens. So we have to speak of two phases temporally contiguous, though ostensibly different.[42]

5.3

Assuming that the picture outlined above is basically reliable, it follows that, during the first two decades of the fourth century BC, two well-defined events took place at approximately the same time: Plato and other Socratics wrote a number of highly innovative or even marvellous dialogues which may well have had remarkable success; and no (or almost no) further philosophical writing happened to be written by the Sophists and other philosophers such as the last naturalistic ones, or the Pythagoreans, so that a sudden loss of weight (possibly an irreversible self-dissolution) of *the* unsocratic philosophical traditions of the time took place. This second point speaks of quite a spectacular event: the break of continuity in the philosophical tradition of Greece (not only of Athens), with the only exception of the Socratics (and the Pythagoreans), the non-existence of further representatives of the Sophistic movement (though with the partial exception of Isocrates) and a fortiori of the naturalistic philosophy outside the Socratic circle. Almost no further philosophical writing happened to be written by the Sophists and other philosophers while Plato and other Socratics were writing a number of highly innovative dialogues. In the fourth century, only the Socratics are known to have preserved a future for philosophy in Athens and elsewhere with a rich offering of new texts, new ideas and eventually new schools.

As a consequence, for a whole century, Greek philosophy consisted (this, at least, is what the available evidence suggests) merely of pupils of Socrates, pupils of Plato and some other Socratics of the first generation (Aristotle and Diogenes the Cynic), and disciples of these pupils. In other words, philosophy ended up being identified merely with the Socratic heritage not only during the first decades of the fourth century BC, but *for the entire fourth century*. Therefore, if during so long a period nobody else succeeded in being acknowledged as a philosopher except a number of intellectuals directly or indirectly linked with Socrates, a massive and almost irreversible 'Socratization' of Greek philosophy took place at the time. And it is worth noting that when, around 450–430 BC, the Sophists imposed themselves as the avant-garde of philosophy in Greece at the expense of the so-called *Physiologoi*, they in no way caused an altogether complete and irreversible dissolution of naturalistic philosophy, which in fact survived for some decades.

So far, historians of Greek philosophy and literature are used to paying very little attention to these events and concentrating rather on individuals, namely, on Plato and his contemporaries. So far as I know, there is no theory that explains how a glorious and extremely rich philosophical tradition, that of fifth-century BC Greece, could have dissolved completely and simultaneously even outside Athens, and be replaced at once by a new tradition. However, the facts are there, and a reasonable line of explanation has to be devised (and eventually challenged). So, according to the points made in the previous subsection, the kind of explanation I dare to submit is that the Socratics (a) flooded Athens and Greece with a surprisingly great flux of new dialogues, (b) impressed most readers with what was new and of good quality (new standards, new kinds of complexity and even new tastes in philosophy) in their writings and (c) attained remarkable success, while (d) the non-Socratics abstained from publishing new texts for whole decades. There is enough here to warrant the conclusion that the engine of these momentous events was the shower of rather creative Socratic dialogues in a moment of penury of new texts and new ideas on the part of other philosophical traditions.

5.4

It is time now to go back to the *explicandum*. The question was: what may there have been behind a period of deep disregard for the naturalistic philosophers of Greece on the part of the 'aporetic' Plato, a disregard which, by the way, was combined with a shower of severe criticisms addressed to the Sophists? One can guess why Plato was so proud of having been a pupil of Socrates, but to see him put aside half of the philosophical tradition of Greece as outdated, and the other half as detrimental, requires something more.

The success of the literary genre, a success beyond any expectations, while in the philosophic arena there was a notable lack of competitors, may have been the decisive factor which reinforced well in time the authors' perception of being truly innovative and doing something very important. Under these conditions, that is, because of the 'new language' Plato and other Socratics brought in as a promising alternative to the customary treatise form, they may well have perceived the whole past of Greek philosophy as more or less outdated and therefore sensed that they should look ahead, rather than back. After all, the Socratics could be particularly gratified by the impression of having had great success within a few years, and this despite the drama of Socrates' trial and condemnation. Whence an uncommon enthusiasm for what they were able to do as well as for the largely favourable reactions they were probably able to observe, and the belief that they were carrying out a first-order revolution in philosophy and communication – as they did, in fact, although their revolution proved to have a relatively short duration. As to Plato, no doubt the most creative of the group, he may well have been even more acutely aware, and proud, of the difference between the new way of doing philosophy and every other modality known at the time.

I would therefore surmise that to account for Plato's rather cold (if not supercilious) attitude towards the whole past of Greek philosophy, an attitude that lasted for some two decades, requires a large context, in particular because such an attitude failed to raise a mistrust on the part of contemporary readers. In other words, if Plato dared to be rather cold towards the Pre-Socratics for a long time, with no wish to conceal such an attitude, this means that the philosophical situation at that time allowed this attitude. Besides, if we compare the disregard towards philosophers with the attention often paid to Homer and some other poets, our explanation appears to be more likely, since the difference of treatment may well have been intentional.

As is apparent, the kind of explanation I am submitting is centred on the invention of a wholly new language for philosophy: the *Sokratikos logos*. This is not the right place for entering into further details about what was new in this new form of written communication, but we may be allowed to recall that the Socratic dialogues used to lead fourth-century BC readers to interact with writing in quite unfamiliar ways. Readers of Plato's aporetic dialogues, and of a number of other *Sokratikoi logoi*, were expected, (1) to decide; who is right and whether Socrates is fair to his interlocutor, (2) to imagine how the interaction of somebody with Socrates will evolve, (3) to experience changes in emotional identification,[43] and (4) to wonder what is the lesson of the dialogue. This is enough to make these dialogues very contagious. Therefore the 'supercilious attitude' mentioned above seems to be a reasonable effect of all these favourable circumstances upon the relatively young philosopher involved in the writing of several aporetic dialogues.

Conversely, could we reach the same conclusions without considering the creativity of the period marked by the aporetic dialogues and the impression of writing a new page in the history of philosophy? And could something like this happen without the self-dissolution of almost every other philosophical tradition taking place at about the same time? Hardly, I would say.[44] As to the following phases of Plato's attitude towards his predecessors, we might conjecture that, for a remarkably long period of time, Plato simply did not imagine he could find enlightening ideas (or, a fortiori, serious 'epistemic obstacles') in these authors of the past. It is tempting, therefore, to interpret the *Cratylus* page mentioned above (section 4.2) where Socrates says he has just sensed a sort of 'swarm of *sophia*', much as if Plato wanted to confess, in an oblique manner quite congenial to him, to having largely underestimated in his earlier dialogues the rich offer of wisdom from the texts of most philosophers from the past, and to announce that he had at last begun to pay more attention to their writings and ideas. For the same reasons it is tempting to imagine that, for the mature Plato, it was surprising to discover that the ancient masters had something important to say, to the point of proving able to push some of his own doctrines into very difficult *aporiai*. As a matter of fact, the core of his 'later' comments on Protagoras (in the *Tht.*), Parmenides (in the whole 'metaphysical trilogy') and Gorgias (in the first part of the *Soph.*) was the admission that he was just striving to escape their strictures. From this point of view his comments bear the mark of a unique intellectual honesty.

And now a rather unexpected corollary: once we accept the idea that, for the greater part his life, Plato did not really love the Pre-Socratics, it becomes possible to account for the impressive lack of passages where he presents us with a sentence by an ancient philosopher that is assumed to be enlightening, or that is treated as a permanent gift. He is in fact prepared to acknowledge such a status for the poets, whom he openly calls 'fathers and guides in wisdom' (*Lys.* 214a). And he is also an emphatic admirer of modern writing on the laws (*Laws* IX 858e–859a), but he has nothing comparable to say about ancient Greek philosophers, nor does he pick up gnomic material from their statements (while he repeatedly comments upon the Delphic *gnothi sauton* with due respect). At most, he exploits a Heraclitean couple of statements on the proportion between monkey, man and god in the *Hippias Major* (289ab) as appropriate for his argument – or another couple of Heraclitean statements just in order to argue that Homer had in fact anticipated the latter's idea of a universal flux (*Cra.* 402a) – but without spending a word on their (altogether remarkable) intrinsic value. And he sincerely praises Thales for his many inventions (*R.* X 600a), but in passing (when talking about Homer) and without a word upon his merits as a philosopher.

This is surprising and would, in fact, be difficult to explain unless we assume that, generally speaking, Plato remained rather cold towards the philosophical heritage of Greece.[45] For the usual approach, centred as it is upon the most important and visible passages devoted by Plato to individual Pre-Socratics, is silent about the phenomenon of disregard which has been put at the centre of this chapter, and therefore suggests the idea that Plato was an enthusiastic admirer of a number of philosophers from the past. But if this is so, how can we explain that these admired philosophers were not acknowledged as 'fathers and guides in wisdom' like (or to a greater degree than) the poets?

6 Who Were the Pre-Socratic Philosophers According to Plato?

A corollary of the above has to do with the role Plato may have played in the identification of a whole group of fifth-century BC Greek intellectuals as philosophers.[46] A more and more definite idea of the beginnings of philosophy in Greece is developed, after Hippias, by Plato and then by Aristotle. There is a basic continuity in their way of outlining such a portrait, and this continuity had the power to give rise to a well-established common opinion which, in its essentials, is still alive (and possibly captures some significant elements of truth).

A noteworthy feature of Plato's role in this process is that he himself was unequivocally a philosopher and a member of a community of writers, the Socratics, most of whom believed themselves (and, in all likelihood, openly claimed) to be philosophers. This is a strong premise for the present investigation, since Plato's belonging to groups strongly related to philosophy supplied some essential guidelines for decisions concerning whether particular ancient thinkers were to be considered philosophers or not. Things were not exactly so in the case of Hippias, but on the other hand the fact that Plato confidently adopted certain leading ideas of Hippias' own historical outline (and that, some decades later, Aristotle did approximately the same) is objectively reassuring not just about the forming of a *communis opinio*, but about the basic reliability of the picture we have painted.

In a recent paper, G.E.R. Lloyd put a number of caveats on the identification of the community of Greek professional philosophers who were active before Plato. He writes: 'Je suis d'accord avec ceux pour qui il existe une réponse brève à la question de savoir ce qu'est la philosophie présocratique, à savoir qu'il s'agit, pour l'essentiel, d'une construction de la science du XIXe siècle.'[47] Well, what emerges from Plato (plus Hippias and Aristotle) is rather a hint in favour of the opposite (and much more traditional) view, for his pages leave very little room to doubt the legitimacy of the qualification of Thales, Xenophanes, Heraclitus and others as philosophers. Indeed, Plato contributed very substantially to the establishment of the canon of sixth and fifth-century BC philosophers, all the more so since he clearly had in mind a tentative but firm hierarchy among the philosophers of the past, so as to point out who, among the naturalistic stream as well as among the Sophists, were the most genuine and the most prominent ones and who deserved to be put at a lower or much lower position on the scale. Now, if we consider how modest Plato's enthusiasm for his predecessors was, his seemingly unhesitating inclusion of several intellectuals in the canon, despite his own prejudices, is likely to suggest that behind his canon there was an already shared idea of who were the philosophers of the past. Indeed, there is plenty of evidence that suggests that the process of assessment of such a virtual canon marked Plato's times in a very special way.

Notes

* For Franco Bianco.
1 W.K.C. Guthrie, *A History of Greek Philosophy*, vol. IV, *Plato. The Man and His Dialogues: Earlier Period* (Cambridge: Cambridge University Press, 1975), p.32; for a remarkably different attitude see M. Dixsaut, 'Platon et ses multiples dialogues', in M. Dixsaut and A. Brancacci (eds), *Platon source des présocratiques* (Paris: Vrin, 2000), p.17: 'Comment Platon pourrait-il contribuer à la connaissance de ceux que nous appelons "présocratiques", alors qu'il ne les cite que très exceptionnellement, les nomme rarement, et expose moins leurs doctrines qu'il ne les fait parler?'
2 Main occurrences: *H.Ma.* 289ab, *Cra.* 402a (cf. 440c), *Smp.* 187ab (cf. 207d), *Tht.* 152e (cf. 179de), *Sph.* 242e. S. Mouraviev, *Heraclitea II.A.1 Traditio (a) Ab Epicharmo usque ad Philonem* (Sankt Augustin: Academia Verlag, 1999), pp. 60–96, has a detailed survey of everything Plato has to say about Heraclitus. See also M. Adomenas, 'The fluctuating fortunes of Heraclitus in Plato', in A. Laks and C. Louguet (eds), *Qu'est-ce que la philosophie présocratique? What is Presocratic Philosophy?* Lille: Presses Universitaires du Septentrion, 2002), pp.419–47.
3 Main occurrences: *Smp.* 178b, *Tht.* 183e, *Prm. passim*, *Sph.* 241d and 258d. The relationship Parmenides–Plato has been the object of impressive scholarly work since F.M. Cornford, *Plato and Parmenides* (London: Routledge & Kegan Paul, 1939). Some recent titles: M. Migliori, *Dialettica e Verità. Commentario filosofico al 'Parmenide' di Platone* (Milan: Vita e Pensiero, 1990); N.-L. Cordero, 'L'invention de l'école éléatique: Platon, *Sophiste*, 242 D', in *Études sur le* Sophiste *de Platon*, ed. P. Aubenque (Naples: Bibliopolis, 1991), pp.91–124 ; J. Frère, 'Platon lecteur de Parménide dans le *Sophiste*', in *Études sur le* Sophiste *de Platon*, pp.124–43. F. Fronterotta, *Methexis. La teoria platonica delle idee e la partecipazione delle cose empiriche. Dai dialoghi giovanili al Parmenide* (Pisa: Scuola Normale Superiore, 2001).
4 The critical passage is *Prm.* 127e–28e. The secondary literature includes notably F. Solmsen, 'The tradition about Zeno of Elea re-examined', *Phronesis* 16 (1971): 116–41; G. Vlastos, 'Plato's testimony concerning Zeno of Elea', *Journal of Hellenic Studies* 95 (1975): 136–62.
5 Empedocles happens to be mentioned twice (*Tht.* 152e, *Sph.* 242de), but his theories are echoed in *Men.* 76cd and three times in the *Ti.* (73d, 77c, 78e: see J.P. Hershbell, 'Empedoclean influences on the *Timaeus*', *Phoenix* 28 (1974): 145–66); N.L. Cordero, 'Platon, Empédocle, et l'origine de l'être human', in *Platon source des présocratiques*, pp.93–106.
6 Main occurrences: *H.Ma.* 281c and 283a, 465d, *Ap.* 26de, *Cra.* 400a and 409ab, *Phd.* 97b–98c, *Phdr.* 270a; L. Pepe, 'Le livre d'Araxagore lu par Platon', in *Platon source des présocratiques*, pp.107–28.
7 *Prt.* and *Tht.* are the dialogues where Protagoras stands out. Minor occurrences are to be found in such dialogues as *H.Ma.*, *Men.*, *Eud.*, *Cra.* and *Phdr.* About Protagoras' relativism and its 'self-refutation' argument in the *Tht.* see L. Rossetti, 'Sulla differenza fra il fenomenismo di Protagora e il fenomenismo scettico', in A.-J. Voelke (ed.), *Le Scepticisme antique: perspectives historiques et systématiques, Cahiers de la Revue de*

théologique et de philosophie, 15 (1990): 55–67; R.J. Ketchum, 'Plato's "refutation" of Protagorean relativism', *Oxford Studies in Ancient Philosophy* 10 (1992): 73–105.

8   Diels-Kranz records fourteen passages from Plato where something is said about Prodicus and his mnemotechnics.

9   Apart of a passing remark in *Ap.* 19e and the secondary role played in the *Prt.*, it is in the twin dialogues attributed to him that Hippias is dealt with extensively. Particularly important is *H.Ma.* 301d–302b (unfortunately not in Diels-Kranz), where Hippias' ontology is outlined. Very little on this passage is to be found outside G.B. Kerferd, 'Plato and Hippias', *Durham University Journal* 42 (1963): 35–6, and *The Sophistic Movement* (Cambridge: Cambridge University Press, 1981).

10 A passing reference in *Phdr.* 270c. The rest can only be a matter of speculation. See J. Jouanna, *Hippocrate* (Paris: Les Belles Lettres, 1992); J. Longrigg, *Greek Rational Medicine. Philosophy and Medicine from Alcmaeon to the Alexandrians* (London and New York: Routledge, 1993); L. Ayache, 'Est-il vraiment question d'art médical dans le *Timée*?', in T. Calvo and L. Brisson (eds), *Interpreting the* Timaeus – Critias [Proceedings of the IV Symposium Platonicum. Selected Papers] (Saint Augustin: Bibliopolis, 1997), pp.55–63.

11 See, however, M.L. Silvestre, 'L'eredità democritea nei dialoghi di Platone', *Atti dell'Accademia Pontaniana* [Naples] 41 (1992): 25-44; L. Pepe, *La misura e l'equivalenza. La fisica di Anassagora* (Naples: Loffredo, 1996), pp.9–24.

12 A notable exception is likely to occur with Cratylus: see S. Mouraviev, 'Cratylos d'Athènes ?', in R. Goulet (ed.), *Dictionnaire des philosophes antiques*, II (Paris: Éditions du CNRS, 1994), pp.501-10.

13 A classical work on this matter is W. Burkert, *Weisheit und Wissenschaft: Studies zu Pythagoras, Philolaos und Platon* (Nuremberg: Carl, 1962).

14 Just consider that Parmenides' theories were the object of widespread scholarly debate over half a century, with the active involvement of almost a dozen qualified intellectuals still known to us (Zeno, Melissus, Empedocles, Anaxagoras, Leucippus, Democritus, Lycophron, Protagoras, Xeniades, Gorgias and Hippias). Given the level of abstraction, we can safely assume that the philosophical status of disputes about Being, Not-Being, the Void and other no less abstract concepts was easily and widely acknowledged by learned contemporaries. If so, we can state that philosophy happened to be counted among the acknowledged specializations, side by side with medicine, astronomy and possibly others, for about two-thirds of the fifth century. Whichever was the inventor of the neologism *philosophia* (as the title of W. Burkert's 1960 paper at *Hermes* indicates: 'Platon oder Pythagoras?'), there is little doubt that the work of Parmenides – or, rather, his ontology – was quickly acknowledged as eminently philosophical in character, and therefore that the whole group of intellectuals involved in a public discussion over Eleaticism could treat themselves (and were taken by others) as philosophers.

15 On the very special status of this passage, see L. Rossetti, 'Platone e la tradizione filosofica pre-platonica', *Atti dell'Accademia di Scienze Morali e Politiche* (Naples), 85 (1975): 180–97.

16 B. Snell, 'Die Nachrichten über die Lehren des Thales und die Anfänge der griechischen Philosophie- und Literaturgeschichte', *Philologus* 96 (1944): 170–82; A. Patzer, *Der Sophist Hippias als Philosophiehistoriker* (Munich: Verlag Carl Alber, 1986). See also G.B. Kerferd, *The Sophistic Movement* (Cambridge: Cambridge University Press, 1981), pp.48ff; J. Mansfeld, '*Cratylus* 402 a–c: Plato or Hippias?', in L. Rossetti (ed.), *Atti del Symposium Heracliteum 1981*, I (Rome: Edizioni dell'Ateneo, 1983), pp.43–55.

17 It is quite possible that Protagoras happens to be mentioned in this context (*Tht.* 152e, which is supposedly inspired by Hippias) not because his name occurred in Hippias' outline too, but because of the important role he plays in this dialogue. In other words: Plato, echoing Hippias, could well find it enlightening to add a new entry to the list of philosophers and poets who share the theory of universal becoming.

18 It may be worth mentioning some of these discrepancies: the place of Thales as *the* beginner is not exactly stated; Plato fails to acknowledge Democritus as the 'last' representative of the naturalistic tradition; nothing is said upon the identification of an Ionian and an Italic tradition (something which, at least for us, began only with Diogenes Laertius and hardly had a future after Eduard Zeller).

19 Section I 6.13–14 of Xenophon's *Mem.* is the *locus classicus* where Socrates argues for this point in full.

20 Something more about Hippias will be said below, section 6.

21 See above, note 9.

22 See for instance the *Phaedo* and *Republic*, where Plato's Socrates feels free to discuss sustained doctrines while his interlocutors become, rather, attentive listeners. For a tentative exploration of this standard, see L. Rossetti, 'Sulla struttura macro-retorica del *Filebo*', in P. Cosenza (ed.), *Il* Filebo *di Platone e la sua fortuna* (Naples: D'Auria, 1996), pp.321–52.

23 See above, note 15.

24 Another passing reference to the same notions (Ocean and Thetys) occurs in *Symp.* 180d.

25 N.-L. Cordero, 'L'invention de l'école eléatique: Platon, *Sophiste*, 242 D', in *Études sur le* Sophiste *de Platon*, pp.91–124, is a notable attempt to deny the reliability of this particular statement.

26 Another point of interest is the passage where Plato's Socrates affects to comment upon Zeno but in fact raises the problem of predication (128e–30a).

27 Indeed, before the *Theaetetus*, the *Parmenides*, and the *Sophist*, we can detect, at most, a period of incubation marked by a display of learning (in the *Symposium* passage as well as in the *Republic*, Book X, passage we have discussed above).

28 One could also mention, *inter alia*, the *Alcibiades I*, where only a passing reference to Anaxagoras and Damon (at 118c) and one to Zeno (at 119a) can be detected.

29 For the sake of the present inquiry, it may be enough to remember that the famous accuser Polycrates (*ho kategoros*, as Xenophon in *Mem.* I2 and Libanius in his *Apologia Sokratous* often write) argues precisely that Socrates is used to take advantage of some texts of the poets in his semi-clandestine battle against Athenian democracy.

30 Let me recall that there is also the virtual disappearance of the Pre-Socratics from the very last dialogues to be accounted for. On this point, see below (towards the end of the chapter).

31 These points have been discussed in greater detail in L. Rossetti, 'Le dialogue socratique *in statu nascendi*', *Philosophie Antique* 1 (2001): 11–35; 'La nascita di un nuovo genere letterario all'inizio del IV secolo a.C.: il *logos sokratikos*', *Classica Cracoviensia* 6 (2001): 187–202; 'Socrate e il dialogo "ad alta interattività"', *Humanitas* (Coimbra) 53 (2001): 171–81.

32 That is, works that satisfy the following three requirements: (a) to be (acknowledged as) works whose main concern is philosophy; (b) to show, at the most, a marginal interest in Socrates, his teaching and his followers; and (c) to be authored during the first three decades of the fourth century or so.

33 The inference exploits his friendly relations with Plato and the supposed existence of 'three books on the philosophy of Archytas' authored by Aristotle (according to Diog. Laert. V 25 and other sources) much more than direct evidence.

34 No exception, so far as I could ascertain.

35 For some additional remarks, see below, section 5.3.

36 Of course we have to make a minor exception to the rule in the case of Plato's *Apology*, epistles and epigrams.

37 We know, at least, that in Xenophon and Aeschines too Socrates is very often portrayed as launching unexpected analogies, comments and ideas, so that interlocutors have to reconsider their previous certainties.

38 Just consider the scholarly debate about the right definition of piety which has often been taken as traceable to the *Euthyphro*. In my own commentary (*Platone, Eutifrone*, Rome: Armando, 1995, pp.170–86), I argued in detail that, towards the end of the dialogue, Plato's Socrates positively obstructs the search for a reasonable definition. Besides, something similar happens elsewhere too.

39 Much more should be said upon this point, in order to mark some distinctions with reference to, for example, M. Frede, 'Plato's arguments and the dialogue form', in J.C. Klagge and N.D. Smith (eds), *Methods of Interpreting Plato and His Dialogues* (OSAP Suppl., Oxford: Clarendon Press, 1992), pp.201–19 and F.J. González, 'Self-knowledge, practical knowledge, and insight: Plato's dialectic and the dialogue form', in F.J. González (ed.), *The Third Way. New Directions in Platonic Studies* (Lanham, MD: Rowan & Littlefield, 1995), pp.155–87. It is clearly impossible to discuss extensively these matters here.

40 For an overview of both standards, see L. Rossetti, 'Sulla struttura macro-retorica del *Filebo*', pp.329–41.

41 It is not difficult to understand what happened with Zeller. In his day the distinction between an earlier phase of the Socratic dialogues and the phase of the metaphysical and doctrinal ones simply was not yet available.

42 This is a point that should be discussed at some length. I hope to do so elsewhere.

43 Especially in aporetic dialogues, readers often tend to feel sympathetic towards the interlocutor at the beginning, but then unfailingly come to feel more and more on the same wavelength as Socrates.

44 It remains to be seen whether the above is concordant with Aristotle's well-known testimony about Plato's teachers other than Socrates. At *Met.* A6, 987a32–b13 (cf. 987b22–5) it is openly said that Plato first studied with Cratylus the Heraclitean and then, once he came to develop his theory of forms, having been under the influence of Socrates, he exploited some Pythagorean ideas, though changing their name ('participation' instead of 'imitation'). In this way Aristotle, who has developed no attitude of appreciating what does not amount to an explicit claim (a *doxa*, a theory, a teaching), clearly concentrates only on the Plato who openly professes theories of his own, and thus on the period of interest for the philosophies of the past, while skipping the period of the aporetic dialogues. Moreover, he does not say how long the period was marked by the prevailing influence of Socrates. Therefore we are permitted to conjecture that the Socratic period and the season of the first *Sokratikoi logoi* written by the group covered a long and important period of Plato's life.

45 It is tempting to add, although only in the simplified manner a footnote allows, that the Plato involved in a dramatic battle with Protagoras (*Tht.*), Parmenides (*Tht., Prm., Sph.*) and Gorgias (*Sph.*) pays great honour to these men of the past and no doubt treats them as subtle and powerful intellectuals, but still the battle remains, a struggle to avoid their

strictures. In these conditions, should not we conclude that he continued to be rather cold towards them?

46 The much disputed problem of the identity of presocratic philosophy cannot properly be addressed here, of course; however, it is equally inconceivable to ignore it. On this subject it is necessary to mention at least the recent exchanges between G.E.R. Lloyd and A. Laks (in Laks and Louguet (eds.), *Qu'est-ce que la philosophie présocratique? What is Presocratic Philosophy?*).

47 G.E.R. Lloyd, 'Le pluralisme de la vie intellectuelle avant Platon', in A. Laks and C. Louguet (eds), *Qu'est-ce que la philosophie présocratique? What is Presocratic Philosophy?*, p.39.

Chapter 3

Aristotle and the Pre-Socratics

Thomas M. Robinson

Given the amount that has been written on the question of Aristotle's attitude towards his various presocratic forbears, it would seem prima facie temerarious even to think, let alone to set out to show, that anything significantly new can be said on the matter, particularly in the compass of a relatively short essay. If there is anything most of us think we know, it is that Aristotle tended to view his predecessors through the lens of his own philosophical preoccupations, with some frequently very skewed results. And it is tempting simply to go over this familiar ground, using perhaps the seminal work of Cherniss[1] as a point of departure and assessing the strengths and weaknesses of his various criticisms, along with attempts of various critics of Cherniss[2] to rehabilitate the master in one way or another.

It is, however, a temptation I plan to resist. Instead, I shall simply state very quickly a couple of major instances where I think Aristotle allows his interests to get in the way of what seems to be a more plausible interpretation, and then pass on to a story of more positive achievements that seems to me remarkable. So let me simply say at once that his preoccupation with *archai* can and does lead him to severe misunderstandings, such as his supposed discovery of two of them in Parmenides, 'hot' and 'cold' (a reference, presumably, to Parmenides B9.1 DK), a misunderstanding he then compounds by ranking them with being and non-being, respectively (*Metaph.* 987a1–2). And the same could be said of his too easy assertion that Heraclitus flouts the principle of non-contradiction (see, for example, *Phys.* 185b19ff; though for a more cautious statement see *Metaph.* 1005b23). The list could be greatly added to, particularly if we follow the lead of Cherniss, but I shall simply leave behind for the moment such well-covered terrain.

Instead, I shall concentrate my attention on Aristotle and the one Pre-Socratic who by common consent is the giant on the scene before the appearance of Socrates, namely Parmenides. Here some remarkable things of a positive nature can be said, in terms of our understanding of Parmenides, the post-Parmenidean philosophers, Plato, Aristotle himself, and in some measure Western philosophy since Aristotle, and I shall spend the rest of the chapter trying to show this in detail.

Let me begin with a verb, *noein*, and its various cognate nouns *noos, noema* and *noesis*. We first run into the word, in presocratic philosophy, in fragment 24 of Xenophanes, where his one god '*oulos noei*', a phrase usually translated as 'thinks as a whole' or 'thinks as a totality' or some such. It is a verb of, in von Fritz's words,[3] 'realizing the situation', at any rate some four fifths of the time that it is found in the Homeric poems. On some occasions it can be used in broader senses, and sometimes can even possibly be best translated as 'think', but in the majority of instances, as von Fritz, Guthrie, Heitsch and others have pointed out,[4] it is a word indicating 'coming to recognize', 'coming to be aware of', 'coming to realize', 'coming to detect' something. Which is to say, it is being used in a large number if not indeed the majority of instances as a verb of cognitive achievement, closely analogous to the verb *gignoskein*.

I have inferred from this that, as an operating principle of interpretation, one should carefully investigate this possibility every time we meet the term in presocratic philosophy, and adopt it as the plausible interpretation if and when the proximate and overall context so suggests. The results, when one looks at the poem of Parmenides, are startling. We learn that, duly instructed by the goddess, Parmenides can 'come to recognize' (*noesai*) two routes of inquiry that are available to him, the 'is and necessarily is' route, the other (which turns out to be a pseudo-route, we soon learn) the 'is not and necessarily is not' route. The subject of 'is' here, which at this early stage can only have as its subject 'whatever this poem turns out to be talking about', is in fact usefully offered to us by contraposition in lines 2.7–8; it is 'that which is' (*to eon*), however we eventually unravel the sense or senses of 'is'.

The same sentence equally usefully tells us that what-is is that which one can 'come to know' (*gignoskein*) or 'point to in words' (*phrazein*, that is, verbalize in ostensive definition). In what seems to be an immediately subsequent sentence of explanation (fragment 3), this time involving the synonym *noein*, we learn that 'to be' and to 'come to know' are 'the same'. The sentence has tied commentators in knots for much too long. We have no need to follow Vlastos in seeing Parmenides as some sort of proto-Berkeley, proclaiming *esse* is *percipi*, or any of the other commentators who try desperately to make sense of a supposed claim that being and thinking are in some way conceptually locked.[5] The much more reputable and straightforward thing being claimed is that coming to know that p and p are 'the same' in that soft, commonsense usage of the word 'same' found frequently in the writings of Parmenides's contemporary, Heraclitus, that is, *conceptually tied* in some interesting and important way, like, in Kirk's words, 'succeeding or being succeeded by, each other and nothing else', or being 'connected through being different stages in a single invariable process'.[6]

The same misunderstandings of the import of *noein* have led commentators into all sorts of misunderstandings of the opening lines of fragment 6, the natural sense of which is surely as follows: 'What is there for *ascertaining* (*noein*) and for *picking out in words* (*legein*) (cf. earlier *phrazein*, "pointing to in words") *is*; for it is *available* for being, whereas *nothing* is *not* available.' That is to say, of two apparently possible candidates for the title 'real' only one turns out to be a genuine candidate, and that is the candidate which is the object of a process of coming-to-know and/or an act of ostensive definition. This on the assumption, naturally, given the time at which Parmenides is writing, of a thing ontology not a fact ontology, and a vision theory of knowledge, not a state of affairs theory. Or, to put it differently, 'If I come to know x (in the sense of "come intellectually to 'see'" x"), then x'; or in more recognizably contemporary terms, 'If I come to know that p, then p'.

This clarified, we can turn to the astonishing fragment 8, which has been interpreted by some to be Parmenides' attempt to describe the real world, by contrast with a world we think to be real but is in fact illusory.[7] But it is the interpretation which has a better claim to be dubbed illusory. While the subject of the poem is indeed 'that which is' or 'the real', the critical limiting factor in the description is that it is the real seen as a whole (*oulon*, 8.4, 8.38) or as a totality (*pan*, 8.5, 8.11, 8.22, 8.24 and so on). Once this optic is established, it becomes clear that, like the rest of his predecessors and contemporaries, Parmenides is interested in the universe. What distinguishes him from them in a very interesting way is his satisfaction that, in contradistinction perhaps to Xenophanes (B34 DK), he is an epistemological optimist in one crucial respect. Knowledge of the universe is possible, he is suggesting, but from a very precise optic: that is, when seen in its totality as a universe, not in terms of its component parts, structures and operations, and also simply in terms of its reality as such, not its reality as qualified in various ways. Simply *qua* real and as a totality it is the following things: *qua* real and as a totality eternal, though everything composing it is in time; *qua* real and as a totality undifferentiated, though differentiated in all other respects; *qua* real and as a totality unchanging and unchangeable, though changeable in all other respects; *qua* real and as a totality unmoving and immovable, though everything composing it is subject to movement; *qua* real and as a totality ungenerated, though everything composing it is subject to genesis; *qua* real and as a totality imperishable, though everything composing it is subject to destruction; *qua* real and as a totality complete, in the sense that there is nothing that could be conceivably added to it that is not already part of it; and finally, *qua* real and as a totality finite, and 'ball-like' in its mass or dimensionality (*onkos*), that is, shaped like what a commonsense viewing of the heavens would suggest, a sphere.

The same universe, viewed this time from the optic of opinion (*doxa*), and by that very token in terms of its hugely variant component parts, structures and operations, is precisely the world of everyday observation. On the details of this, philosophers will have their own particular views, and these will have varying degrees of plausibility, while being of their nature never something beyond *doxa*. The version outlined to Parmenides by the goddess, of which only a few tantalizing fragments exist as what is now called the Way of Seeming, is, in the very *kosmos* (ordering? structure?) of the language the goddess must use to articulate it, deceptive (*apatelon*, 8.52, 8.60). But what emerges is nonetheless, she says, something *plausible* (*eoikota*, 8.60) as such a *diakosmos* (arrangement) of language, and sufficient to overcome the attempts of any competing *doxai* to better it (8.61), though its basic weakness, shared with other *doxai*, will still be its pluralist stance. In it *two* forms for reality have been named (night and day), whereas *knowledge* will have as its object *one* form, whose name to cover the totality (*pan*) is *to eon* ('the real', or 'that which is') (8.53–4, along with 'Cornford's fragment'; see D. Gallop, *Parmenides of Elea,* Toronto, ON: University of Toronto Press, 1984, p.91).

With this by way of background we can finally turn to Aristotle. At *Physics* 1.2 we have a discussion of Parmenides, in which he is taken to task for failure to appreciate some critical ambiguities in the verb 'to be'. In so criticizing, Aristotle is in the company of a long line of commentators, but what is seldom adverted to is the fact that he sees Parmenides to be talking about the cosmos, and moreover the cosmos we know (185b6); there is no hint that he sees him to be saying that the cosmos we know is illusory and/or that Parmenides is committed to any form of monism, numerical or otherwise. And in this he has surely got Parmenides right; his attacks, whatever their strengths or weaknesses, are not directed at a straw man.

If what I am saying here has an air of paradoxicality, in that commentators since the beginning have tended to see Parmenides as nothing if not a monist, this is because of a misunderstanding, I would argue, of the basic epistemological stance of the poem, starting with a misunderstanding of the import and importance of the verb *noein*. And it is a misunderstanding, I will further argue, that Aristotle very effectively avoids. But I must of course justify my own heterodoxy of interpretation here, and will attempt to do so without further ado.

In a remarkable and much-read (and, more importantly, misread) passage of the *De anima*, Aristotle talks of perceiving (*to aisthanesthai*) as being analogous to 'coming to know' (*to noein*), and on the strength of this distinction builds his case for a description of rational soul as being receptive of an 'object of knowledge' (a *noeton*) in the way that the faculty of sense is receptive of an 'object of sensation' (an *aistheton*) (3.4.2–3). On the face of it, given the large-scale use of the verb *noein* as a verb of cognitive achievement, as we have just been seeing, this is an effective and potentially very fruitful analogy to draw, and in so doing Aristotle has a predecessor, it seems, in Democritus, who according to John Philoponus took the further step of actually *equating* the two (A 105 DK).

If I have called this famous passage 'much misread', however, it is because English-language translators, from Hicks to the most recent,[8] invariably take Aristotle's analogy to be between 'thinking' and perceiving, rather than between 'coming to know' and perceiving, with results that Aristotle himself would surely have rejected out of hand. On the face of it there is no analogy whatever between the discursive *process* that is thinking and the specific *act* of coming-to-awareness that is perception, and a translation which suggests that there *is* irretrievably obscures Aristotle's intention. So intellect is 'nothing at all actually before it comes to know/comes to be aware', not 'nothing at all actually before it thinks' (429a24). Or again, intellect is 'at this stage ... capable of coming to know/coming to be aware of itself', not 'at this stage ... capable of thinking itself' (429b9). Or '[a]ssuming that the intellect is something simple and impassive, how will it come to know/come to be aware <of something>, if coming to know/coming to be aware of <something> is to undergo/be subjected to (*paschein*) something?', not 'How will it think, if to think is to be acted upon?' (429b23–5). Or 'mind is in a manner potentially those things that are knowable, but none of them in actuality until it comes to know them', not 'mind is in a manner potentially all objects of thought, but is actually none of them until it thinks' (429b30–31).

One could go on with examples like this, but enough have been cited to make the point. The translators are missing a crucial and beautifully clear analogy because they have failed to see that Aristotle is building his case upon the time-honoured use of the verb *noein* as a verb of cognitive achievement, a case that Greek readers, fully aware of this use, would have understood at once for the very forceful, and prima facie very plausible, thing that it is. Let me reinforce the point with a brief look at the *Metaphysics*, before returning to the Pre-Socratics.

In so doing I should like to begin with a question. Aristotle, like any other philosopher, is allowed to make mistakes, so why could he not be making the mistake of indeed claiming that *thinking* and perceiving are analogous activities, so proving all our English-language translators right after all? But this will not work. As it turns out, Aristotle has some excellent fail-safe techniques to protect his Greek-language readers at any rate from any possible misunderstanding of his intentions. Already, in the *De anima* (429b9) he had made it clear that synonymous verbs for *noein* were 'to discover' (*heurein*) and 'to learn' (*mathein*), both verbs of cognitive achievement, not of simple thinking. And here in the *Metaphysics* he strengthens the point by referring to the act of *noein* as one of 'coming into contact with (*thinganon*), that is, coming to be aware of (*noon*)' its appropriate object (1072b21).

If this is right (and I think it is), important clarity has been achieved on how right Aristotle is in his understanding of a major crux in the thinking of Parmenides and just what he was able himself to build as a philosopher upon that understanding. On the Parmenidean base that 'coming to be aware that p entails p' he is able to construct his own case that the Pure Act which is the Prime Mover is an eternal moment of coming to awareness of its appropriate object which is itself. Using the synonyms Aristotle has himself supplied us with, this Act must be described as something along the lines of 'eternal self-discovery', 'eternal self-ascertainment' or the like, where we try, impossibly, to imagine such discovery or ascertainment as without antecedent process or consequent state, and also as occurring at that eternal *moment* which is eternity rather than across some eternal *period of duration* which for most people passes as eternity.

Just how hard it is to think this way becomes clear when we see Aristotle affirming that this eternal Act is also 'life' (*zoe*) (1072b26), where the very word suggests continuity. In this context he is prepared to talk of the eternity of the Prime Mover as an act of continuous (*syneches*) eternity (1072b29), but it seems to me it would be a mistake to allow this single use of the word, in which the term 'continuity' might understandably be taken to suggest sequential duration, to override what he has elsewhere established with a good deal of philosophical rigour as his genuine intention in the matter.[9] In an earlier passage (407a7), for example, he talks of *noesis* as being *syneches* ('continuous') in a way analogous to the continuity and oneness one ascribes to intellect (*nous*). That is, one must imagine it in its single momentariness as an act, and in its therefore being indivisible – even, as we would say, logically – into further separable moments of before and after.

So far I have mentioned how Aristotle has done two things, getting Parmenides right on a key point, possibly *the* key point, in his epistemology, and being able to build something extraordinary of his own on the basis of it. But a third achievement, of which Aristotle could not possibly have been aware, must be pointed out too, and that is the light all this throws on some hitherto obscure passages of presocratic (and, for that matter, Platonic) writings. Now, finally, we can see some clear reason why Diogenes of Apollonia chose to call his supreme principle *noesis*, by contrast with the choice of his contemporary Anaxagoras to call it *nous*. In a choice of term which is no accident (that is not an Aristotelian pun), he stresses the eternal *activity* that is divine intellection (B3 DK), just as it is no accident (again, no pun) that he goes on, in a phrase replete with consequences, to state for the first time in the history of philosophy a doctrine of teleology (things are 'disposed in the best possible way'), and to clearly link the two (ibid.).

If, like the Socrates of the *Phaedo*,[10] Aristotle had problems finding the teleology he sought in the activities of the *nous* of Anaxagoras, he must undoubtedly have found it in the *noesis* (and with it, the teleological stance) of Diogenes. As for his description of the Prime Mover as *noesis noeseos* ('ascertainment of ascertainment', *Metaph*. 1074b34–5), it seems clear that he is consciously opting for the contribution of Diogenes to our understanding here, rather than that of Anaxagoras.

Turning to an earlier thinker, Xenophanes, we can now with much greater clarity see what he was after in claiming that his one supreme divinity 'sees as a totality, *noei* as a totality, and hears as a totality' (B24 DK). English-language translators have invariably translated *noei* here as 'thinks',[11] as we saw them doing when they met the same verb in Parmenides. But enough has now been said, thanks not least to the guidance provided by Aristotle, to suggest that this is not what Xenophanes would have had in mind at all. The supreme god, he is much more likely to be saying, 'comes to know' as a totality, or 'comes to be aware' as a totality. If there is any residual doubt that he means this, it is surely put to rest by the use of the other two verbs in the quotation, 'see' and 'hear', both of them verbs of perception and both of them in that regard, as Aristotle stressed, precisely analogous to a fundamental verb of cognitive achievement, *noein*.

What all this means is that, in getting Parmenides right on a fundamental epistemological point, Aristotle has allowed us to see what has long remained hidden, and that is an extraordinary dynamism in what one might call the cosmotheology and epistemology of Xenophanes, Parmenides and Diogenes of Apollonia, a dynamism that Plato in turn builds upon in the *Republic*, where *noesis*, the fourth stage of cognition in the Line, represents the final stage of the mind's intellectual progress, in which the mind/soul comes to know/comes to be aware of the Forms, and where Plato in his turn employs three striking metaphors to describe it as the act of apprehension that it is: *opsis* ('catching sight of', 507b9ff), *haphe* ('catching hold of', 490b3) and, dramatically, *mixis* ('copulating with', 490b5).[12] It is Plato's fail-safe technique, analogous to the use of *heurein* and *mathein* that we saw in Aristotle, to ensure that his readers know exactly what he has in mind by his use of the dynamic verb *noein*.

It also allows us to start achieving clarity on just what Parmenides' immediate successors in cosmology, Empedocles, Anaxagoras and Democritus/Leucippus were supposed to be reacting to. Accepted wisdom (challenged most recently by Curd, though on grounds very different from the ones I am myself proposing[13]) has it that Parmenides held to an unconscionable cosmological monism, a 'radical critique of commonsense belief in the world about us', which needed to be responded to by particular devices, such as the affirmation of pluralism or the affirmation of empty space or the affirmation of eternal motion.[14] But the trouble with this theory is that it is almost impossible to find evidence in their writings that they had found anything unconscionable about Parmenides at all. On the contrary, they show every evidence of accepting from him with gratitude a couple of principles which, once articulated, were perceived to be self-evident ('Why didn't we think of that?') and incorporated without comment into their own and most subsequent philosophical theory. I am thinking, of course, of the principles that (a) if there is something, there has always been something, and (b) if there is something, there will always be something. Apart from that, they simply take issue with him as a cosmologist, accepting this point, rejecting that, and building up their own cosmological systems.

On the reading of Parmenides that I have argued to be that of Aristotle, none of this is surprising. If Aristotle is on the right track, as I think he is, especially in the area of Parmenides's epistemology, they would have seen the content of the two ways of Parmenides as being one and the same universe viewed from two different optics, and moreover exactly the same universe that they were themselves trying to describe. They would I think have been totally mystified by the later tradition which credited him with two universes, one of them illusory. So, as a bonus, getting a clear understanding of just how insightful Aristotle's understanding is, especially, as I have indicated, of Parmenides's all-important and much-misinterpreted epistemology, turns out to be valuable as a guide to the understanding of the something which is itself *prima facie* very strange, and that is the relative calmness with which his supposedly hair-raising doctrines appear, from what evidence we have, to have been greeted.

It might be suggested, at this stage, that there is evidence that two of Parmenides' possible pupils, Zeno and Melissus, show little sign of understanding Parmenides in the way that has just been described, and in fact appear to argue that the world of sense is indeed illusory. But this too seems to be doubtful. To take the case of Melissus first, he too, with Parmenides, clearly understands the real as 'all of it', using Parmenides' own term *pan* (D2, DK), and agrees with him that this *pan* is eternal (ibid.). Where he disagrees is on its supposed limitedness, arguing instead that it is without a boundary (B3) in space as well as in time. In a further fragment (B9) we learn that, again in disagreement with Parmenides, he infers from the oneness of *to eon pan* that it has no 'body' (*soma*) or 'bulk' (*pachos*). This is certainly a puzzling statement by any reckoning, but considerably less so if we understand him to mean by the phrase 'not having bulk' that it is not a physical object. This would also, as it happens, be a natural conclusion to draw from its unlimitedness in space, and as such it serves as a very useful counterweight to the tendency of most Greek cosmologists other than the atomists to put a curved boundary to space, and hence to assume that it is a physical object on an ontological par with its own component parts (for a significant example, see the argument of Timaeus at *Tim.* 28b–c).

If this is true, Melissus is in effect agreeing that, if we are talking about *to eon pan*, Parmenides is right on all but one point, its supposed possession of bulk. And in this, Melissus appears to be saying, Parmenides works against himself, since, if the real as a totality has a boundary, as Parmenides asserts, it is as such a physical object and hence by that very token in possession of parts.

The same can be said of the famous fragment 8, once we realize that, in talking about 'the one <reality>', Melissus is following Parmenides in talking about 'the real in its totality'. 'If < the real in its totality> were a plurality,' he says, each of these plural things would have to be like what he says 'the *one*' <real as a totality> is. As for his further attack on the senses in this fragment, he appears to reiterate in his own terminology what Parmenides had been saying about the world of sense, that is, that it is a world of opinion (*doxa*) not truth (*aletheia*). It is simply the one real *qua* real and in its totality that is for him 'genuinely real' (*eon alethinon*) and 'unchanging'; the objects of the world of sense perception, by contrast, 'seem to us' (*dokei hemin*) to be subject to change, and hence can never be genuinely real in the way the one, unchanging <real as a totality> is.

What this appears to mean is that Melissus, like Parmenides, is attacking, not plurality as such, but the claim that a world of plurality will offer us anything more than *doxa*. It is in no way a claim that such a world is illusory, but rather a claim, foreshadowing Platonism, that, on a scale of reality, it is less genuinely real than that same world seen simply in terms of its reality and as a totality. As for his final claim that, if the real were a plurality, 'things would have to be of just the same nature as the one' (that is, as the one reality as a totality), this seems to be fully in line with Parmenides, fragment 8: if viewed simply in terms of their reality, a putative multiplicity of such realities would, by the law of the identity of indiscernibles, constitute that *single* reality the existence of which it was Parmenides' aim to demonstrate.

Similar things can be said of Zeno's claims too, from what little survives of them. On the assumption that what is under discussion is Parmenides' 'reality as a totality', we find Zeno arguing (B1 DK) that, if it were multiple, any particular within it would both have a size and not have a size, and that the total number of such particulars would be both finite and infinite (B3). The points being made are logical ones, and serve to corroborate, to Zeno's satisfaction, a case that I have previously mentioned in terms of the identity of indiscernibles: if what is under discussion is reality as a totality, any putative 'parts' or components thereof will be seen to be just that, putative, thanks to the contradictory characteristics with which they would necessarily be endowed.

The same might be said of the so-called 'arguments against motion', for the details of which we must rely on Aristotle; but the picture here is less clear. Whether we see space and time as infinitely divisible or composed of indivisible *minima*, either way, argues Zeno, paradoxical consequences will be produced. Whether this meant, however, that he believed (or thought Parmenides believed) that the world of sense perception is illusory is very doubtful. As a skilled debater, probably against

Pythagoreans, he is interested in scoring points, not in describing the world. And Parmenides' claim that the real as such and as a totality is immobile will of course be shown to be true *a fortiori* if even the world of apparently moving sense-objects can, by a suitable display of logical gymnastics, be demonstrated to be characterized, paradoxically, by immobility. Or so one might, I hope reasonably, speculate; the exact nature and objectives of Zeno's paradoxes are still a matter of scholarly dispute, and they will continue to constitute somewhat hazardous evidence, one way or the other, in any attempt to put together the *Rezeptionsgeschichte* of Parmenides' poem.

Let me conclude with what seems to me a fourth major achievement of Aristotle, and that is his ability, using Parmenides as his base, to set in place procedures for further constructive philosophizing, even, paradoxically, when he himself may not fully have understood an argument at issue. I shall offer just two examples, the details of which deserve a study in themselves, but the main point they exemplify seems instructive.

The first has to do with that old chestnut the verb 'to be'. On this, like so many who have followed him, Aristotle has problems making sense of the detail of Parmenides' claims, but his great contribution to philosophy, and to the search for a solution to the puzzle, is his recognition of just how ambiguous the verb is (see, for example, *Phys.* 185a20ff). The point here is the recognition of the ambiguity, not the clarification by reference to substance and accident that Aristotle himself takes to be the most philosophically instructive way to elucidate the problem, and it is further work *investigating* such ambiguity in recent decades, led by some splendid research by Kahn,[15] that has probably thrown more light on Parmenides than was thrown in the previous two millennia.

The second has to do with the concept of sameness, a concept that undoubtedly puzzled Aristotle, as it puzzles us, as we struggle to make sense of some of the more paradoxical-looking claims of both Heraclitus and Parmenides. Again, it is Aristotle's *recognition* of ambiguity in the use of the word 'same' rather than his own particular *analysis* of the ambiguity in terms of substance and accident that is of lasting value, a recognition thanks to which, as I have tried to show, we can now make sufficient sense of the peculiar use of the word 'same' by both Heraclitus and Parmenides as to absolve both of them from any suspicion of either breaking the law of non-contradiction (Heraclitus) or prefiguring Berkeleyan idealism (Parmenides).[16] So in this regard, too, Aristotle turns out to be illuminating as a critic of his predecessors in ways he might not perhaps have imagined. And the philosophical enterprise has, thanks to him, as a result moved perceptibly further forward.

Notes

1 H. Cherniss, *Aristotle's Criticism of Presocratic Philosophy* (Baltimore, MD: Johns Hopkins University Press, 1935).
2 See, for example, M.C. Stokes, *One and Many in Greek Philosophy* (Washington, DC: Center for Hellenic Studies, 1971), pp. 24–6.

3   K. von Fritz, '*Noos* and *noein* in the Homeric poems', *Classical Philology* 38 (1943): 86.
4   von Fritz, ibid.; W.K.C. Guthrie, *A History of Greek Philosophy* (Cambridge: Cambridge University Press, 1962), vol. 1; C.H. Kahn, 'The thesis of Parmenides', *Review of Metaphysics* 22 (1969): 700–724; A.P.D. Mourelatos, *The Route of Parmenides* (New Haven, CT: Yale University Press, 1970); E. Heitsch, *Xenophanes: Die Fragmente* (Munich: Artemis Verlag, 1983). For a thoughtful discussion of the matter see J.H. Lesher, *Xenophanes of Colophon* (Toronto, ON: University of Toronto Press, 1992), p.103 n.2.
5   See G. Vlastos, 'Review of J. Zafiropoulo, *L'Ecole éléate* (Paris 1950)', *Gnomon* 25 (1953): 168.
6   G.S. Kirk, J.E. Raven, and M. Schofield, *The Presocratic Philosophers*, 2nd edn (Cambridge: Cambridge University Press, 1983), p.189.
7   Mourelatos, *Route of Parmenides*, pp.359ff.
8   For example, R.D. Hicks, *Aristotle: De anima* (Cambridge: Cambridge University Press, 1907), J.A. Smith (in Richard McKeon (ed.), *The Basic Works of Aristotle*, New York: Random House, 1941), and H.G. Apostle and Lloyd P. Gerson, *Aristotle: Selected Works* (Grinnell, Iowa: The Peripatetic Press, 3rd edn, 1991).
9   A reference to the supposed 'continuity' of *noesis* at 1074b29 can be discounted, since it refers to the non-state of affairs that *nous* (= the Prime Mover) is supposedly potency rather than actuality. Since it is in fact actuality, its *noesis* is the same, an act that involves no process and is as a result not subject to the type of continuity that could ever be described as 'wearisome' (*epiponon*).
10 *Phaedo*, 97bff.
11 See, for example, Kirk, Raven, and Schofield, *Presocratic Philosophers*, and Lesher, *Xenophanes*.
12 That the reference of *mixis* is to sexual intercourse, not to some generalized 'intermingling', seems clear from the whole account of the soul's drive towards knowledge in terms of the pains and travail of eros.
13 Patricia Curd, *The Legacy of Parmenides* (Princeton, NJ: Princeton University Press, 1998), pp.4–5.
14 See, for example, the account offered in *Presocratic Philosophers*, p.351.
15 C.H. Kahn, 'The Greek verb "to be" and the concept of being', *Foundations of Language* 2 (1966): 245–65, 'The thesis of Parmenides' (1969); *The verb 'be' in ancient Greek* (Dordrecht: Reidel,1973); 'Retrospect on the verb "to be" and the concept of being', in S. Knuuttila and J. Hintikka (eds), *The Logic of Being* (Dordrecht: Reidel, 1986).
16 See above, pp.37–38.

Chapter 4

Nietzsche on the Beginnings of Western Philosophy

Gareth B. Matthews

As almost any student of philosophy will be able to tell you, Western philosophy begins with the Pre-Socratics: Thales, Anaximander, Anaximines, Xenophanes, Heraclitus, Pythagoras, Parmenides, Zeno, Empedocles, Anaxagoras, Leucippus and Democritus. The extant writings of these philosophers are canonically collected in that great classic of philosophical scholarship, *Die Fragmente der Vorsokratiker*, put together by Hermann Diels and Walther Kranz at the end of the nineteenth century and first published in 1903.

Lecturers on the history of ancient Greek philosophy today, like me, may be embarrassed by having to call all the philosophers in Diels and Kranz 'presocratic philosophers'. That embarrassment may have more than one source. First of all, it may be embarrassing to have to tell students that philosophy began when someone said that everything is water. After all, that claim is so obviously false that it is hard to understand why anyone should get everlasting credit for making it. There is another problem with the water claim, besides its implausibility. However it is understood, it hardly seems to be philosophical at all; therefore it is not, it seems, even a plausible candidate for being the first philosophical pronouncement in Western culture.

Nietzsche shows sympathy for this first sort of embarrassment when, in his *Die Philosophie im tragischen Zeitalter der Griechen*, he writes: 'Greek philosophy seems to begin with an absurd notion, with the proposition that water is the primal origin and the womb of all things. Is it really necessary for us to show respect for this proposition and take it seriously?' (TZ 16, 38–9).[1] Nietzsche also tries to deal with the second source of embarrassment, as I shall explain in a moment.

There is, however, quite a different source of embarrassment in store for anyone who feels called upon to announce to students that all the figures in Diels and Kranz are presocratic philosophers. They are obviously not all *pre*socratic, at least not in the obvious sense of living and teaching before the time of Socrates, or even being born before Socrates. Thus Democritus, for one, was born almost a decade after Socrates, as was the Sophist, Prodicus, who also appears in Diels and Kranz. What many of us do in response to this 'calendar' or dating worry is to mumble something about the towering importance of Socrates himself and the extremely close connection between Socrates and Plato. The term 'presocratic' then becomes, we may say, a term of mere taxonomical convenience.

When Friedrich Nietzsche delivered his lectures on the earliest Western philosophers at the University of Basel in the summer semester of 1872,[2] he insisted on putting Socrates together with the Pre-Socratics into the group of earliest Western philosophers. Thus the topic of his lectures was 'The Pre-*Platonic* Philosophers'. Coming to understand why Nietzsche grouped Socrates with the presocratic philosophers will be part of coming to understand Nietzsche's ideas about the beginning of Western philosophy.

However, before we consider the question of whether Socrates should be lumped together with his predecessors, or allowed to take his customary place of honour beside his great pupil, Plato, and Plato's great pupil, Aristotle, I want to raise some issues about what it might mean to think of someone as the very first philosopher. How does there ever come to be a first – the first artist, the first musician, the first scientist or the first philosopher? There are several interesting issues here. One issue we might call the 'Self-Conception Issue'. Does one have to think of oneself as an artist or scientist or philosopher to count as the first person of that sort? Does one even have to have the concept of an artist, scientist or philosopher to count as the first artist, scientist or philosopher?

My old teacher, Donald Williams, once told those of us in his lecture class on seventeenth-century philosophy about an exam he had set that included the question, 'Discuss Descartes's claim to be the father of modern philosophy'. One waggish student had responded to this question with the one-sentence answer, 'Descartes didn't claim to be the father of modern philosophy', and then gone on to answer the next question. Williams, after waiting a moment for the laughter in the class to die down, then went on to add, in his appealingly breathless lecture style, 'But he did!' That is, according to Williams, Descartes did claim to be the first modern philosopher.

In a certain way Williams seems to have been right. Descartes did think of himself as making a new beginning in philosophy. Even if he did not have much of a conception of what modern philosophy would turn out to be, he certainly did want to make a break with philosophy's past. But can we reasonably think of Thales as aiming to be the first exemplar of a whole new type of thinker, the philosopher? Does it matter? Might he have a reasonable claim to be the first philosopher, even if he himself did not make any claim to that distinction, or even show any evidence that he thought of himself as exemplifying a new *typos*, that is, a *typos* never before exemplified in Western culture?

I once saw a remarkably imaginative show at the Museum of Modern Art in New York, the MOMA, called 'Primitive Art and Twentieth Century Art'. The curator who put the show together, William Rubin, had juxtaposed, on the one hand, paintings and pieces of sculpture by the most prominent twentieth-century artists and, on the other hand, masks and figurines produced by indigenous people in Africa, Asia, Australasia and South and Central America. In some cases Rubin was able to claim that the Picasso or Giacometti, or whatever it was among the twentieth-century works displayed, had been directly influenced in its production by the artist's having actually seen the juxtaposed tribal mask or figure. In other cases Rubin could plausibly claim at least a great and obvious affinity between the modern work and the tribal piece.

Some critics have questioned whether we should think of, say, a ceremonial mask or a fertility doll produced by a tribal artisan as a work of art at all, since it was not made to be displayed in an art gallery or in the home or castle of a wealthy art patron. Proponents of the 'museum theory' of what makes something count as a work of art can respond to this worry by saying that the tribal pieces are clearly works of art because they have been shown in some of our best and most prestigious art museums. On this view, it does not matter what was in the mind of the tribal artisan when he produced the mask or figure; the work is art because it has found a recognized place in an art museum.

Applying this test to Thales, Anaximander, Anaximines and the other so-called 'presocratic philosophers', we could say that it does not matter how they thought of themselves or conceived what they were doing. When Plato and Aristotle and other self-described philosophers reached back to Thales and his Milesian confrères to incorporate them into their own philosophical discourse, those early thinkers came to count as philosophers. We could dub this 'the museum theory' of what counts as a philosopher.

One trouble with the museum theory, whether of art or of philosophy, is that it seems to leave no room for any interesting discussion of what *ought* to be counted as art or philosophy, that is, a discussion of what truly belongs in the art or philosophy museum. That seems wrong, or at the very least, unfortunate. Even if we are prepared to count as art some, or much, or even most of the tribal masks and figures that have been displayed in the most prestigious art museums, we should still be able to have a reasonable discussion about whether this or that piece is, not just inferior art, but not even art at all.

The parallel in philosophy is obvious. Not everyone whose sayings Plato or Aristotle discusses in an admittedly philosophical context deserves to count as a philosopher. Solon does not. Nor does Homer or Aeschylus. So what about, say, Xenophanes? Is he a real philosopher? Or is he at most a borderline philosopher who should be included in our philosophy museum just in case someone turns something up by him that is arguably philosophical?

Perhaps what gives us the best justification for thinking of Thales as the first philosopher is that he was the first member of the Milesian school. Even if he did not think of himself as exemplifying the type, philosopher, the type was well established by the triumvirate, Thales, Anaximander and Anaximines, and he was the first member of that group. We could call this issue the 'Demarcation Issue'. What, in the end, distinguishes philosophy from science and the philosopher from the scientist? Could one as easily say that Thales was the first scientist in our Western tradition as say that he was the first philosopher? After all, he is credited with having predicted the solar eclipse in 585 BCE. Can one offer a reasonably plausible set of necessary and sufficient conditions for counting as a genuine philosopher, conditions that Thales, and no one before Thales, would satisfy?

A first thing to notice about Nietzsche's lectures on preplatonic philosophy is that he rejects the museum theory. Here is the way he begins his very first lecture:

Greek philosophy is usually considered by asking oneself, How far, in comparison with more recent philosophers, did the Greeks recognize and advance philosophical problems? We want to ask, What do we learn from the history of their philosophy *on behalf of the Greeks*? Not, What do we learn on behalf of philosophy? (VP 211 (3))

Two paragraphs later, Nietzsche says this:

So we want to show first that the Greeks, from out of themselves, had to do philosophy, and to what end. Secondly, we want to observe how *the philosopher* emerged among the Greeks, not just how philosophy emerged among them. To get to know the Greeks it is particularly important [to recognize] that some among them came to conscious reflection about themselves. Almost more important still than conscious reflection is their personality, their behavior. The Greeks created *philosopher types*. Think of the individually differentiated society of Pythagoras, Heraclitus, Empedocles, Parmenides, Democritus, Protagoras, and Socrates. The inventiveness in this group distinguishes the Greeks from all other peoples. (VP 212 (3–4))

So how does Nietzsche have any hope of understanding that, say, Thales was the first Western philosopher, if he does not work back from what we might call 'the philosophy museum of the nineteenth century', that is, the canon recognized by nineteenth-century European universities; or even from the philosophy museum of Plato's Academy or Aristotle's Lyceum, that is, from the list of philosophers Plato and Aristotle quote or refer to as philosophers? Surely he does not think that Thales and Anaximander and Anaximines already proclaimed themselves to be philosophers.

On this point Nietzsche makes a clever move. He notes that Greek culture recognized a type of figure, the Wise Man, or Sage, σοφὸς ἀνήρ, even as early as the seventh century BCE. Thus the 'Seven Sages', as spoken of by the Delphic Oracle, included Solon, as well as Thales. Nietzsche's idea seems to be that, once the figure of the sage, the σοφός is established in Greek culture, we can have a real philosopher as soon as we have a sage who thinks in a way that meets the criteria for doing philosophy.

According to Nietzsche, the figure of the wise person, the σοφὸς ἀνήρ, developed in Greek thought in these stages: (1) The Mythical Pre-Philosophical Stage, (2) The Sporadic-Proverbial Pre-Philosophical Stage, (3) The Pre-Philosophical Stage of the Wise Man, (4) The Philosopher. Whereas the proverbs Nietzsche has in mind when he talks about 'The Sporadic-Proverbial Pre-Philosophical Stage', Stage 2, are not really especially philosophical, those of Stage 3 are. They include such maxims as 'Moderation is best' (μέτρον ἄριστον) and 'Know Thyself' (γνῶθι σαυτόν).

What, according to Nietzsche, marked off Thales from thinkers at these earlier stages? Here is what he says:

Thales posits a principle from which he makes deductions; he is foremost a systematizer. It might be objected that, on the contrary, we already find the same force [*Kraft*] in much older cosmogonies. We need only think of the cosmogonical ideas in the *Iliad*, then the *Theogony*, then the Orphic theogonies ... [But] Thales is distinguished from these in that he is *unmythological*. His reflection is carried out in concepts. The *poet*, who represents a stage preliminary to the philosopher, was to be overcome. Why does Thales not fit together completely with the [other so-called] Seven Sages? He does not [just] philosophize sporadically, in separate proverbs; he not only makes one great scientific discovery but he also makes connections; he wants the whole, a world picture [*Weltbild*]. Thus, Thales overcomes (1) the mythic preliminary stage of philosophy, (2) the sporadic–proverbial form of philosophy, and (3) the various sciences – the first by thinking conceptually, the second by systematizing, and the third by creating one [unified] view of the world. Philosophy is therefore the art that presents an image of universal existence in concepts; this definition fits Thales first. Of course, a much later time recognized this. (VP 216–17 (7–8))

According to this passage one could say that the following is Nietzsche's definition of 'philosopher':

(D) x is a philosopher = df x is a wise person who thinks conceptually and systematically and who creates a unified picture of the world.

There is much one could quarrel with in this definition. For one thing, it seems to exclude Nietzsche himself from counting as a philosopher, since he does not think systematically. But what I want to focus on is a different sort of objection. This definition does not help us understand how it can be that the preplatonic philosophers are philosophically interesting to us today. In a way Nietzsche has already tried to disarm this objection by saying that his question is 'What do we learn from the history of [Greek] philosophy on behalf of the Greeks?' and not 'What do we learn on behalf of philosophy?' My reply is that we can only *recognize* these figures as philosophers insofar as we can find them interesting to philosophize with. The historian of philosophy who has not made reasonably clear what makes these figures worthwhile philosophizing with has not made clear why we should respect them as philosophers.

Both Plato and Aristotle suggest that philosophy begins in wonder (*thaumazein*). As I argue in *Socratic Perplexity and the Nature of Philosophy*,[3] the wonder, or astonishment, Plato and Aristotle have in mind is not anything like Kant's awe at the starry heavens above and the moral law within. Instead it is the surprised recognition that one does not know how to deal with puzzles about basic concepts one had thought were quite clear, concepts such as the concept of coming to be, of change, of passing away, of virtue and of weakness of will.

It is important to Nietzsche to insist that philosophy begins in the Western world when there are first examples of a certain type of wise person. What difference does it make whether one thinks of philosophy as something that begins with the appearance of a systematic conceptual thinker who creates a unified picture of the world or, as I should say, with a thinker whose thought is a response to the puzzled recognition that there is something basic in our way of thinking about ourselves and the world that is puzzling, even perplexing? Let me try to explain.

When I teach survey courses in ancient philosophy in which I begin with the presocratic philosophers, I try to point out general issues that I think these philosophers are interested in. Thus I tell my students that the first philosophers were focused on what I call 'the Problem of Change', which I might explain in terms of this reasoning:

1 If there is such a thing as change, one thing becomes another thing.
2 If one thing becomes another thing, one thing is replaced by another thing.
3 If one thing is replaced by another thing, nothing undergoes change.
4 If nothing undergoes change, there is no change.

Therefore

5 If there is such a thing as change, there is no change.

Clearly, the self-contradictory conclusion of this bit of chain reasoning is unacceptable. What has gone wrong? Which premise is to be rejected?

In fact, each of the above premises is ambiguous. Thus, for example, the consequent of the first premise, 'one thing becomes another thing', might mean 'one thing is replaced by another' or it might just mean 'something that was F is (now) G, where being F at any time, t, is incompatible with being G at that same time, t'.

But it is not just that each premise of this argument is, taken by itself, ambiguous. Any attempt to read each of the premises in such a way as to make it true, or at least plausible, will yield the result that there is equivocation from premise to premise and the argument as a whole will illustrate the fallacy of equivocation.

In the course of analysing this argument, my students and I come to realize that we need to distinguish between what Aristotelians call 'alteration' and what they call 'substantial change'. Having made some such distinction, we move towards the realization that the Milesians (Thales, Anaximander and Anaximines) can be seen as groping towards the idea that at least some change can be understood as alteration in a persisting substratum. Thus Thales might have noted that water comes in three different forms: solid, liquid and gas. And Anaximines seems to have realized that alteration might result from the compression or decompression of some air-like stuff. Such theoretically charged observations might lead to the thought that either change in temperature or change in pressure may, in a way, change one thing into another, even though, in another way, there is no new thing that results, since the underlying stuff persists throughout the change.

My approach to Thales, Anaximander and Anaximines is, of course, quite different from what we find in Nietzsche. Instead of focusing on a philosophical problem of change, he focuses on the philosophers, indeed, on types of philosophers, even, where possible, on philosopher-archetypes.

Both Nietzsche and I have to face the question, 'What relevance does preplatonic philosophy have for us today?' For Nietzsche the relevance arises from the special purity of the philosophical types that preplatonic philosophy offers us. For me its relevance arises primarily from the directness with which the preplatonic philosophers confront seemingly acceptable yet, as investigation shows, highly problematic theses. Thus, lest I become smug in thinking that distinctions later philosophers draw, for example, the Aristotelian distinction I used above between alteration and substantial change, I remind myself and my students of the metaphysical challenge that quantum physics seems to pose for us today. In a certain way, quantum physics, by telling us that quanta are not well-behaved, persisting particles, takes us back to the preplatonic philosophers and their efforts to deal with the problem of change.

To try to tease out what difference this contrast between Nietzsche and me might make I propose to concentrate for a while on what Nietzsche has to say about the last of the preplatonic philosophers, Socrates. Socrates, as it turns out, is a figure of unending interest for Nietzsche, as he is also for me. As I have already mentioned, I recently wrote a book, *Socratic Perplexity and the Nature of Philosophy*, in which I try to bring out something of the continuing significance of Socrates. Nietzsche, although he did not write an entire book on Socrates, discusses him in many of his works. 'Socrates, let me confess it,' he writes at one point, 'is so close to me that I am almost constantly doing battle with him.'[4] Here, in his lectures on the preplatonic philosophers, are some of the ways Nietzsche characterizes the philosophical archetype, Socrates.

1   He is not an aristocrat, but a plebeian. He is uneducated or, at least, as Nietzsche sometimes puts the matter, Socrates is self-taught.
2   He is ugly. He has a flat nose, thick lips and bulging eyes. Moreover, he suffers the greatest from natural passions.
3   The force of his considerable will, his *Willenskraft*, is directed towards ethical reform. This, Nietzsche claims, is his *single* interest.
4   What distinguishes his philosophical character is his belief that knowledge (επιστήμη), acquired through *dialectic* ... is the only path to the ethical reform he seeks.
5   In sum: he is the first philosopher of *life*, and all schools deriving from him are first of all philosophies of life. A life ruled by thought! Thinking serves life, while among all previous philosophers life had served thought and knowledge. Here the proper life appears as a purpose; there proper knowledge is the highest thing. (VP 353–4 (144–5))

My own conception of the philosophical type, Socrates, is quite different from this. For me, Socrates is the first and most striking example of a philosopher who finds all our basic ethical concepts philosophically problematic. Although he, like Meno in Plato's dialogue of that name, once thought he understood well enough what, say, virtue is, he is now immobilized by perplexity and does not know what to say in reply to some of the most basic questions about virtue. But, of course, he is not so immobilized that he cannot use elenctic examination to reduce his interlocutors to an equally paralysing perplexity. As he admits in reply to Meno's protest that he is a stingray, he is a stingray that also stings itself, a self-stinging stingray.

This image of Socrates as a self-stinging stingray is, I think, seminal to Western philosophy. Much, if not most, Western philosophy is either an attempt to show how problematic our concepts of time, change, causality, justice, knowledge, weakness of will and so on are, or else an attempt to produce theories and analyses that offer some hope of dissolving the Socratic perplexity.

Plato, of course, portrays Socrates, not just as a philosophical inquirer, but also as a proponent of philosophical theses, for example the thesis that knowledge is virtue. But Nietzsche understands this Socratic view of knowledge and virtue, not as a thesis that can be examined and criticized, but rather primarily as an expression of Socrates' character. 'Knowledge as the path to virtue differentiates his philosophical character,' he writes (VP 354 (145)). On my picture, the moral seriousness of Socrates' character is indeed linked to his elenctic pursuit of a satisfactory definition-style analysis of virtue, and the various specific virtues; but, in my view, Socrates is also extraordinarily good at bringing out the difficulties, the perplexities, that arise from trying to understand the very thesis that knowledge is virtue.

What philosophical difference does it make whether one accepts my picture of the philosophical type, Socrates, or Nietzsche's? For Nietzsche, the type, Socrates, and the other preplatonic philosopher types as well, are fascinating, intriguing, sometimes infuriating, philosophical personalities. 'I am going to tell the story of those philosophers, simplified,' he writes in the Preface to *Die Philosophie im tragischen Zeitalter der Griechen*. He continues:

> I will extract from each system only the point that is a piece of *personality* and belongs to what is incontrovertible and non-debatable, which history must preserve ... The task is to bring to light that which we must always love and honor and which no later enlightenment can take way: the great human person [*der grosse Mensch*]. (TZ 5–6(24))

If we follow Nietzsche and concentrate only on what is incontrovertible and non-debatable about these remarkable people, what will there be about them that we will be able to analyse, criticize or explain? It will be precisely their personalities. We will offer psychological analyses, critiques and explanations of those personalities, as well as historical analyses, critiques and explanations.

I certainly agree that these remarkable philosophers can be analysed psychologically and can also be fitted into their historical context. But if psychological analysis and historical positioning are the chief intellectual challenges they pose for us, their philosophical thinking will be largely lost on us. And to fail to enter into philosophical dialogue with them does them no honour.

What sorts of analysis of Socrates, in particular, does Nietzsche offer us? In the section on 'The Problem of Socrates' in *Twilight of the Idols*, a work published seventeen years after the lectures on preplatonic philosophy, Nietzsche expresses the 'irreverent thought that all the great sages are *types of decline* [*Niedergangstypen*]' (GD 61 (12)). He goes on to say that, already in his *Birth of Tragedy*, he had 'recognized Socrates and Plato to be symptoms of decay [*Verfalls-Sumptome*], tools of the Greek dissolution, pseudo-Greek, anti-Greek' (GD 62 (12)).

It turns out that the decay, or degeneration, Nietzsche has in mind, at least with respect to Socrates, is both individual and communal. He links what he calls the 'depravity and anarchy' [*Wüstheit und Anarchie*] in the instincts of Socrates, as well as the 'overdevelopment of the logical faculty' [*die Superfötation des Logischen*] (GD 63 (14)). 'I seek to understand,' he writes, 'what idiosyncrasy begot that Socratic equation, reason = virtue = happiness, that most bizarre of all equations, which, moreover, is opposed to all the instincts of the earlier Greeks' (ibid.).

Here is a further discussion, in *Twilight of the Idols*, of what one might call 'Socratic rationalism':

> One chooses dialectic only when no other means is available. One knows that it arouses mistrust and that it is not very persuasive. Nothing is easier to erase than the effect of a dialectician: the experience of every meeting at which there are speeches proves this. It can only be *self-defense* in the hands of those who no longer have any other weapon....
>   Is the irony of Socrates an expression of revolt? Of the mob's *ressentiment*? Does he, as one oppressed, enjoy his own ferocity in the knife-thrusts of his syllogisms? Does he avenge himself on the noble people whom he fascinates? As a dialectician, one holds a merciless tool in one's hand: one can become a tyrant by means of it; one compromises those one conquers. The dialectician leaves it to his opponent to prove that he is no idiot: he makes one furious and helpless at the same time. The dialectician renders the intellect of his opponent powerless. Is dialectic only a form of *revenge* in Socrates? (GD 64 (14–15))

Admittedly, these psychological judgements on the personality of Socrates are harsher than what one finds in the much earlier lectures, or in the manuscript, *Die Philosophie im tragischen Zeitalter der Griechen*. But they are similar in type to the earlier assessments.

As I have already allowed, there is certainly a place for psychological and historical analysis of philosophers, and not only of preplatonic philosophers, but even of philosophers of your personal acquaintance and mine. But if our primary response to any philosopher, whether ancient, modern or contemporary, is to analyse that thinker psychologically or historically, then, I maintain, we have shown no real respect for what that thinker most basically is, namely, a philosopher.

For many of us who love philosophy, it will not be enough to identify, classify and then analyse, psychologically and historically, the philosophers we study. So Nietzsche's approach to the beginnings of Western philosophy can be for us, at most, a first step in coming to terms with the preplatonic philosophers. To say it is only a first step is not, of course, to say that it is no step at all. But I am not myself going to spend much time thinking about Thales, or Anaxagoras, or Parmenides, or Socrates, unless I can find something in what they wrote or, according to testimony, something they said that engages me philosophically. In fact I find much in the preplatonic philosophers that engages me philosophically. Nietzsche seems not to have found much that engaged him philosophically. I think that is a pity.

There is, however, one exhilarating exception to Nietzsche's general treatment of preplatonic philosophy as a story of philosopher-types, that is, of types of philosophical personalities, rather than a story of philosophical argumentation in response to the recognition of philosophical perplexity. This is the treatment he affords Parmenides. I am thinking especially of what he says about Parmenides in *Die Philosophie im tragischen Zeitalter der Griechen*, rather than the earlier lectures on the preplatonic philosophers. The eleventh of those earlier lectures is devoted to both Parmenides and what Nietzsche calls 'his forerunner, Xenophanes'. Thus Parmenides gets only half a lecture and is not even included in the short lists of prize Pre-Platonics Nietzsche comes up with from time to time in those lectures.

In that half a lecture on Parmenides Nietzsche uses part of a long paragraph to present Parmenides's 'Way of Truth', which is meant to lead us to the immovable, indivisible and eternal One. Nietzsche's exposition is, in fact, quite straightforward, though very brief. His evaluation of the Parmenidean Way of Truth in that 1872 lecture is decidedly mixed, but much more negative than positive. 'Here we have an unnatural ripping apart [*Auseinanderrissung*] of the intellect,' he writes:

> the result must finally be [a dichotomy between] mind [*Geist*] (the faculty of abstraction) and body (the lower sensory apparatus), and we recognize right away the ethical consequences in Plato: the philosopher's task to liberate himself as much as possible from the bodily, that is, from the senses. [This is] the most dangerous of false paths, for no true philosophy can construct itself from this empty hull; it must proceed from the intuition of reality, and the more it consists of fruitful individual aperçus, the higher it stands. (VP 294 (86))

On a much more positive note, Nietzsche adds this:

> As a critique of the cognitive faculty, however, this raw distinction is of the greatest worth; it is the original source, first, of dialectic (though there is no philosophy from a [mere] combination of concepts), and later, of logic (ibid.).

The treatment of Parmenides in *Die Philosophie im tragischen Zeitalter der Griechen* is strikingly different from all this. To be sure, chunks from the lecture on Xenophanes and Parmenides are simply repeated in the later work, but much more is added – two or three times as much. Moreover, in the later work, Nietzsche treats the philosophical reasoning of Parmenides with much more seriousness and personal involvement than he had done in the lecture, indeed, with more seriousness than he accords the reasoning of any other preplatonic philosopher, including Socrates. Here is one of several important passages in which he presents some of Parmenides's reasoning:

> That which truly is must be forever present; you cannot say of it 'it was', or 'it will be'. The existent cannot have come to be, for what could it have come out of? Out of the nonexistent? But the nonexistent is not, and cannot produce anything. Out of the existent? This would produce nothing but itself. It is the same with passing away. Passing away is just as impossible as coming to be, as is all change, all increase, all decrease. (TZ 46 (78))[5]

Using this Parmenidean reasoning as a basis, Nietzsche draws the following picture of the Parmenidean One:

> The existent is indivisible, for where is the second power that could divide it? It is immobile, for where could it move to? It can be neither infinitely large nor infinitely small, for it is perfect, and a perfectly given infinity is a contradiction. Thus it hovers:

bounded, finished, immobile, everywhere in balance, equally perfect at each point, like a globe, though not in space, for this space would be a second existent. But there cannot be several existents. For in order to separate them, there would have to be something which is not existent, a supposition which cancels itself. Thus there is only eternal unity. (Ibid.)[6]

One could, of course, quarrel about this or that detail in Nietzsche's exposition of Parmenides' reasoning and the conclusion he thinks Parmenides reaches from that reasoning. But one can hardly deny that this discussion of Parmenides is a serious and responsible attempt to present, not only Parmenides' conclusion about reality, but also the reasoning that leads him to that conclusion. Nor do these two passages exhaust Nietzsche's presentation of the reasoning of Parmenides.

Even more remarkable than Nietzsche's comparatively full treatment of Parmenidean reasoning is his own philosophical attempt to refute Parmenides. Although Nietzsche is somewhat defensive about this attempted refutation, he is clearly very serious about it. Let me mention briefly several of the lines of reasoning that Nietzsche tries out in an attempt to defeat the reasoning of Parmenides.

First, in a passage that draws on Aristotle's distinction between essence and existence and on Kant's attempt to use that distinction to refute the ontological argument, Nietzsche maintains that we cannot infer the existence of anything from its essence. 'Now against all similar arguments Aristotle has shown,' Nietzsche writes, 'that existence [*Existenz*] never belongs to essence [*Essenz*], that the existence [*Dasein*] of a thing never belongs to its essence [*Wesen*]' (TZ 49 (82)).

Second, explicitly following Kant, Nietzsche maintains that concepts without percepts are bare, and so the logical truth, 'What is, is; what is not, is not' is, unless completed, as in 'What is a tree, is a tree; what is not a tree, is not a tree' [his example], simply empty of content (TZ 49–50 (82–3)).

Third, turning to the famous first line of fragment 6, 'What there is to be said and thought must be' [χρὴ τὸ λέγειν τε νοεῖν τ' ἐὸν ἔμμεναι], Nietzsche focuses on the claim that thinking and being are identical (TZ 54 (87)). 'Thinking and that bulbous–spherical being,' he writes, 'wholly dead-inert and rigid-immobile must, according to Parmenides' imperative, coincide and be utterly the same thing. What nonsense!' [*Das Denken und jenes knollig-kugelrunde, durch und durch todt-massive und starr-unbewegliche Sein müssen, nach dem Parmenideischen Imperativ, zum Schrecken aller Phantasie, in Eins zusammenfallen und ganz und gar dasselbe sein. Mag diese Identität den Sinnen widersprechen!*] (ibid.).

Fourth, following up this critique of the Parmenidean identification of thinking with being, Nietzsche says this in the next chapter: 'If the thought of reason in concepts is real, then plurality and motion must also have reality, for rational thought is moved' (TZ 54 (88)).

Each of these four lines of reasoning, plus a few others from this section of *Die Philosophie im tragischen Zeitalter der Griechen*, could appropriately be discussed at some length. But perhaps I have said enough about this remarkable passage to highlight its uncharacteristically dialectical character, that is, uncharacteristic for Nietzsche.

Why should it be that Nietzsche shows so much interest in the philosophical reasoning of Parmenides – more, I think, than he shows for the philosophical reasoning of any other preplatonic philosopher, Socrates included? And why should it be important for him to respond in kind, that is, with an attempt at philosophical refutation, indeed a refutation in the very form that Parmenides taught us, namely, *reductio ad absurdum*?

Part of the answer must be, I think, that, although Parmenides is the most austere and abstract of philosophers, there is something heroic about his uncompromisingly intellectualist asceticism, a heroic character that Nietzsche comes to admire, as well as abhor. Nietzsche describes Parmenides as fleeing, 'not like Plato into the land of eternal ideas, into the workshop of the world-creator, feasting [his] eyes on the unblemished unbreakable archetypes, but into the rigor mortis of the coldest, emptiest, concept of all, the concept of being' (TZ 48 (80–81)). To Nietzsche this flight is, I suspect, both thoroughly repulsive and yet somehow highly admirable.

Nietzsche goes on to add that this Parmenidean flight was not only not like Plato's, it was also not like the 'flight taken from the world by the Hindu philosophers' either. Nietzsche explains:

> Parmenides' thinking conveys nothing whatever of the dark intoxicating fragrance of Hindu wisdom ... No, the strange thing about his philosophic feat at this period is just its lack of fragrance, of color, soul, and form, its total lack of blood, religiosity and ethical warmth. What astonishes us is the degree of schematism and abstraction (in a Greek!) above all, the terrible energetic striving for *certainty*... 'Grant me, ye Gods, but one certainty,' runs Parmenides' prayer, 'and should it be but a log's breadth on which to lie, on which to ride upon the sea of uncertainty, it is wide enough to lie on. Take away everything that comes to be, everything lush, colorful, blossoming, illusory, everything that charms and is alive. Take all these for yourselves and grant me but the one and only, poor empty certainty.' (TZ 49 (81))

Again, the reader gets the sense that Nietzsche is both thoroughly repulsed and yet somehow attracted by the heroic, intellectualist asceticism of Parmenides.

In Part Two of *Also sprach Zarathustra*, written a decade after *Die Philosophie im tragischen Zeitalter der Griechen*, the prophet-figure, Zarathustra, brands all talk of the one, the plenum, the unmoved, the sated and the permanent as *menschenfeindlich*, inimical to humanity. In a striking inversion of the famous first line of the concluding chorus of Goethe's *Faust*, Zarathustra insists that it is the (idea of) the *intransitory*, rather than the idea of the *transitory*, that is only an image or parable, *ein Gleichnis*.[7] Through this inversion of Goethe, Nietzsche reverses Plato's idea that this world of coming to be and passing away we now inhabit is only a hall of mirrors, mirroring the eternal and unchanging Platonic Forms. According to Zarathustra, it is the eternal and unchanging that is the image, the figment of human conjecture, and an evil one at that.

But whatever the exact motivation for Nietzsche's comparatively extensive philosophical and dialectical response to Parmenides, the upshot is that he treats Parmenides as a thinker who is trying to deal with the most perplexing puzzles of being and non-being. He shows his respect for the problematic issues that challenged Parmenides, and challenge us today, by offering reasoning to defeat the Parmenidean claims. Thus he treats Parmenides in the way I think all preplatonic philosophers, indeed, all philosophers, should be treated, that is, by seeking what those philosophers found astonishing, by engaging critically in the reasoning they use to deal with their astonishment, and by assessing the theses they came to accept.

So what should we conclude? What should be our judgement on Nietzsche as a historian of preplatonic philosophy? First, through Nietzsche's concept of the sage, the wise person, in ancient Greek culture, plus his list of stages through which the idea of the sage develops in Greece, Nietzsche gives us a good way of understanding how it could be, conceptually, that Western philosophy had a beginning. I regard this as a good response to what I called the 'Self-Conception Problem' and the 'Demarcation Problem'. Moreover, by treating the first philosophers as archetypal philosophers, he also helps us to appreciate their striking individuality and variety.

On the other hand, by treating these philosophers primarily as personalities, Nietzsche discourages us from trying to discover what they found philosophically perplexing and from assessing the adequacy of their response to the perplexity they discovered. This is even true of Socrates, with whom Nietzsche obviously feels a great kinship. Nietzsche derides the philosophical thesis he attributes to Socrates (that virtue is knowledge), but without considering the reasoning that might lead one to suppose that, for example, one cannot be virtuous without being able to say, in some formally satisfactory way, what virtue is, or know what virtue is without actually being virtuous.

The one exception to Nietzsche's rather disengaged treatment of the preplatonic philosophers is his discussion of Parmenides. Although Parmenides does not enjoy very extensive treatment in Nietzsche's preplatonic lectures, he does get such treatment in the somewhat later, but only posthumously published, manuscript, *Die Philosophie im tragischen Zeitalter der Griechen*. There Nietzsche seems himself to get caught up in the perplexities of being and non-being, of coming to be and of passing away, and he responds philosophically, that is, argumentatively. I have speculated that this special show of respect for the thinking of Parmenides may arise from the belief that it was Parmenides who first argued for the, to Nietzsche, emasculating and enervating thesis that true reality is one, eternal and unchanging, whereas the forever changing world of sense experience, the world in which we live, talk, strive, suffer and sometimes win, is mere illusion. But whatever it is that motivates Nietzsche to take Parmenides seriously by responding to him dialectically, his response honours Parmenides, it honours Nietzsche, and it honours philosophy.

Notes

1   Page numbers will be given, first for the German edition, and then for the English translation. The translations used in this paper are my own adaptations and modifications of the cited English translations. Here are the details of the editions used: (henceforth GD) *Götzen-Dämmerung, Nietzsche: Werke*, 6. Abteilung, 3. Band (Berlin: Walter de

Gruyter, 1969), pp.49–154; English title, *Twilight of the Idols*, R. Polt, trans. (Indianapolis, IN: Hackett, 1997); (henceforth VP) *Die vorplatonischen Philosophen, Nietzsche: Werke*, 2. Abteilung, 4. Band (Berlin: Walter de Gruyter, 1995), pp.207–362; English title, *The Pre-Platonic Philosophers*, G. Whitlock, ed. and trans. (Urbana, IL: University of Illinois Press, 2001); (henceforth TZ) Die Philosophie im tragischen Zeitalter der Griechen (Stuttgart: Reclam, 1994), pp.5–76; English title, *Philosophy in the Tragic Age of the Greeks*, M. Cowan, trans. (Chicago: Henry Regnery, 1962); (henceforth Z) *Also sprach Zarathustra* (Berlin: Deutscher Taschenbuch Verlag de Gruyter, 1988); English title, *Thus Spoke Zarathustra*, W. Kaufmann, trans. (Harmondsworth: Penguin Books, 1996).

2 He may have delivered these lectures, or an earlier version of them, already in his first year as professor at Basel, in 1969. See Nietzsche, *The Pre-Platonic Philosophers*, pp.xxii–vi.
3 Matthews, *Socratic Perplexity and the Nature of Philosophy* (Oxford: Oxford University Press, 1999). See especially chapter 2, 'Perplexity and the beginning of philosophy'.
4 Quoted in the English translation of TZ, p.13.
5 This passage is quite similar to one in the lecture.
6 This passage expands a bit on the lecture.
7 Z, p.110 (86–8).

Chapter 5

Aristotle's Reading of Plato

Daniel W. Graham

When Plato began to write, there was no philosophical establishment in Athens, or anywhere else in Greece. The only higher education available consisted of occasional courses taught by itinerant lecturers, conveying whatever the teacher wished to teach with a liberal dose of what the audience wanted to learn, namely, how to speak well in public forums and how to manage business and government affairs. Competing theories of scientific explanation were widely disseminated but not, apparently, widely respected. Intellectual expertise was suspect and intellectuals were distrusted, despised, or both. At the death of Socrates, a small but ardent band of his followers retired to Megara, vowing to keep their master's memory alive.[1] Out of that band came a new kind of literature, *Sokratikoi logoi*, presenting to the public in a new format a new style of thought emanating from a new kind of thinker.

From what we can tell, Plato was at first a minor figure in this Socratic movement, overshadowed by Antisthenes, with his anti-conventional understanding of Socrates. But as the fourth century BC progressed, Plato emerged as the dominant figure, the author of dialogues without parallel in their stylistic polish and dramatic impact, a friend of potentates abroad, and founder of a grand centre of learning at home.[2] To his Academy came the brightest minds of the time, including leading mathematicians and astronomers.[3]

Plato had taken a despised and suspect subject of study that existed intermittently at the margins of Greek culture and had made it the wonder of its time. In a dazzling show of argument and drama, Plato had silenced critics of Socrates such as Polycrates the Sophist and countered enemies of the dialectical method such as Isocrates.[4] Combining moral gravity, religious devotion and, sometimes, scientific and logical precision, Plato transformed philosophy into a discourse central to everyday life and yet beholden to the highest ideals of excellence. If anecdotes can be believed, ordinary citizens began to flood into the Academy: farmers leaving their ploughs and women disguising themselves as men to sit at the feet of Plato and his colleagues. Plato was courted by tyrants and his students were invited to write laws for newly-founded cities. Philosophy had come of age, as a result of the writings of Plato more than of any other individual. He had given philosophy a human face – that of his master – and had made virtue the beginning and end of the philosophical quest. Science and mathematics could now be admitted as subjects of a liberal education because they had been moralized.

Into this centre of learning unlike any the world had known came an orphan from an obscure city in the Thracian Chalcidice. Aristotle of Stagira would spend twenty years in the Academy as student and then lecturer, and then go on to be the only member of the Academy to rival, and indeed eclipse, his master in the breadth and depth of his learning. If Plato invented philosophy as we know it, Aristotle either invented or put on the secure path of a science the studies of informal logic, formal logic, physics, zoology, meteorology, psychology, metaphysics, ethics, political science, poetics and even rhetoric. In the future history of philosophy, much of Western thought would be a dialectic between Platonic and Aristotelian philosophy. For twenty years Plato and Aristotle interacted in the rarefied atmosphere of the first university. We know virtually nothing of their personal interactions beyond what we can infer from the philosophical works they wrote.

Clearly Aristotle was a critic of Plato. Harold Cherniss has written a great study of Aristotle the critic,[5] and even if he never finished the projected second volume of his work, he amply demonstrated that Aristotle could be a severe and even uncharitable critic of the man who invented the principle of charity. Books have been written on Aristotle the Platonist, Aristotle the anti-Platonist, and Aristotle the philosopher whose thought evolved away from Platonism, or variously towards Platonism.[6] What can we say in a brief chapter about Aristotle's reading of Plato? I propose here to look at what Aristotle learned from Plato: the ways in which he is indebted to his master. To be sure, Aristotle could at different times and in different contexts be all of the things his interpreters have attributed to him: a harsh critic of Plato, a naïve follower, a formidable or inept adversary, a thinker with evolving attitudes. But he always went back to Plato for the starting point of his own investigations. Plato was his inspiration as well as his straw man and his *bête noire*, his ever-present interlocutor.

In the succeeding sections of this chapter I shall examine three areas in which Aristotle learned from Plato: physics, ethics and philosophy of language. I hope that in the process of this examination we may appreciate better both philosophers and their philosophical relationship with each other, and perhaps also in some measure how philosophical texts can have life long after their authors are dead.

Physics

The obvious place to go in Plato for a discussion of physics is the *Timaeus*, but that would be to miss the most profound of Plato's contributions to Aristotle. We must start with the *Phaedo*, and indeed an unlikely part of that work. Plato's first argument for immortality of soul is an argument from opposites. The beautiful comes from the ugly, the just from the unjust, the smaller from the larger, and so on. In general every state comes from its opposite state. In particular, what is dead comes from what is living. But by parity of reasoning, what is living must come from what is dead. Furthermore, if there were not symmetrical and balanced processes, soon one opposite would disappear. For instance, if everything that was awake went to sleep, but nothing that was asleep woke up, soon everything would be asleep and nothing would be awake. Similarly, if life and death were not balanced symmetrical processes, soon everything would be dead and nothing alive.

But some things are living, some are dead, so there must be a continual interchange among the living and dead (70d–72d).

Socrates appeals to this argument from opposites to prop up the argument from recollection when Simmias objects to the latter, but he seems to shelve both arguments as only provisional (77b–d). Yet Socrates comes back to the earlier argument when an anonymous interlocutor raises another objection to Socrates' claim that opposites cannot come from opposites: the argument from opposites claims that this is precisely how opposites do arise:

> Inclining his head and listening, Socrates said, 'You do well to remind us of what was said, but you do not understand the difference between what we are saying now and what we said then. For then we were saying that the contrary *thing* [*pragma*] comes from the contrary thing, but now we are saying that the contrary *itself* can never become contrary *to* itself, neither the property in us nor the reality in nature. Then, my friend, we were talking about things that *have* contraries, calling them after the name of those others; now we are talking about those very things which, being present, bear the name we apply to them.' (103a–c)[7]

Plato makes a crucial clarification of the concepts he is dealing with. We must distinguish the bearers of the properties from the properties themselves. The bearers can come to exemplify or participate in different opposites, but the opposites themselves cannot change in their character. Plato here makes a distinction between a thing and its property for the first, or almost the first, time in recorded philosophical literature.[8]

What Plato gives us here is less than a theory of change. He introduces the notion of a change from opposite to opposite ad hoc, in an inductive argument to provide a framework for showing that the soul is immortal. He forgets the distinctions he makes until they become relevant to an argument for immortality based on the Forms. He then disambiguates the notion of an opposite, distinguishing bearer from property, but he does not do so until more than thirty Stephanus pages have passed since he introduced the opposites themselves. His focus remains on proving the immortality of the soul, not on providing a conceptual or scientific account of change itself.

In *Physics* I, Aristotle sets out to provide a general theory of change. After criticizing the Eleatics for doing away with change, he turns to the positive accounts of his predecessors. He finds that all the Pre-Socratics who allow change recognize contraries (chs 4–6). But the two contraries cannot account for change by themselves: 'For it is problematic that density should act by nature on rarity or vice versa, and similarly with any other contrariety whatever' (189a22–4). Giving what is essentially Plato's argument for a *tertium quid*, Aristotle concludes that besides the two opposites there must be a substratum, a thing that has properties, which in his ontology will be a substance.

In chapter 7, Aristotle takes an example which he will generalize to account for change. A non-musical man becomes musical. By a kind of linguistic analysis, he determines that the various ways of describing this situation ('the man becomes musical', 'the not-musical becomes musical' and so on) are different and, in modern terms, transformationally equivalent ways of saying the same thing. The essential ingredients are the terms 'man', 'unmusical' and 'musical'. The former refers to the substratum which undergoes the change, the latter two terms to the contraries the substratum exemplifies at different times. For the change to take place the subject must be now unmusical, now musical. Generalizing, Aristotle holds that change instantiates a scheme consisting of a subject or substratum s and contraries (here contradictories) *not-F* and *F*. At one time *not-F* belongs to s, at another time *F* belongs to it. In the case of primary substances coming to be, it is difficult to say what the s is, but, on the model of a statue made out of bronze, we can say that some material goes from being not-formed to being formed. By extension, for a primary substance there is some material or matter m which is now *not-F*, now *F*, fitting the general scheme of change.[9]

With a deceptively simple train of reasoning drawing on presocratic accounts of change and Platonic considerations, Aristotle has gone from concrete explanations of changes to a fully general theory of change: in any change a substratum changes from exemplifying a property to exemplifying an opposite property. Change is an exchange of opposite properties by a subject. This account fits, of course, Aristotle's fundamental ontological view that the ultimate subject is the ultimate reality, and that everything else depends for its existence on the ultimate reality. But the original insight is the one supplied by Plato in the *Phaedo*. In Aristotle it provides the fundamental analysis of change. Going on to discuss causes, nature, chance, time, place, motion and other topics of natural theory, Aristotle eventually elaborates eight books of natural theory, or physics – *ta physika*.

The *Phaedo* provides much more than the scheme of change. In an important digression, Plato has Socrates tell about his study of causes, in a quasi-autobiographical passage. Confused by the mechanistic causes proposed by the Pre-Socratics, Socrates hears someone reading from a book by Anaxagoras, who proclaims that everything is organized for the best. That seems like an epoch-making insight to Socrates, and he rushes out to read the book for himself. But he finds that Anaxagoras does not make use of his own insight, but rather falls back on mechanistic causes to account for the world.[10] Although it would be rash to attribute this train of thought to Socrates, Plato's analysis of science is deeply Socratic in another way: Plato is applying Socratic principles to natural science and announcing that, if these principles, such as a consideration of what is best, can indeed be applied, then science (which Socrates had ignored) is worth pursuing. But science must be reconceived along Socratic lines. Aristotle echoes Plato's assessment of Anaxagoras: the principle is absolutely correct, but the philosopher of Clazomenae fails to exploit his principle.[11] He is like a sober man among his muddled colleagues, yet he brings in the account of what is best only as a *deus ex machina* when he has nothing else to offer. Plato's dialogue provides a kind of scientific manifesto proclaiming the pursuit of what is best as the goal of scientific explanation. Aristotle enlists in the scientific quest, and gives a name to this kind of explanation: that for the sake of which something happens, or *final cause* explanation.

At least one more insight of the *Phaedo* informs Aristotle's scientific programme. In developing his more sophisticated kind of explanation, Plato points out that some properties are always accompanied by others. Snow is always cold, fire always hot, three always odd.[12] Thus we can infer additional properties from a given property. What Plato seems to be getting at is the notion of logical entailment.[13] This notion will become enormously productive in Aristotle's theory of syllogism, as finally laid out in the *Prior Analytics*. The regular inferences Plato notices and identifies as necessary connections, Aristotle develops into the first logical system.

In all of this, Aristotle is deeply indebted to Plato. Yet his own theory is no mere borrowing or adaptation of his master's theory. In each case Aristotle seizes on an important insight, making it a principle for further elaboration, and embeds it in a sophisticated theory of his own designing: the theory of change, the theory of causes, the theory of logic. Plato is aware of truths about each of these subjects, but he does not develop a full-blown theory for any of them. Aristotle takes the insight and elaborates it within a theoretical framework to account for a wide range of phenomena, so that he can claim that his several theories explain all the phenomena falling within the domain of the theory.

Ethics

At the end of Book I of the *Republic*, Socrates asks if a horse has a work or function (*ergon*) (352d ff). A function, he explains, is what one does best or only with a given thing. Thus one sees only with the eyes and hears only with the ears, so that seeing and hearing are the respective functions of eyes and ears. There is also a corresponding excellence or virtue for each thing that has a function. But the soul has a function, namely to 'take care of things, direct, and plan' (353d5), so, accordingly, it must have an excellence or virtue, namely justice. And if a soul is virtuous, it must live well and be happy, whereas if it is vicious it must live poorly and wretchedly. So the life of justice is more advantageous than the life of injustice. This argument from function defeats Thrasymachus and establishes that justice is better than injustice, and, as against the sophist's last position, that justice rather than injustice is a virtue.

Aristotle surveys views about what the goal of all action, the good life, consists of, in his *Nicomachean Ethics*, Book I. Everyone agrees in calling the good life happiness, but there is no general agreement about what kind of life actually achieves human happiness. At this point Aristotle leaves off reporting others' views and giving preliminary criticisms and begins an argument to establish what, in general terms, happiness is. The argument from function goes as follows:

1   If x has a function (*ergon*), a good x is one that functions well.
2   Man has a function.
3   The function of man is determined by what is (a) peculiar [(b) proper] to x.
4   What is (a) peculiar [(b) proper] to man is his (a) reasoning capacity [(b) soul].
5   The life of activity (*energeia*) is better than the life of inactivity.
6   The excellences or virtues represent the potential for perfect functioning.

7   Hence the good for man is the activity of [(a) the reasoning part in conformity with the theoretical virtues] (b) the soul in conformity with virtue (1097a22–1098a7).

This argument is evidently an argument from function very much like Plato's argument in *Republic* I. It is a bit more elaborate than Plato's argument and has a different focus, for it seeks to identify the function of man as a species rather than of the human soul in particular. It also defines man's function in terms of his soul or capacities within the soul, and so we may say that it keeps within the general framework of Plato's argument, perhaps as seen from a more biological perspective.

Aristotle's argument also seems somewhat schizophrenic insofar as it seems to present two different interpretations of the function, here represented by the (a) and (b) versions. (I think both must be presented because Aristotle seems to settle for (b) the weaker conclusion after he has gone to some trouble to set up the premises for the (a) conclusion. This wavering has to do with Aristotle's larger strategy, I believe, rather than any uncertainty about the soundness of the argument. Aristotle realizes that he is getting ahead of himself in anticipating the conclusions of Book X, and backs off to give only a general and preliminary characterization of happiness here.)

One further feature of Aristotle's argument is his use of the concept of *energeia*, activity or actuality, a concept he himself seems to have invented.[14] But in one sense the notion of activity is just an extension of the notion of function, as the Greek terms themselves suggest. And in any case, we can trace back to Plato's *Euthydemus* the insight that grounds the distinction between potency and activity, so that, even if the terminology is new, the distinction would be congenial to Plato.[15]

Now we could spend some time analysing the different nuances of these two arguments from function, and we would probably notice that Aristotle's argument is more technically grounded and more sophisticated than Plato's, but that it continues the spirit and insight of Plato's argument. But what is most important about the two arguments is not fine differences in their content and structure, but their place in the larger context of argument. Plato's argument provides a neat refutation to Thrasymachus' position, and it seems an appropriate stopping place for a successful debate. But of course it does not end the debate; Socrates points out that the inquirers have failed to define justice, and so they have not settled the problem at all, but given only a provisional answer to the questions about justice. Book II begins with a more formidable attack on justice, put in the mouths of Glaucon and Adimantus, and Socrates responds with a whole new strategy for meeting the attack. The argument from function, it turns out, is a mere throwaway move in the quest to understand justice.

By contrast, Aristotle uses the argument from function as the centrepiece of his first book on ethics, and as the foundation for all that comes after. The essence of the good life is determined by the argument from function, which even anticipates the argument of the final book. To understand human action in general we must understand the goal of all action. The goal of all action is the good life. The good life is the actualization of human potentiality. The soul is the seat of human potentiality. Thus the good life will consist in the activity of human psychic capacities in accordance with the appropriate virtues (Book I). In this part of the exposition, Aristotle's ethics appeals to principles of metaphysics, biology and psychology. To understand the good life presupposes understanding what kind of being, that is, what species of thing we are discussing; to understand the species we must understand the range of psychic functions, their respective importance, which ones the species in question has and so on.

Once we have determined the functions in question, we must identify the relevant excellences or virtues. There are two kinds of virtues, moral and theoretical. Moral virtues are habits realized by practice of the appropriate kind (Books II–V). Theoretical virtues are intellectual capacities realized in ways other than by practice (Book VI). In achieving the good life we must avoid weakness of will and master pleasures (Book VII). Friendship is an important component of the good life (Books VIII–IX). And finally the good life consists of contemplation, the most godlike of states (Book X). Aristotle's conception of ethics is an architectonic scheme built on the foundation of the good life, as determined by the proper definition. In Aristotle the stone rejected by the builders has become the head of the corner.

Plato, to be sure, has a grand conception of ethics too. The ten books of the *Republic* rival the *Nicomachean Ethics* in length and exceed it in the range of topics. But we can see a kind of demerit in Plato's very exuberance. Whereas we can define the general topic of Aristotle's treatise as ethics, we cannot define Plato's topic, at least not satisfactorily. Plato sets out ostensibly to define justice; in the process of pursuing the nature of justice, he designs an ideal state, complete with rulers, education system, comparison with different constitutions and a prospective history of its decay. Along with ethics we get political science, epistemology, metaphysics, philosophy of education, psychology, value theory, aesthetics, some philosophy of science and a myth about the afterlife. Plato's vision is governed not so much by a foundational argument as by analogies like that between the soul and the city, images like the divided line, metaphors like the Sun, allegories and parables like the Ship of State and the Cave, and mythical images like that of the cosmic whorl. Plato's argument is a fluid dialectic in which few, if any, arguments stand fast until the end. We are asked to understand human nature, human society and the world itself by reference to flights of fancy which purport to represent how things are, or better yet, how they should be but never quite are in the realm of experience. Plato's picture of the world is a series of images that, like the objects of his perceptible world, can never be held within a single vision. Plato's arguments supply insights, but he never trusts them to tell the whole truth. There will be another argument, perhaps with another analogy, and another, and another. In the end we remember his images more than his arguments.

Aristotle, we begin to see, mines the writings of Plato for arguments, and some of these give him the foundations of a philosophical edifice. The distinction of a subject exchanging contrary properties gives him the definition of change and the foundation of all natural philosophy. The argument from function provides the principle for human motivation, the foundation for all ethical theory. For Plato the argument from opposites is the first, expendable argument in a series of at least five major arguments for the immortality of the soul (of which perhaps only the last is really defensible). The argument from function provides only a temporary resting place in the pursuit of a definition of justice, a pursuit which leads to the Mother of all Digressions. Ultimately Plato's *disiecta membra* become the skeleton of Aristotle's theory.

Language and Ontology

Plato's *Phaedo* may have been written at a time before Aristotle was born, and the *Republic* when Aristotle was a child or a youth, but in the last case, the writings Aristotle reacted to appeared at a time Aristotle was a member of the Academy. This raises some difficult but intriguing questions about the philosophical interactions of Plato and Aristotle that I will come back to briefly later. For now suffice it to say that in his later dialogues Plato was exploring the nature and reality of the Forms, and looking for ways in which they connect with the world. Plato broached problems about knowledge in his aporetic dialogue *Theaetetus*. The sequel was his *Sophist*, a dialogue that in trying to define what a sophist is travels into new territory concerning the nature of the Forms and their relation to the world, in particular the world of language and communication.

The *Sophist* is not an easy dialogue to understand; the argument is long and complex, and more technical than those found in most of Plato's works. But we can isolate a few important landmarks. Plato wishes to show how it is possible to make false statements without 'saying nothing'. For if false statement is possible, the sophist can be a liar or deceiver, and we can judge his statements to be unsatisfactory; if there is no false statement, any utterance he or anyone else can make cannot be criticized or evaluated negatively. In order to deal with the question of false speech, Plato identifies five Ultimate Kinds, *megista genê*, namely Sameness, Difference, Motion, Rest and Being. He shows that these Kinds are distinct from each other and have their own unique characteristics. He carefully goes through the connections between them to note relationships such as incompatibility (for instance between Motion and Rest), compatibility ('mixture' between Sameness and Difference) and inclusion (between Being and any other class). The Kind Difference has the unique characteristic of describing how anything *is not* something else. Thus Not-being can be explicated in terms of Difference. Not-being is not the contrary of Being or existence, but something's being other than or different from something else (257b–c). Specific applications of Not-being, for instance the not-beautiful, are just as much as their positive counterparts. The concept marks off a section of the domain of Being which contains not-beautiful things (257d–258b).

To emphasize the importance of the subject Plato maintains that to disconnect each thing from everything else would completely do away with discourse. 'For discourse arises for us by means of the interconnection of Forms (*tôn eidôn symplokê*) with each other' (260e). Plato regards the claim that Forms connect with each other as the foundation of speech and thought (since thought itself is a kind of inner speech, 263e). Much remains unclear and controversial about how Plato understands the Ultimate Kinds and their connection with language and thought.

But it does appear that for him speech and communication presuppose some kind of logical–semantic relationships prior to the speech acts we perform. To put it another way, there are a priori conceptual relations that make communication and rational cognition possible. Like Kant, Plato seems to think that percepts without concepts are blind.

In order to show how speech can connect with what is not, Plato analyses the sentence. It is composed of a noun (*onoma*) and a verb (*rhêma*) as the minimal components, which can form the most simple, or atomic, sentence such as 'Man learns' (262d). Nouns or verbs by themselves do not produce sentences, for instance 'walks runs sleeps' or 'lion stag horse' (262b). When one connects (*sumplekein*) a noun and a verb, one does not simply name (*onomazein*) but accomplishes something (*perainein ti*), so that one states (*legein*) something and utters a statement (*logos*) (262e). Just as in the world some things (*pragmata*) fit together (*harmottein*) and some do not, so among linguistic signs (*tês phônês sêmeia*) some elements fit together and some do not (262e–263a). Plato notes that speech must be about something (263a), and so intentionality enters the picture. The sentence 'Theaetetus is sitting' is about Theaetetus. So is the sentence 'Theaetetus is flying'. The former says something that *is* about Theaetetus, the latter something that is not; hence the first is true, the second false. Since thought is inner speech, the same analysis applies to thought: false or true belief is the result of incorrect or correct correlations between facts and signs representing them. Because Plato's analysis accounts for false statement and false belief, it allows us to distinguish between false and true theories, and to refute those sophists who claim that there is no falsehood, *quod erat demonstrandum*.

Aristotle begins his analysis of language and reality by saying, 'Of things said, some are said with connection (*kata sumplokēn*), some without connection. Those with connection are expressions such as "man runs", "man wins". Those without connection are expressions such as "man", "ox", "runs", "wins"' (*Categories* 1a16–19).

Using a term familiar from Plato's *Sophist*, and using the notion of an atomic sentence composed of noun and verb, Aristotle makes the distinction between a connected string of words and unconnected words basic to his theory in his *Categories*. In the *De interpretatione* he further defines the noun and the verb (chs 2, 3), which he finds are components of a sentence (ch. 4). Like Plato (though using slightly different terms) he goes on to define affirmation and denial (ch. 6). Aristotle makes the significance of connecting noun and verb clear in the *Categories*:

> None of the things said makes an affirmation just by itself, but affirmation arises by the connection of these words with each other. Every affirmation is apparently either true or false, while no word said without connection is either true or false, such as 'man', 'white', 'runs', 'wins'. (2a4–10)

Only by connecting the right kinds of single words, such as a substantive and a verb, can one make a sentence. Only a sentence can be an affirmation and make a statement.[16] Only sentences are bearers of the properties of truth and falsity.

Aristotle divides up simple words into ten classes according to what they signify (*sêmainein*) or refer to (1b25–2a4). Referring words indicate either being (*ousia*), how much, of what sort, in relation to what, where, when, disposition, having, acting, or being acted on. The ten classes of words correspond to the ten categories or types of thing in the world. Aristotle gives examples: being or substance is like man, horse; how much like two cubits long, three cubits long, of what sort like pale, literate. We are reminded of another passage in Plato's *Sophist*:

> Visitor from Elea: Let's say in what way we refer to the same thing in each case when we use many names.
> Theaetetus: Such as what? Give me an example.
> Visitor: I suppose we are referring to a man when we give him many names, assigning colors to him, shapes, sizes, vices and virtues, in all of which cases and a thousand others we say he is not only a man, but good and countless other things. And at the same time we are supposing each thing is one, by the same token we take it to be many as we refer to it by many names. (251a–b)

Plato envisages several ways in which we can describe a man; Aristotle enumerates and classifies those ways. The picture is Plato's, the analysis Aristotle's.

Plato sees linguistic utterances as somehow representing the world: the true ones present things as they are, the false ones situations different from the way things are. The utterances of language presuppose a pattern of Forms woven together (*sumplekein*), a patchwork or texture of overlapping domains like a great Venn diagram. Every member of the domain at the same time is and is not, in different senses. But by appreciating different logical and semantic relationships, we can see how speech, thought and understanding are possible.

Aristotle uses many of the same devices and some of the same vocabulary. But instead of settling for a few Ultimate Kinds, he attempts to give an exhaustive inventory of the kinds of things there are. He makes vertical divisions between universals and particulars (although he does not use a term for the former in the *Categories*) and a horizontal division between substances or things and accidents or attributes. He further envisages vertical subdivisions of universals: there are genera and species (using Plato's terms for Kinds and Forms, respectively). And he subdivides accidents into the nine non-substantial categories. Thus he replaces a vague conceptual map with a precise architectonic structure: every object of reference has its place in his scheme, and every statement gains its meaning by the way it links objects together.

Again Plato is satisfied with a sweeping insight into the nature of things and the possibility of language and thought. Aristotle is out to analyse, inventory and dissect the several classes of things, then to assemble them into a perspicuous system. Plato seems vaguely to be presupposing Forms of the same kind or similar to those he posited in the Middle Dialogues. Aristotle carefully distinguishes form-like entities from the things of our experience, and he also distinguishes types of substances from types of accidents. Using the terminology of other Aristotelian treatises, we may say he distinguishes universals from particulars, and he subdivides universals into universal substances and universal accidents. Not content to make distinctions, he claims that there is an order of priority among his ontological classes. Primary substances, that is, particular substances, are self-existent; everything else depends for its existence on primary substances.[17] Thus the really real things are particulars of the most concrete sort. Universals are always posterior and dependent.

Aristotle does not draw the conclusion, but it is obvious: those things that Plato calls Forms are universals. And they are not the ultimate realities, but only their dependencies, their ontological satellites. The Theory of Forms is false. Order in the world of experience does not depend on there being Forms, but there being universals depends on there being discrete particulars in the world of experience, particulars which have determinate features. As to an argument for his ontology, Aristotle tells us that primary substances underlie everything else, as if that were an argument. In the end he too resorts to images. But they are images of the One Under Many, not the One Over Many. If he has not won the argument, he has at least turned Plato's world upside down and made us see things from a new perspective.

Aristotle takes one more important step beyond Plato. For Plato, at least roughly, there is one Form for every word, more specifically, for every referring term. It is, in fact, a major departure for Plato when he sees he can gloss 'is not' with 'is different from'. It turns out that 'is not' is a misleading expression that sounds like it functions as an opposite when it is in fact more like the opposite of 'is the same as'. Still, this semantic insight applies only to one rather peculiar, if problematic, expression. Aristotle, by contrast, begins his *Categories* by recognizing the difference between synonyms and homonyms (ch. 1). For Aristotle two things (not words, as in modern English usage) are synonyms if they are called by names that mean the same thing, such as Socrates and Fido are both animals, where 'animal' means the same thing. But a wooden chair and a department Chair are homonyms. By this doctrine Aristotle recognizes the many meanings words can have, and he raises a problem for Plato's One Over Many principle. The fact that two things have the same name is not a sufficient condition for their participating in the same Form, or having the same universal predicated of them. They must have the same meaning.

Thus Aristotle recognizes that there are semantic ambiguities. Even more important, he recognizes that there are ambiguities of syntax. Although the sentence 'Socrates is a man' looks similar to the sentence 'Socrates is pale', the former represents a necessary truth (if it is true at all) and the latter a contingent truth. The former expresses an essential predication, the latter an accidental predication. Predication, *katêgoria* (a term invented by Aristotle) properly holds between entities in the world, but it is reflected in the grammar of language, at least the logically perspicuous language of Greek. Aristotle's table of entities shows how they are related to one another and reflected in verbal descriptions of the world. Plato hints that language can reveal true relationships; Aristotle makes language isomorphic with the world (or, perhaps more correctly, makes the world isomorphic with language).

For Aristotle language shows the priority of the subject to the predicate, and hence of substance to accident, and presupposes the priority of the concrete, particular subject to the collective or abstract, universal subject. The fact of language becomes a kind of tacit argument for the One Under Many point of view. Thus Aristotle uses the tools Plato introduced to undermine Plato's theory. While Plato sees language as depending on the interconnection of Forms for its efficacy, Aristotle sees it as making reference to individuals and generalizing from individuals.

In one arena we can see one particular disagreement between Plato and his student. In the *Sophist*, Plato clearly recognizes that the connection of a noun and a verb makes possible an assertion that is true or false. Aristotle makes a stronger claim in the *Categories*: only a statement can be true or false.[18] Truth and falsity are qualities of statements, Plato notes. Truth and falsity is a quality only of statements, Aristotle maintains. The claims are not in themselves incompatible, but in the *Philebus* we find Plato arguing that there are such things as true and false pleasures.[19] His tacit antagonist is, I suspect, Aristotle. Aristotle does not allow truth and falsity to apply to non-linguistic entities. The arguments Plato gives Aristotle would counter by saying that, to the degree we commonly call things such as pleasures true or false, we are using the terms in an equivocal manner. Statements and pleasures are homonyms, not synonyms.

Aristotle goes on to develop philosophical grammar and logic, based on the insights Plato makes in the *Sophist*. Again Plato is the innovator, Aristotle the system builder. Plato moves on to other topics without exploiting the insights of the *Sophist*. Aristotle uses them as the logical–linguistic foundation for philosophical theory. Ultimately, he sees every science as a logical structure with a set of axioms which entail theorems. The terms of the axioms refer to the basic realities the science deals with. They link them together in logical relationships that have implications for how the world is connected. Our own knowledge of the world depends on our ability to arrive at patterns in universals through an inductive process. The broad picture is Plato's as sketched in *Republic* VI,[20] but the details are Aristotle's, as is the insistence that the objects of knowledge are ordered into compartmentalized units. Science is modular to reflect the structures of the world. Accordingly, Aristotle's treatises are divided by subject matter: physics, cosmology, the structure of matter, meteorology, zoology, psychology and so on. When Plato composes a dialogue, as we have already seen in the case of the *Republic*, even if it deals with a limited question, such as arguments for immortality, it is likely to include a host of other topics: epistemology, metaphysics, scientific explanation, and so on.

Conclusion

It is clear from the examples we have explored that Plato is a major, and probably the major, source of inspiration for Aristotle. In physics, metaphysics, ethics, logic and language, as certainly also in political science and other areas, Aristotle is deeply influenced by Plato, even when he strongly disagrees with him. For even when he most strongly disagrees with his master, Aristotle takes from him explanatory schemes, elements of theory and even his conception of the problems.

But where Plato is heuristic and dialectical, Aristotle is systematic and apodictic. Plato develops interesting insights in dialectical arguments, then passes on to grand visions; Aristotle dusts off elements from the arguments, generalizes them as principles in an appropriate domain, and builds grand theories on them.

Aristotle uses the concepts and schemes he has borrowed from Plato to criticize him, and yet by his use of them he reveals his indebtedness. In some moods he acknowledges the great influence Plato had on him, yet his most characteristic response may be the one in which he says, alluding to his master:

> Perhaps it would be best to examine and discuss the meaning of the general good, even though the task is complicated by the fact that our friends have introduced the Forms. Yet it would seem best and even requisite for the defense of the truth to reject these familiar doctrines inasmuch as we are lovers of wisdom. For though both are dear, it is our sacred duty to choose the truth in preference to our friends. (*Nicomachean Ethics* 1096a11–16)

Here at his most personal, Aristotle gives a poignant reminder of the tension every scholar feels between loyalty to a beloved mentor and his own pursuit of truth. There is then a special irony in the fact that Aristotle's attitude towards the truth was also learned from Plato. As his master says, 'A man should not be esteemed above the truth' (*Republic* 595c). For a philosopher like Aristotle, a classic is a work that continually teaches and inspires the reader by its advances, and challenges him by its shortcomings. But the philosopher's first commitment is to truth. And he must be led on by the truth itself, as Aristotle sometimes says, even if that leads him beyond the familiar doctrines of a beloved mentor.

Notes

1. Diogenes Laertius 3.6; 2.106.
2. The picture of Plato's progress emerges most clearly from his continuing conflict with Isocrates, as demonstrated by C. Eucken, *Isokrates* (Berlin: Walter de Gruyter, 1983).
3. Theaetetus, theorist of irrational numbers and of regular solids; Amyclas of Heracleia; Menaechmus, discoverer of conic sections; Dinostratus, who applied Hippias' quadratix to the squaring of the circle; Theudias of Magnesia, author of an early Elements of Geometry; Leodamus, another geometer; Athenaeus of Cyzicus; Philip of Mende; Philip of Opus, alleged author of the *Epinomis*; Heraclides of Pontus, author of an astronomical theory with a revolving earth and of philosophical romances; Eudoxus of Cnidus, who brought his whole school with him, a mathematician who invented the theory of proportions as well as the method of exhaustion, a philosopher who subscribed to a hedonistic theory, a geographer who described the known world, and an astronomer who invented the first mathematical model of the heavens. Speusippus, Plato's nephew, would be his successor as head of the school, followed by Xenocrates of Chalcedon. Hestiaeus of Perinthus, Erastus and Coriscus of Scepsis, Timolaus of Cyzicus, Evaeon of Lampsacus, Python and Heraclides of Aenus, Hippothales and Callippus of Athens, and Demetrius of Amphipolis were also his students. Two women, Lastheneia of Mantinea and Axiothea of Phlius, are reported to have studied in the Academy also. See Diogenes Laertius 3.46 for a partial list of students.

4   The *Euthydemus* and *Gorgias* seem to be in part responses to Isocrates; the *Gorgias* and *Symposium* responses to the *Katêgoria Sôkratous* of Polycrates.
5   H. Cherniss, *Aristotle's Criticism of Plato and the Academy*, vol. 1 (Baltimore, MD: Johns Hopkins University Press, 1944).
6   For example, F. Solmsen, *Aristotle's System of the Physical World* (Ithaca, NY: Cornell University Press, 1960); I. Düring, *Aristoteles: Darstellung und Interpretation seines Denkens* (Heidelberg: Winter,1966); W. Jaeger, *Aristotle: Fundamentals of the History of his Development*, 2nd edn, trans. R. Robinson (Oxford: Oxford University Press, 1948); D.W. Graham, *Aristotle's Two Systems* (Oxford: Clarendon Press, 1987).
7   My own translations throughout.
8   For treatments, see M.M. McCabe, *Plato's Individuals* (Princeton, NJ: Princeton University Press, 1994); W.-R. Mann, *The Discovery of Things* (Princeton, NJ: Princeton University Press, 2000). The former deals with Plato's treatment of individuals, while the latter denies that Plato really had a concept of individuals; I tend to agree with the latter treatment.
9   See D.W. Graham, 'Aristotle's discovery of matter', *Archiv für Geschichte der Philosophie* 66 (1984): 37–51; *Aristotle's Two Systems*, ch. 5.
10 *Phaedo* 96a–99c.
11 *Metaphysics* 984b15–22, 985a10–21.
12 *Phaedo* 104bff.
13 See P. Shorey, 'The origin of the syllogism', *Classical Philology* 19 (1924): 1–19; G. Vlastos, 'Reasons and causes in the *Phaedo*', *Philosophical Review* 78 (1969): 291–325.
14 See D.W. Graham, 'The etymology of *entelecheia*', *American Journal of Philology* 110 (1989): 73–80.
15 *Euthydemus* 280c–282a; 288e–289b.
16 *De interpretatione* 17a2–5.
17 *Categories* 2b4–6.
18 *Categories* 2a7–10.
19 Discussion at 38e–40e, conclusion at 40c.
20 510b–511e.

Chapter 6

Augustine and Platonism: The Rejection of Divided-Soul Accounts of Akrasia

Scott MacDonald[*]

Augustine's debt to Plato is enormous. (We might better say 'to Platonism' here than 'to Plato' because Augustine most likely knew Plato almost entirely indirectly, through the texts and ideas of late ancient authors.[1]) The indisputable magnitude of Augustine's debt has led many scholars to think of Augustine as a derivative thinker and, for that reason, as not among the greatest Western philosophers. Moreover, it has caused a good deal of the scholarship on Augustine to focus on trying to sketch the derivations: on identifying which Platonist texts Augustine may have read (Porphyry? Plotinus?) and which Platonist doctrines undergird and explain his characteristic positions. But I am convinced that that way of reading Augustine systematically obscures his greatness, which very often consists precisely in what Augustine does *with* and *to* the Platonism he inherits.

In this chapter I consider an example of Augustine's encounter with Platonism that I think illustrates his philosophical genius and originality. It is a case in which Augustine clearly draws on the tradition but is also subtly and sharply critical of it. I am going to look at his famous account, in Book 8 of the *Confessions*, of the final stage of his conversion to catholic Christianity. At the centre of the account is his compelling examination of the intense inner conflict that characterized that final stage. He is puzzled by the conflict he experiences, and it is clear that part of what puzzles him is that he takes himself to be suffering a sort of akrasia or weakness of will. Of course, that is a puzzle bequeathed to late antiquity (and to us) by the Socrates of Plato's *Protagoras*. But Augustine's case turns out to be akrasia with a twist, a distinctively Augustinian twist that gives the old problem a new dimension. Moreover, Augustine's analysis of his case draws on a Platonist idea for explaining akrasia: the idea that the possibility of akrasia requires multiple sources of motivation.

But Augustine's pluralism about motivation differs in surprising ways from the pluralism expressed by Socrates in *Republic* Book 4 (the main text where Plato is thought to be replying to the position articulated in the *Protagoras*) and that is because Augustine's peculiar case has given him reason for thinking that a multipartite soul cannot adequately account for a crucial feature of human action. As I will suggest, Augustine's encounter with these elements of Platonism leads him to some original results, results that are informed by Platonism but that also criticize and reshape it.[2]

Psychological Conflict

Before turning to Augustine's text, I want briefly to sketch a kind of general framework for thinking about psychological conflict that will help us see what is at stake in Augustine's account. Conflict or competition within an agent's practical life is utterly routine and, for the most part, not particularly puzzling. On a recent evening Alice, my teenage daughter, wanted to watch TV but was also desperate to spend the evening at her computer downloading music from the web. It was clear to her on this particular evening that she could not manage both of these things. Her desires in this case conflicted in the straightforward sense that she could not satisfy both and she knew it. She had to settle on one and leave the other to wither (or fester, or do whatever unfulfilled teenage desires do). Inner conflicts of this sort are often fairly trivial, as Alice's was. But they are also sometimes important and can force painful choices, as they do when the objects of our competing desires are goods each of which we care about profoundly.

Whether they are trivial or significant, cases in which an agent's desires conflict in this routine sort of way do not pose any deep philosophical puzzles about agency. Agents, of course, face the *practical* problem of deciding how to proceed in these cases. And they do this typically by deliberating, totting up and comparing prospective quantities of pleasure, flipping a coin or employing some other sort of decision procedure. But that sort of practical problem is a problem that agents themselves face; it is not a problem about agency as such.

Some sorts of conflict in agents' practical lives, however, have special features that raise worries about our understanding of agency itself. Cases involving the phenomenon that is sometimes described as akrasia are of this sort. When we ask *whether* it is possible – as those cases might seem to suggest – or *how* it is possible for an agent to choose or act against her better judgement, we are asking about the nature of agency itself. There are two crucial extra features in these cases: they involve not just competing desires or motivations but, first, the fact that one of the competitors is certified or endorsed by reason (embodies a better judgement) and, second, the fact that motivation stemming from or associated with the better judgement is ultimately defeated in the competition: the agent chooses or acts *against* her better judgement. Cases of this sort can seem puzzling from a theoretical standpoint; the Socrates of the *Protagoras* thought that human agency would be utterly unintelligible if actions of this kind were really possible. But they can also appear puzzling from a first-person point of view. To suffer akrasia on some occasion is to experience a kind of resistance to one's own agency, a kind of intransigence arising from within oneself. It can feel as though one has acted but without the sort of autonomy and control that typically characterize one's agency. These are cases of inner conflict in which one of the competitors is recalcitrant or unruly and in a certain way manages to force itself on us.

There are cases of inner conflict that fall on the same spectrum as cases of simple competition and akrasia but farther out, so to speak. These are cases in which the affront to agency is so severe that we are fairly certain that the conditions for moral agency, whatever those are, have been undermined. Cases of thoroughgoing addiction and psychological compulsion are examples of this sort. Imagine a deeply loving mother – let us call her Anna – who suffers from a psychological compulsion. When her small child returns from school each day Anna literally cannot bring herself to touch the child, is physically repelled by the thought it, out of a compulsive fear of being contaminated by the germs she believes to have accumulated on her child's clothing and body during the school day. When she is in the grip of her compulsive fear Anna seems to us really not to have control of her actions in the sort of way necessary for genuine agency. Unlike our ordinary desires and even the deeply entrenched motivations in the face of which we suffer akrasia, the compulsive's and the addict's motivations render their possessors crucially passive. When her compulsions are driving her behaviour, Anna is not *acting* in the relevant sense. She is instead passive, in the grip of a force that is alien to who she is. We can imagine that she is desperate not only to escape the grip of the compulsion but also, and perhaps especially, to help her child understand that, when she recoils from the child's touch or refuses to provide a comforting hug or loving caress, it is not really *she* who is recoiling or refusing.

Augustine's case in *Confessions* 8 seems to me interesting precisely because it falls somewhere between cases of weakness of will and cases of addictive or compulsive behaviour. For that reason it is a kind of test case that forces us to think about the boundary separating cases of internal conflict that nevertheless exemplify genuine moral agency and cases where internal conflict undermines it entirely. By helping us think about where and how to draw that boundary, Augustine's case and Augustine's own analysis of it can help us think more clearly about the nature of human agency itself.

Augustinian Divided Will

So now let us look at Augustine's case.[3] In the preceding book of the *Confessions* (Book 7) Augustine, with the help he claims to have found in certain Platonist books, has come to believe that the Christian account of reality is true. That is, he has come to see that the Christian God is the ultimate source of reality and the highest good in whom ultimate human happiness is to be found.[4] But he has also discovered that that significant and hard-won cognitive achievement has left him still short of his goal. Knowing where happiness is to be found is not the same thing as possessing it, and so at the end of Book 7 Augustine is left with a problem that the events of Book 8 finally resolve for him. Here is how he puts it at the beginning of Book 8:

> All doubt had been taken from me ... My desire was not to be more certain of you but to be more stable in you. But in my temporal life everything was wavering, and my heart needed to be purified from the old leaven. I was attracted to the way, the Savior himself, but was still reluctant to go along its narrow paths. (*Conf.* 8, 1)

As a first approximation it is fair to say that Augustine sees himself at this juncture as facing a moral challenge. He sees that being stable in the enjoyment of God is going to require that he undertake a Christian way of life: he needs to 'go along [Christianity's] narrow paths'. Moreover, he sees that it is going to require of him a kind of moral transformation: as he puts it here, his heart will need to be purified and, in particular, he will need to give up the sexual desires and activities that are weighing him down.[5] That moral challenge grows into the deep moral difficulty at the centre of Book 8. Briefly put, the difficulty is that Augustine wants – indeed wants desperately – to meet the moral challenge he is faced with, but he is unable to. He discovers in himself a deep intransigence. He discovers that the sort of control that normally characterizes agency is lacking to him in this crucially important case, the case on which his ultimate happiness depends.

At the end of Book 8, Augustine describes the dramatic resolution of his problem, the events in the Milanese garden that might be thought of as his final religious conversion.[6] The details of this final resolution are crucial to the *Confessions* and to Augustine's theology more generally. But that part of the story is not what interests me here. Since I am interested in the phenomenon of internal moral conflict that Augustine compellingly draws to our attention, I leave aside altogether questions about whether or not and how his conflict might be resolved.

As we have seen, at the very beginning of Book 8, Augustine describes himself as 'reluctant' to go along Christianity's narrow paths. About a third of the way into Book 8, when he first begins to consider his moral difficulty in detail, we learn that reluctance has given way to utter inability. Augustine has just heard the story of the conversion of the famous orator Marius Victorinus. Here is his reaction to it:

> I was longing [to devote myself to you, as Victorinus had done] but was bound not by any external iron (*ferro alieno*) but by my own iron will. An enemy had a grip on my will and so made a chain for me and bound me. Lust is the product of a misdirected will; and when one follows lust, habit is produced; and when one offers no resistance to habit, necessity results. By these links, as it were, connected one to another (that is why I called it a chain), a harsh bondage held me under restraint. But the new will (*voluntas nova*) that was beginning to be within me, so that I might serve you freely and will to enjoy you, God, the one certain joy, was not yet strong enough to conquer my older will (*priorem*), which had been strengthened by age. So my two wills (*duae voluntates*), one old (*vetus*), the other new (*nova*), one carnal, the other spiritual, were in conflict with one another, and their discord was dissipating my soul. (*Conf.* 8, 10)

Augustine here reports having a new will to serve God (his desire for the sort of moral transformation that will allow him to be stable in God) but his new will is utterly ineffectual. His new will is opposed in the harshest possible way by another, older will. His old will binds him with the force of iron chains. He has two wills, he tells us, and they are in conflict.

There is a lot in this passage that deserves close attention, but I want to begin by looking at the nature of the inner conflict it introduces. Augustine may have been surprised or disappointed or even frustrated to discover that implementing his new will was not going to be easy. But what seems to puzzle him and what he seems to think needs explanation is not the experience of conflict itself but the severity of the conflict in this case. The first stirrings of his new will encounter not merely resistance but the cold, hard iron of necessity. His new will is bound as a captive, and he is utterly unable to move himself in the direction in which his new will points him.

The conflict is so severe, in fact, that Augustine is tempted to view the necessity that shackles his new will as somehow an alien force, distinct from himself and imposing itself on him from without. The old will might seem in reality to be no longer really his will but a sort of alien will. He tells us that 'an enemy had a grip on my will'. Adopting the language of the Apostle Paul he describes his new and old wills as spirit and flesh, respectively, and suggests that, insofar as the flesh battled against the spirit, the flesh (that is, his old will) 'was no longer I'.[7] The habit in which his old will is embodied acts with violence, dragging down his unwilling mind.[8]

The language of necessity, bondage, passivity and violence is intended to make clear the severity of Augustine's internal conflict. It is no doubt also meant to tempt us to conclude that Augustine's old will was no longer his will. But I think it is fairly clear that Augustine tempts us in that way only for affect. (And he has special reason for wanting to lead us on in this way: he is concerned about the Manichees in particular who want to dissociate themselves from the evil wills that are in them.[9]) Despite his flirting with the idea of alienation, however, he is careful to deny that his old will is to be thought of as having become a purely external force in his life. Each time he is on the verge of making that point, he carefully stops just short of it.

There are at least five pieces of evidence in the texts that show Augustine taking care to qualify his seemingly bold claims about alienation. First, he is eager to reject any suggestion that the necessity imposed by his old will excuses him of moral responsibility. He tells us that despite the fierce opposition of habit 'it was my own doing because I had arrived willingly at a place where I did not want to be' (*Conf.* 8, 11, quoted below). Similarly, the unwilling mind dragged down and bound 'deserves to be, since it slipped into the habit willingly' (*Conf.* 8, 12, note 8 above).

His idea in these passages is that he remains morally responsible for his condition but that the responsibility devolves to his present self from his past choices and actions. The state of bondage he is in now, which renders him unwilling and passive, is the result of prior actions that he undertook willingly (*volens*). Given this notion of what we might call indirect responsibility, Augustine's account here might be thought to resemble the account we would be inclined to give of the cocaine addict who, having first experimented with cocaine voluntarily, now finds herself with an addiction that she hates but that nevertheless rules her life with iron necessity. Her current addictive motivations and actions are no longer hers, although she remains (indirectly) morally responsible for what she does insofar as she is (directly) responsible for having got herself into the state she is in at present.

It might seem that this manoeuvre allows Augustine to claim moral responsibility for his present condition, but does nothing to lessen the impression that his old will is *now* wholly external to him and not *his* will at all. After all, that is what we would be inclined to say in the case of the currently unwilling addict. But there is a second piece of evidence. Although he claims to be bound, he tells us that it is 'not by any external iron but by my own iron will' (*Conf.* 8, 10, quoted above).

Third, when he invokes the Apostol Paul's striking claim from Romans – 'it was no longer I' – Augustine is careful to hedge it in a way that Paul does not:

> In this way I understood in my own experience what I was reading, how 'the flesh lusts against the spirit and the spirit against the flesh' (Gal. 5:17). It was, of course, I in each of them, but I was more in that which I approved in myself than in that which I disapproved. For in the latter case it was more the case that 'it was no longer I' (Rom. 7:17), since for the most part I was undergoing it unwillingly, than it was the case that it was I doing it willingly. Nevertheless a fiercer habit opposed me – it was my own doing because I had arrived willingly at a place where I did not want to be. (*Conf.* 8, 11)

Where Paul says 'it is no longer I', Augustine introduces a qualification: '*it was more the case* that "it was no longer I" ... than it was the case that it was I.' And he goes on in the next clause to explain that '*for the most part* I was undergoing it unwillingly'.

Fourth, when he introduces the contrast between his new and old wills (at *Conf.* 8, 10) he makes it clear that by 'old will' he does not mean a will that existed at one time in the past, that gave rise to habit, but that now no longer exists. His view is not that his new will is his only will and that the necessity that now binds it is merely the legacy of another will, not that other will itself. As Augustine describes his experience, his new will and his old will coexist in the present. When he says that his new will was not sufficient for overcoming his older will now strengthened by age (*Conf.* 8, 10), he pretty clearly does not mean that his older will is now gone, having left in its place something else, a kind of habit born of repetition over time. He claims instead that the old will remains and that it (the old will) is itself stronger by virtue of time-worn habit. After all, that is the point of his striking claim that he is being torn apart by the conflict of his two wills.

Finally, it is significant, I think, that Augustine portrays his inner struggle in this case as a conflict between two *wills*. He does not say, as the philosophical tradition he had inherited leaves it open to him to say, that his situation is characterized by the presence of a new will that struggles ineffectually against his appetites or animal drives, something arising from the body or non-rational part of the soul rather than from the rational mind. That is to say, it is noteworthy that Augustine does not conceive of his will as pitted against some other distinct internal source of motivation, some other part of the soul. He conceives of his new will as pitted against another will, another will that is also his.

We can see the significance of this way of thinking of the conflict if we look at the particular role Augustine assigns to the will in the complex of psychological events that give rise to ordinary choice and action. He holds that actions for which we can be held responsible are those we perform by will (*voluntate*). Moreover, every act of will has an object, aims at something: 'Obviously,' he says in *De libero arbitrio*, 'in order to will at all, one must will something' (*De libero arbitrio* 3, 75). How, Augustine asks, do these objects come before our consciousness? How do they arise as candidates for will? His answer is that they arise by various means, many of which are outside our control. They intrude on our senses, someone suggests something to us, a thought pops into our head. But an object's having entered into our consciousness in one of these ways makes it merely a *possible* candidate for will; that constitutes what Augustine calls a 'suggestion'. Our will enters into the story in the crucial way relevant to agency only when we consent to a suggestion that has some initial attraction for us (or reject something for which we have an initial aversion). Augustine makes this idea clear in a well known passage from his commentary on the Sermon on the Mount.

> There are three steps by which sin is brought to completion: suggestion, delight, and consent. A suggestion comes about through memory or a bodily sense (when we see, hear, smell, taste, or touch something). If the enjoyment of this thing delights, then if the delight is illicit, one ought to refrain from it. For example, when we are fasting and an appetite for something to eat arises in us at the sight of food, this occurs only by virtue of delight. Nevertheless we do not consent to it, and we restrain it by a command of reason which has control. But if consent had been given, the sin would be complete. (*De sermone Domini in monte* 1, 34)[10]

A suggestion's having some attraction for us is the stage in this process to which Augustine gives the name 'delight'. Consent occurs only after suggestion and delight, and only consenting to what has been suggested and what we have taken delight in constitutes the relevant act of will. To consent to something in this way is to make it (or allow it to become) our will; and if we then act accordingly, we will have acted by will.

This three-part schema (suggestion/delight/consent) is central to Augustine's ethical theory.[11] It gives him the structure he needs to distinguish and explain the phenomenon he takes to be distinctive of and essential to moral agency, namely, the act of will: consent. Moreover, given this three-part schema, we can see how Augustine's thinking of his old will as will entails a significant commitment. He thinks of urges, inclinations and desires that arise from the non-rational part of the soul – what he sometimes refers to generically as 'motions (or disturbances)' in the non-rational part – as doing their work at the stage of delight. They are the sorts of things that render attractive to us the objects that cross our radar screens, as it were, thereby making them candidate targets for will. But we can be said to will one thing or another only when we have consented to our delight in it. We can of course consent to what some urging of the non-rational soul makes attractive to us. But to do so is to make that urging (or what it urges) our will. And to make something our will in this sort of way is what Augustine thinks makes it ours in the sense relevant to moral agency.[12]

So when Augustine calls that part of him that remains recalcitrant in the face of his new will 'his (old) will' and when he suggests that his old will and new will somehow coexist and conflict, he is committing himself to robust ownership of his old will. If it is will, it embodies consent, and if it embodies consent, then it belongs in the most intimate way to the person who is that moral agent. By contrast, movements and disturbances in the non-rational soul, the brute desires and attractions a person experiences, are not as such features of her insofar as she is a moral agent, that is, insofar as she is appropriately subject to praise or blame. Augustine has seen that a motivation's being internal to us is not sufficient to ensure that it belongs to us as moral agents; not all our internal motivations are relevant to who we are from the moral perspective. Some of them may be alien to us and force themselves on our consciousness. When they do so we are crucially passive in the face of them. Only when we consent to them, only when they have been transformed into what Augustine calls our will, do they enter into the circle of our moral agency.

What I think all this evidence shows is that the fit between Augustine's case and that of the unwilling drug addict we considered briefly above is not exact. The two cases are alike in that, in both, prior fully voluntary choices have given rise to a bondage from which the agents cannot now free themselves. For that reason both agents are responsible (if only indirectly) for their present choices and actions. But the two cases come apart in the following way. In the case of the unwilling drug addict we are inclined to say that the desires and actions expressive of her addiction have become entirely external to her. She – that is, the moral agent that she is – remains connected with them only by virtue of features of her history. By contrast, Augustine, I think, wants to deny that the only connection tying him to his old will is his past. His old will remains his own, remains part of who he is from the perspective of moral agency, remains *his* will.

This is part of what is intriguing about Augustine's case. If I am right about it, he is staking out an interesting part of the spectrum of moral agency. The internal conflict he experiences on the way to his final conversion has features common to akrasia: he finds himself doing by virtue of his old will what he no longer thinks best.[13] But the case is more extreme than ordinary weakness of will because he takes himself not merely to act contrary to his new will but to be bound or necessitated to act in that way. But Augustine does not want to lump this case together with other extreme cases, such as that of unwilling drug addiction or pathological compulsion, where the necessity involved really undermines present moral agency. He is proposing for consideration a case in which the agent is (1) internally conflicted in a significant way, (2) bound against his will by one party to the conflict, (3) morally responsible, and (4) in an important sense *not* alienated from what it is that binds him.

Augustine's case shares features (1) and (3) with akrasia, features (1) and (2) with some cases of pathological compulsion, and features (1), (2) and (3) with the unwilling addict. The presence of all of features (1)–(4) uniquely locates Augustine's case on the spectrum of moral agency. This is what I meant when I said that Augustine's case is one of akrasia *with a twist*.

Augustine's Rejection of the Divided-soul Account

I want to interrupt my development of Augustine's understanding of his special case for a moment to consider how what we have seen bears on related Platonist themes. First, although Augustine shares with the Socrates of *Republic* 4 the belief that the soul has rational and non-rational parts, Augustine does not appeal to those distinct parts as distinct sources of motivation in order to explain akrasia (as Plato seems to intend to do in *Republic* 4).[14] Indeed Augustine insists that the conflict in his case is between two *wills*; it is within a single part of the soul, the will itself, where the will is understood to belong to the soul's rational part. Augustine, then, does not attempt to explain his case as one in which the rational part of the soul finds itself in conflict with some other part of the soul.

Second, Augustine's understanding of the role of the will in moral agency gives him reason to reject the multiple-sources explanation of akrasia as inadequate. We are morally responsible for and not merely passive in the face of the motivations that render our actions akratic. But motivations grounded in a non-rational part of the soul – appetite, say – considered just as such may be wholly alien to us, as the addict's and compulsive's motivations are. Appealing simply to multiple sources of motivation, then, gives us no way to distinguish akrasia from pathological compulsion and unwilling addiction. It gives us no way to distinguish cases in which the conditions of moral agency are satisfied, and the agent is therefore morally responsible for his actions, from cases in which moral agency is undermined and the agent is in fact a passive victim of alien forces that happen to be in some sense internal to him. As Augustine sees it, then, appealing to multiple sources of motivation as an explanation of akrasia will fail to carve reality at its joints. Hence his insistence that his case is characterized essentially by the presence of two conflicting *wills* is an implicit rejection of one important strand of Platonism.

It is an implicit rejection of Platonism, but the opponents Augustine has immediately in mind are more likely the Manichees.[15] Platonism and Manichaeism, however, are instructively alike. As Augustine understands it, the Manichees hold that we have within ourselves two souls: a good soul, which is in fact a small piece of the divine substance, and an evil soul. On this view our psychological conflicts are to be understood as the result of two opposing motivational forces within us. Moreover, *we* are in fact to be identified only with our good souls; our evil motivations and actions are the manifestation of a force that is alien to who we are.[16] Augustine rejects this Manichaean analysis of inner conflict and rejects it precisely because it undermines a crucial feature of the relevant conflicts, namely, that both conflicting motivations belong to me in the important moral sense. Augustine roundly excoriates the Manichees, accusing them of delighting in the view precisely because it exonerates them of any culpability for their actions. He himself feels acutely the pinch of moral responsibility.

> When I was deliberating so that I might serve the Lord my God, as I was already disposed to do, I was the one who was willing, I was the one who was refusing – it was I. But I was neither willing fully nor refusing fully. [*Ego cum deliberabam ut iam servirem domino deo meo, sicut diu disposueram, ego eram qui volebam, ego qui nolebam: ego eram. Nec plene volebam, nec plene nolebam.*] (*Conf.* 8, 22)

Augustine's striking repetition of the first person pronoun 'I' (*ego*) in this passage constitutes his emphatic insistence that both the relevant conflicting wills belong to him as a moral agent. The relevant cases of conflict, therefore, are not to be thought of on analogy with psychological compulsion. Our akratic motivations, even our twisted akratic motivations, cannot be alien to us in such a way that they cease utterly to be ours. Augustine can reasonably be seen as recognizing that appealing to distinct parts of the soul offers no essential advantage over the Manichaean appeal to distinct souls in this regard.

The Augustinian Divided Will

Let us return to the details of Augustine's case. Augustine thinks that his case is deeply puzzling, and he expends a good deal of effort trying to bring the puzzle clearly into focus. It is generated by the fact that in his case, as he conceives of it, what he longs for, what he wills but is unable to do, is primarily to have a certain sort of will. In this part of the *Confessions* he describes the object of his new will in several different ways, all of which, I think, come to essentially the same thing. Let us simplify matters by adopting the terms suggested by the first passage we looked at (*Conf.* 8, 10): Augustine's new will is the will to devote himself to God. To be devoted to God, however, is for one's will to be in a certain state; hence Augustine's new will is that his will be of a certain sort, the sort that constitutes being devoted to God. Now, in order to bring out the peculiarity in cases of this sort, cases in which an act or state of one's will is the object of one's will, he contrasts his puzzle case with more straightforward cases in which the object of one's will is a bodily movement:

> If I tore my hair, if I struck my forehead, if I clasped my knee with interlaced fingers, I did it because I willed to. Now I could have willed it and not done it (*potui autem velle et non facere*) if the mobility (*mobilitas*) of my limbs had not cooperated. I did so many things, therefore, in which willing (*velle*) was not the same as being able (*posse*). And I was *not* doing what [1] was pleasing to me by virtue of an incomparably greater affection and [2] I would have been able [to do] the moment I willed [it] (because the moment I willed [it], I would of course be willing [it]). For in this case the ability (*facultas*) was the will (*voluntas*), and to will [it] (*velle*) was already to do [it] (*facere*). Nevertheless it was not happening. The body obeyed the slightest will of the soul (so that its members were moved at its pleasure) more easily than the soul obeyed itself with regard to carrying out, by the will alone, the will's own ultimate will. (*Conf.* 8, 20)

Augustine expresses his puzzlement here in both a general and a specific way. There is his surprise at the general observation that his body should conform readily to the will of his soul whereas the soul should utterly fail to conform to its own will. And then there is the more focused astonishment at the paradoxical results of his analysis of the two different cases. He suggests that, when one wills to perform a certain action and then succeeds in doing it, three things must be in place: the will to do the action, the ability to do the action, and the action itself (*velle, posse, facere*). In the case of bodily movements, the willing and the bodily movement are clearly distinct. For one thing they are in different locations, so to speak, the mind and the body. For another, their distinctness can be made apparent by observing that in certain cases, where the relevant ability is lacking, the willing can occur without the bodily movement's ensuing. By contrast, Augustine points out that, in the case he is trying to fathom, the willing just is the action in question. That is because in this case the ability to do the relevant action is the will itself (*voluntas*), which of course is necessarily present when one wills. So in the peculiar case at hand, there does not appear to be any room for slippage between the willing and the doing; to will it just is to do it. Given that result, the particular case that led him to this investigation seems not just exceedingly odd, but impossible.[17]

> What is the source of this absurdity (*monstrum*)? How does this happen? The mind gives a command to the body and it is immediately obeyed; the mind gives a command to itself and it is resisted. The mind commands that the hand be moved and it is done so easily that the command and the obedience are almost indiscernible – and in that case the mind is mind whereas the hand is body. But when the mind commands that the mind will [something], the mind is not something distinct and nevertheless it does not do [it]. What is the source of this absurdity? How does it happen that someone who would not command [something] unless he willed [it], wills [it], and does not do what he commands? (*Conf*. 8, 21)

Augustine has an answer.

> But he does not *completely* will [it] (*non ex toto vult*); therefore he does not completely command [it]. For he wills it to the extent that he commands it, and insofar as what he commands does not occur, to that extent he does not will [it]. This is because the will commands that the will should be – and it is not something else but the will itself. And so it does not command fully (*plena*), and that is why what it commands does not occur. If [the will] were full, it would not command that it be, because it already would be. So there is no monster here, partly willing and partly nilling, but a kind of illness in the mind because, weighed down by habit, the whole mind does not rise up toward the truth. And so there are two wills (*duae voluntates*) because one of them is not whole (*tota*), and what is present in the one is lacking in the other. (*Conf*. 8, 21 continued)

It is easy to appreciate the strategy here. If, in the case at hand, the willing just is the doing, then it is impossible that Augustine will and that he not succeed in doing what he wills. So Augustine suggests an alternative principle to the claim that the willing just is the doing, a principle that is weaker than the original but in the same spirit. What is true, he suggests here, is that in the case at hand to will something *completely* just is to do it.[18] Given the alternative principle, Augustine's failure to will completely opens up the possibility of his failing to do what he wills. The absurdity vanishes.

We might think of this as Augustine's bipartite or multipartite conception, not of the soul but of the will. The will is a single whole that can give some or all of itself to its particular acts and states. Insofar as it gives less than all of itself to a particular act of will, there is the possibility that the will will give what remains of itself to another act. This sort of portioning out of the will opens the door to conflict: there can be distinct acts of will that conflict with one another, each of which has some part of the will behind it. Moreover, the partitioning is what gives rise to the need for commands of the sort Augustine imagines the soul giving to itself. When the will gives itself completely to a particular act, no wayward part of the will could remain that might need to be brought into line by means of a command. Platonism is right, then, about this: if there is conflict within a single thing, it must be by virtue of the thing's having distinct parts. Platonism was wrong to think that partitioning the soul could account for the essential features of akrasia, but it was right to think that partitioning of some sort is necessary.

The Puzzle of Moral Idenfication

So Augustine's preference for the multipartite will over the multipartite soul for explaining akrasia seems well motivated. But the idea of partitioning in the will raises plenty of difficulties of its own. I want to conclude by developing (without resolving) just one of them, one that is particularly important for Augustine himself.

The way in which the last passage (*Conf.* 8, 21) ends suggests a straightforward way of understanding how conflicts will play out in the multipartite will. We might suppose that when there are two wills, neither of them complete, such that what is present to one is lacking to the other, the one in which there is more of the will will carry the day, overcoming the one in which there is less. That way of thinking of it seems to fit some of the things Augustine has said about his internal conflict. He has told us that his new will was just beginning to be, and so presumably would not yet have had very much of the will present in it, and that his old will had the accumulated strength of entrenched habit, which might plausibly suggest the presence of a significant portion of the will's total resources.

But this straightforward way of extending Augustine's idea will not do. If the relative strength and weakness of Augustine's old and new wills is to be explained by the fact that more of his will is present in his old will than in his new, then it might also seem that more of Augustine – that is, more of the moral agent whose wills these are – is in the old will than in the new. If that were the case, we would expect Augustine to identify most strongly with his old will, but, as we have seen, he does just the opposite:

> It was, of course, I in each of them, but I was more in that which I approved in myself than in that which I disapproved. For in the latter case it was more the case that 'it was no longer I' (Rom. 7:17), since for the most part I was undergoing it unwillingly, than it was the case that it was I doing it willingly. (*Conf.* 8, 11)

What grounds can Augustine have for claiming that more of him was in his new will than in his old, if not that a greater portion of his will was in the new will than in the old? Augustine has got hold of and seen clearly the significance of the concept of what we might call 'moral identity'. His insistence that our conflicting motivations in important cases must be conflicting wills is his attempt to provide room for it. But he needs to do something more to account for the peculiar feature of moral agency that this passage draws our attention to: the agent's experience of identifying himself with what is in fact only a part – and perhaps only a minority part – of what nevertheless constitutes him as a moral agent.

There is a suggestion in this passage of how Augustine might answer that question; it has to do with the notion of his *approving* one of his two wills.

Moreover, it is a suggestion that points down another Platonist pathway, towards the idea that one's *reason* is definitive of one's moral identity. Augustine's exploration of that pathway must be left for another occasion, but I hope to have shown here how his reflections on the phenomenon of inner moral conflict constitute both Augustine's embracing and his radically transforming an important element of the Platonist heritage. His analysis of that phenomenon, the problems his analysis uncovers and the solutions he develops and advances are compelling, sophisticated and philosophically acute. Moreover, far from being simple-mindedly derivative, they are breathtakingly original: they introduce us for the first time in the history of philosophy to a genuine, psychologically deep and complex moral self, someone who looks unmistakably and uncannily like us.

Notes

* I read versions of this paper at a conference, 'Uses and Abuses of the Classics', at the State University of New York at Buffalo, at the Cornell Summer Colloquium in Medieval Philosophy, and at Nazareth College. I am grateful to the audiences on those occasions for helpful discussion. I am also grateful to Jeffrey Brower for comments on a draft.

1 For a useful survey of the state of the scholarship on this issue, see 'Plotinus', chapter 3 in S. Menn, *Descartes and Augustine* (Cambridge: Cambridge University Press, 1998).
2 I do not mean to suggest that Augustine's encounter with these elements of Platonism involved his direct acquaintance with the *Protagoras* or *Republic*.
3 I use the Latin text in J.J. O'Donnell, ed., *Augustine: Confessions (Vol. 1): Introduction and Text* (Oxford: Clarendon Press, 1992). All translations here are my own. I have profited from consulting M. Boulding, trans., *The Confessions* (Hyde Park, NY: New City Press, 1997) and H. Chadwick, trans., *Saint Augustine: Confessions* (Oxford: Oxford University Press, 1991). References are to the book and standard paragraph numbering; omitting the (redundant) chapter numbers.
4 For an account of the events in Book 7, see S. MacDonald, 'Divine nature', in E. Stump and N. Kretzmann (eds), *The Cambridge Companion to Augustine* (Cambridge: Cambridge University Press, 2001), pp.71–90.
5 See *Conf.* 7, 23 for a specific reference to the burden of sexual desire.
6. *Conf.* 8, 28–9.
7 See the passage from *Conf.* 8, 11 quoted below.
8 'I was certain that it was better for me to give myself to your love than to surrender to my own cupidity. The former, however, pleased me and won me over whereas the latter enticed me and bound me ... In vain I "delighted in your law in respect of the inner man; but another law in my members fought against the law of my mind and led me captive in the law of sin which was in my members" (Rom. 7:22). Now the law of sin is the violence of habit by which even the unwilling mind is dragged down and held, as it deserves to be, since it slipped into the habit willingly' (*Conf.* 8, 12).
9 See *Conf.* 5, 18; 8, 22–4; and the third section of this chapter: 'Augustine's Rejection of the Divided-soul Account'.
10 Compare: *De libero arbitrio* 3, 29; 3, 74–5; *De Trinitate* 12, 17–18.
11 In the passage from *De sermone Domini in monte*, Augustine focuses on suggestion, delight and consent; presumably there is a phenomenon mirroring this one that consists in suggestion, aversion, and rejection.

12 Notice that in *Conf.* 8, 12 (note 8 above) Augustine speaks of 'surrendering to cupidity'. 'Surrendering' there captures the notion of consent, 'cupidity' the notion of delight. To surrender to cupidity is to consent to some suggestion in which one takes delight.
13 That is clear from *Conf.* 8, 12: 'I was certain that it was better for me to give myself to your love than to surrender to my own cupidity. The former, however, pleased me and won me over whereas the latter enticed me and bound me.'
14 For useful discussion of Plato's position in *Republic* 4, see T. Penner, 'Thought and desire in Plato', in G. Vlastos (ed.), *Plato II: A Collection of Critical Essays* (Notre Dame, IN: University of Notre Dame Press, 1971), J.M. Cooper, 'Plato's theory of human motivation', *History of Philosophy Quarterly* 1 (1984); T.H. Irwin, Plato's Ethics (New York and Oxford: Oxford University Press, 1995), pp.203–22.
15 As *Conf.* 8, 22–4 shows.
16 See *Conf.* 5, 18; 8, 22–4.
17 It is not entirely clear how to understand the precise nature of the puzzle about willing that Augustine presents here. When he says that 'to will [it] was already to do [it]' he may be (illicitly) inviting us to conflate *willing to will X* with *willing X*, so that he supposes that when he has done the former, he has already (thereby) done the latter. Or he may simply be inviting us to reflect on the oddity of a first-order act of will's recalcitrance in the face of a second-order act of will. Augustine presses a similar sort of puzzle with a similar ambiguity in his famous discussion of the compatibility of free will and divine foreknowledge (*De libero arbitrio* 3, 1–11).
18 Compare *Conf.* 8, 19: 'But to travel to that destination one does not use ships or chariots or feet. It was not even necessary to go the distance I had come from the house to where we were sitting. For not only to go but also to arrive there was nothing other than willing to go, but willing firmly and wholly (*fortiter et integre*), not swerving and lurching this way and that, like a half-crippled will struggling along with one part trying to get up while another part is falling down.'

Chapter 7

Heidegger's Hermeneutic Reading of Plato

Kah Kyung Cho

Plato's Allegory of the Cave opens with the following statement of Socrates to Glaucon: 'Here is a parable to give an aspect (of the essence) of education as well as the lack of it, which fundamentally concerns our Being (nature) as man.'[1] From this passage, it is apparent that the allegory is intended to be an exposition of the essence of *paideia*, which is usually translated rather loosely as 'education'. Though Plato appears to be in no hurry to give an advance definition of the essence of *paideia*, he comes closest to doing so by bringing *paideia* together with its opposite notion, *apaideusia* ('uneducatedness'). For neither the positive attributes normally found in an 'educated' man (such as refinement in arts and letters) nor the absence thereof in an 'uneducated' man are in themselves a sufficient index of what *paideia* truly is. It is only when we comprehend the transitional character through which these two formally opposed concepts are intrinsically connected that we realize why and how their relationship, as a transition from *paideia* to *apaideusia*, and vice versa, 'fundamentally' affects the nature of man.

Heidegger's interpretation of Plato's Allegory of the Cave heavily focuses on this 'transitional' character of 'education'. He reminds us that for Plato the essence of *paideia* does not consist 'in pouring mere knowledge into an unprepared soul as if it were an empty, arbitrarily held out container'. Rather, soul itself must be prepared for change, and precisely for that purpose, *paideia* has to be first and foremost that which 'leads to turning the whole man around in his nature or essence' (*E* 256, *H* 23).[2] Specifically, the series of events reported in the Allegory are transitions (*Übergänge*) from the cave out into the light of the day and back again from the daylight into the cave. Heidegger asks, 'what occurs during these transitions? .... What is it about these transitions that matters?' (*E* 255, *H* 22).

What occurs during the transition is an 'inversion' (*Umwendung*) of man's entire attitude. What matters about these transitions is that they 'demand each time a reorientation of the eyes from the darkness to the light and from the light to the darkness. Hence the eyes are confused every time for two contrary reasons' ('Twofold confusions occur for twofold reasons', 518a, 2). Heidegger then gives the following exegesis:

> A man can either be transported from an ignorance which he hardly notices to a state where beings (*to on, das Seiende*) show themselves more essentially, but unable to appreciate this essential aspect; or a man can fall from a position of essential knowing and

become confined in a region under the power of ordinary reality, without still being able to accept as the real what is here usual and customary. (*E* 225 ff)

Based on the question raised by Heidegger above and our preliminary reading of his discussions, four themes stand out which, taken together, serve as the guiding light of his interpretation of Plato's Allegory. First, Heidegger draws a close parallel between the varying degrees in which reality or beings show themselves and the changing physical locations of the prisoner. Starting from the depth of the cave, moving past an elevated area lit by an artificial fire and finally exiting to the open air, the successive movements of the prisoner are played out in a series of striking flashbacks under one central theme: light. Any light or fire, and ultimately the sun itself, are the cause and source of the way reality shows itself, and it is therefore what gives 'visibility' to what has been sighted. This situation surrounding the prisoner's experience in the cave is fraught with symbolism of light and vision that requires a further clarification.

Secondly, the failure of man in appreciating the 'more essential' aspect of reality after being moved to this new stage is due to the power of the 'ordinary reality' that still holds him under its sway. Hence the aim of *paideia* is to get to the root of the matter and turn around the whole being (soul) of man. This involves literally 'uprooting' man from the familiar milieu of his habitation.[3] But even after being freed from the old abode, the threat of lapsing into the state of *apaideusia* is quite real. This is shown by the fact that the narrative of the Allegory does not end with the ascent of man to the highest stage. The descent of the freed man back to the cave is not an incidental epilogue. To make the task of *paideia* complete, he must now lead the chained prisoners to freedom at the risk of being misunderstood and even persecuted by them. Did not the fate of Socrates show what price he had to pay for trying to convert the soul of the ignorant? With this passing reference to Socrates (*E* 260), Heidegger emphasizes that *paideia* 'contains in itself the essential relationship [of falling back] to *apaideusia*'. This means that the matter of enlightening uneducated people is not external to one's own 'education'.[4]

Thirdly, the inversion of man is never completed in one step or as a linear, forward moving process. There is always a blind side to the laboriously gained access to new reality. The knowledge of new reality is adequate only in relation to the realm to which a man is designated. For instance, the knowledge of objects illuminated by fire may be 'more real' than the perception of the shadow, but this knowledge is available only to the prisoner who is freed to come near the fire. The cave dwellers, on the other hand, have no way of even suspecting that there could be any other reality than the one to which they are inextricably bound. By the same token, the 'more real' knowledge of objects obtained under artificial light is still a far cry from the glance at the 'things themselves' lying in the splendour of daylight. At this point, Heidegger distinguishes between 'the mere act of getting free from the chains' and 'the actual liberation' (*E* 259). The latter 'lies in the steadiness with which one turns toward what manifests itself in its outward appearance and is in this manifesting the most *unhidden*' (italics mine). We shall come back later to this crucial passage and clarify its still hidden link to Plato's theory of Idea.

So far Plato has only given us the point that the essence of *paideia* is 'turning the whole man (soul) around'. Now Heidegger articulates this process of 'turning around' (*periagōgē*) in several stages: 'transition' (*Übergang*), 'inversion' (*Umwendung*) and 'reorientation of habit' (*Um- und Eingewöhnung*). They are interconnected, but carefully shaded and contrasted stages in which it becomes obvious that the eye and what it sees as real are just as intensely involved and tested as the soul itself. Thus, in terms of affecting both vision and soul, 'transition' is at its most crucial and painful when one makes the very first step to break with the old, ingrained habit. The pain of being transported from the familiar to an unknown reality, albeit in the name of a 'more essential' reality, is so great that people would not ordinarily risk such transition on their own. Nevertheless, if cities were 'to have respite from evil' (473c–d), that is, to avoid repeating the same errors of the older generation, Plato feels it necessary to remove children early on from their parents' home.

As distinguished from 'transition' in the sense of being physically transported from one location to another, 'inversion' has to do more with 'turning around' man's entire attitude. It means not only freedom from 'uneducatedness', but also positively directing the attention of the freed man towards the 'most real', or the 'most unhidden' in Plato's expression. The essence of *paideia* can be fulfilled only when the 'inversion' brings a man to unflinchingly face the highest reality. This culminates in the part of education called 'reorientation' of habit. A sustained effort is necessary for a man to remain 'oriented to' and 'dwell in' the newly opened realm with the intent of 'getting used to it'. To this Heidegger adds the following explanation: 'Just as one's own eye must reorient itself slowly and steadily, whether to the brightness or to the darkness, so also must soul, with patience and with a relevant series of steps, get used to staying in the realm of being to which one is exposed' (*E* 256, *H* 23). Without a slow, painstaking formation of this new habit, the liberation from 'uneducatedness' will be short-lived. For the shock of being exposed to an unfamiliar reality, and possibly the pain affecting the sight would simply drive the confused man back to the comfort of his old habit[5] and the safety of dwelling in the 'ordinary reality'. It is only after enduring some time in the uncomfortable situation that the eye gets adjusted to the surrounding and begins to appreciate 'the more essential reality' that reigns in the new realm.

Fourthly, and most importantly, while Heidegger admits that Plato's stated purpose in the Allegory was to give an illustration of the essence of education, he would consider 'essence of truth' rather than 'essence of education' as the central, albeit unstated, theme of this classical piece of Plato. Hence he explicitly elevates this unstated, theme to the title of his work: *Plato's Doctrine of Truth*. The adventurousness of Heidegger's interpretation is not diminished by his assurance that the centrality of the topic of 'truth' does not come at the expense of the validity of 'education'. He even goes so far as to say that his essential redefinition of 'truth' in fact serves the purpose of 'making possible' Plato's theory of education 'in its fundamental structure' (*E* 257). Conversely, he argues that the essence of 'education', just as Plato's Allegory has illustrated it, 'opens up a glimpse into a change in the essence of "truth" as well' (ibid.). Thus it is Heidegger's overall contention that his own essay, 'Plato's doctrine of truth', and Plato's Allegory of the Cave *qua Doctrine of Education*, must belong together in a mutually complementing relationship. Only when the pure storyline of the Allegory of the Cave is isolated as a self-contained text may there be between Plato and Heidegger prima facie two different ways of reading the same text. Yet Heidegger sees those two different readings ultimately collapsing into one at the level of 'problem-centred' hermeneutic interpretation. For the real issue unfolds itself in the context of 'the problem of history', not necessarily within the bounds of the subjective consciousness of an author. The problem-historical approach is a 'bird's-eye' point of view, from which the two positions could be historically mediated as accentuating and validating each other.

But there remains the undeniable problem that Heidegger is offering *his* interpretation of the Allegory of the Cave in the name of Plato as Plato should have read it. What he is offering is fully dressed and is entitled '*Plato*'s Doctrine of Truth' (italics mine). After initially declaring that he has no quarrel with Plato on Plato's own ground, Heidegger has in effect carried his 'dialogue' onto a different plane. More specifically, the subject matter was switched from 'education' to 'truth', and also the terms of the discourse of 'truth' were referred to a higher court (of *Being*), where a 'dialectical' unity between 'truth' and 'education' could be rendered plausible. Hence we must ask the inevitable question: what is Heidegger's justification in 'overriding' Plato's own thesis, both at the level where Plato was talking about 'education' and at the level where Plato's view of 'truth' is subjected to criticism? Before we try to respond to this challenge, it is worth a moment's pause to listen to what Heidegger has to say about this matter in a prefatory remark: 'The "doctrine" of a thinker is that which is left unsaid in what he says, to which man is exposed in order to expend himself upon it' (*E* 251).

The need for us to 'expend ourselves' on what is unsaid by a thinker can arise only in proportion to the gravity of a larger, overarching issue that we perceive should have been duly addressed but was overlooked, or less than satisfactorily answered. The criteria with which to measure this perceived inadequacy have to be contextual either within the total framework of an author's work or with reference to a still larger historical development to which his thought is related in an important way. Heidegger places Plato primarily in the latter framework. But this framework itself is surpassed by Heidegger's own conception of the entire tradition of Western metaphysics in terms of the *History of Being*. Imposing such a theme on Plato or other thinkers has been perceived by critics as extraneous or context-alienated, especially when Heidegger was practising a highly concentrated *parole* analysis, reading his own, single thought into or out of selected words and texts of other authors.

His first major work that drew negative criticism[6] was *Kant and the Problem of Metaphysics* (1929). Foraging the 'Transcendental Analytic' of the *First Critique* for clues, Heidegger tried to show that Kant had a fleeting awareness of the 'finite' temporality of human *Dasein*. Although his 'suspicion' could not be directly corroborated by the text, Heidegger was led to conjecture that no sooner had Kant glimpsed the 'abyss' (of finitude) at the root of the faculty of 'Imagination', that he must have 'cringed' and turned away from this unsettling phenomenon. Heidegger ingeniously reconstructed his thesis about Kant's 'awestricken retreat' (*Zurückschrecken*) on the observation that the revised second edition of the *Critique of Pure Reason* assigned a greater role to understanding at the expense of imagination than did the first edition. In plain text, this means that Heidegger had to rekindle that briefly flickering insight Kant had into the problem of existential temporality of human being.

Nevertheless, to an avowed rationalist metaphysician who implicitly shared Newton's universal space and time as *sensorium Dei*, such a contingent factor as the existential human temporality was surely an alien vocabulary. As it happened, Heidegger admitted years later (1950) that he found his earlier position on Kant no longer tenable.[7] Needless to say, this one isolated open gesture did little to allay the rather deep-seated scepticism among his readers. Their critical voice was raised pointedly against Heidegger's interpretative practice in which philosophers and poets, both classical and modern, were *nolens volens* brought in line with his own speculative conception of Being. His usual defence consisted in separating 'the method of historical philology' from '*a dialogue between thinkers*' which is '*bound by other laws* ... [which] are more easily violated; the possibility of going astray is more threatening, the shortcomings are more frequent' (ibid., italics mine).

Anticipating a similar criticism for his interpretation of Plato, Heidegger now argues, *ex privativo*, that he may be placing 'too much of an alien burden' on Plato's 'allegory'. But all the same, he asserts in the next breath that the unsaid, namely the underlying Doctrine of Truth, 'governs the hidden law of what Plato says as a thinker' (*E* 257). Now we have here the obvious choice of critically examining either Heidegger's treatment of the 'unsaid' of Plato on the basis of what is said by Plato, or Plato's discussion of 'education', which is what is said by Plato, with reference to Heidegger's theory of 'truth', which is what is unsaid by Plato. The first topic would focus on Heidegger's own doctrine of 'truth', with Plato merely serving an ancillary role to provide whatever Heidegger can make out of Plato's text.

In choosing to consider the second problem, we actually follow Heidegger's own lead, at least half of the way. That is to say, Heidegger's dictum that 'in order to learn and henceforth know what a thinker has left unsaid, whatever it may be, it is necessary to consider what he has said' (*E* 251), is to be modified and articulated as follows: 'In order to learn and henceforth know more clearly what Plato meant to say, it may be useful to consider what Heidegger says Plato had left unsaid.' There is no mystery, however, about what was left unsaid by Plato, since we know it is none other than Heidegger's own interpretation of 'truth' as 'unconcealment'. To speculate whether and under what different circumstances Plato might have agreed with Heidegger in embracing this particular theory of 'truth' as his own would be an exercise in futility. This is so because, firstly, Plato did state his case positively in terms of 'education theory', which Heidegger himself does not dispute. Secondly, where Heidegger deviates from Plato is on a different plane, from which Plato could be excluded, inasmuch as it is at the level of 'depth psychology' where Heidegger could indulge in analysing Plato's motives against Plato's own self-knowledge.

A wider contextual horizon encompassing both Heidegger's 'truth' and Plato's 'education' has to be secured, if Heidegger's exposition of the 'Doctrine of Truth' is to lay claim to compatibility with Plato's essential description of 'education'. Furthermore, it will serve Heidegger's interest better if he can desist from putting himself at the centre of this expanded horizon and render Plato's proximity to the common overarching issue more readily visible. Purely in terms of the breadth of historical perspective, *physis* may qualify as such a common horizon. It is broadly shared by Heraclitus, Parmenides and even Aristotle, who could all bear witness to Heidegger's reading of *physis* as Being. This in turn would directly conflate with the notion of 'unconcealment', so basic to Heidegger's definition of 'truth'. But all this is an advantage Heidegger should not simply take for granted, if he were to meet Plato's argument at its strongest, without any abridgment. As it stands, *physis* had already lost its full meaning for Plato and was relegated as *physika* (science of nature) to an academic discipline, side by side with logic and ethics. Heidegger now has to address Plato's central concept, which has the broadest possible basis *within* the framework of his philosophy. The one and only such concept that appropriately meets the eye and possibly bears the burden of horizon could be *Idea*. But could it offer precisely the framework for bridging *paideia* and *alētheia*? It is certainly not enough that Idea subsumes under itself the essence of both *paideia* and *alētheia*, for essences are in themselves ideas, which subordinate themselves of their own accord to their highest genus. It is a different matter when two heterogeneous categories, such as the act of seeing and the object seen, have to be brought together. Plato and Heidegger are, in point of their 'truth' theory, at odds with each other by holding onto the model of 'being' and that of 'saying', respectively.

Before we turn to this intricate issue, let us make one brief and another more expanded observation for a better overview of the layout of our discussion. The first is related directly to the problem we have just raised and serves as a preliminary index to the way Heidegger sees 'education' and 'truth' linked 'together into an original and essential unity' (*E* 257). The second observation is meant to provide a broader background knowledge of Heidegger's hermeneutical approach, as he has been often, both rightly and wrongly, criticized for doing 'violence' to historical texts of other authors.

Concerning the first point, Heidegger has already stated that Plato's aim of 'education' is to change the whole personhood, instead of merely filling a person's mind with knowledge. Such a change, as shown above, is inseparably tied to the change of 'region' from which man is 'uprooted' or into which he is 'transplanted'. Now, with each change of the region, 'beings themselves make their appearance' in such a way that 'everything commonly known to man up to this time and the way it was known become different' (ibid.). In other words, the educational reform of a person is correlated to changing aspects of reality as well as to the ways such change of reality is perceived and known. Reality in general, we are told, refers to 'what is always openly present in the region in which man abides'. It is important to note here that what is openly present is never a pre-existing state of things lying passively before our eyes. Rather, its opposite, namely, the hiddenness, is the original state, and only when this original state is overcome does there emerge something like the open presence of things into full view. Thus reality in its most real sense is 'unhiddenness', made accessible only by 'overcoming' the initial, resistant state of 'hiddenness'.

An artfully conceived 'etymological' commentary on Heidegger might throw some light on this matter. According to him, openness as unhiddenness is the consequence of a 'privation', a constantly wresting extortion of the 'unhidden'. In the Greek word *a-lētheia* as 'truth' there is the hint of the 'privative' *a-* which indicates that something like 'concealment' belongs to the essence of 'truth'. It is from this primary word with the dual meaning of 'unhiddenness in relation to the hidden' that what we ordinarily call *truth*, which we nowadays understand in flat opposition to and in abstract separation from *untruth*, has derived. Heidegger then emphatically states that 'where unhiddenness is not a component of the definition of "truth", an "allegory of the cave" has no basis from which it can be clarified' (*E* 261). We may also ask ourselves: could Plato have employed the extraordinary imagery of a subterranean cave simply to explicate the essence of 'education'? Even if movement and transition from abode to abode must essentially belong to the design of a pedagogy to produce a certain desired effect on man's soul, such need could have been fulfilled by a number of other mundane models or physical settings. But with the 'allegory' – with its built-in contrast and interplay between light and dark, the visible and the invisible, ascending and descending levels of dwelling place – the significance of 'truth' as *the basic realm* on which the openness and hiddenness of reality presents itself could not have been more dramatic.

If the changing ambience with increasing and decreasing accessibility to reality holds the key to educating the human soul, there could hardly be a more effective allegory than the one built on the aspect of the cave. The cave, in every respect, is nature's custom-designed setting for *paideia*. But Heidegger is quick to point out that the unified title of what plays itself out on the various stages of this setting is none other than *alētheia*. In other words, the 'essence of education is founded in the essence of "truth" (unhiddenness)' (*E* 260). Education cannot directly mould man's soul. It has to go through the experience of reality (Being) which in various ways profoundly impinges on his soul. The highest goal of education is accomplished when the highest reality, that is, the highest state of unhiddenness, is grasped. This is how Heidegger sees ultimately the inner unity of *paideia* and *alētheia*. Upon closer analysis, however, it turns out to be one possible version of the unity, in which *ontological* 'truth' constitutes the foundation, and 'education' emerges as the upper, founded layer. Clearly, Heidegger is making 'education' dependent on 'truth'. Against this, a defence of Plato's version of the unity should be possible, insofar as Idea can be considered as the foundation on which the experience of truth and untruth depends.

Now with regard to the larger methodological question, Heidegger's manner of reading his meaning of 'truth' into the text of the 'allegory' is actually nothing new. He proceeds here very much as he did with the now familiar fable of *Cura* in *Being and Time* (para. 42). He confers on the 'allegory', irrespective of the way Plato himself appropriates it, the status of a 'preontological' testimony about *man's being*. He frees it of any theoretical constructions, including Plato's interpretation, and lets it speak as though it is coming out of the pristine depth of man's soul. In a style reminiscent of depth psychology, Heidegger would sooner take stock in a statement made without intention than in a deliberately constructed theory. This distrust of cerebral concoction, as opposed to things that have their base in *phenomena* as pure 'self-showing', does not stop before the bar of reason, even if it is reason which speaks through the language of Plato. Therefore, when Heidegger says that 'it (allegory) illustrates not only the essence of education, but at the same time it opens up a glimpse into a change in the essence of *truth*' (*E* 257), there is no question for him which of these 'two things' should carry a greater weight. Since it is phenomenally more evident, the theme of 'truth' must prevail.

Still, Heidegger's preference for the theme of 'truth' cannot rest exclusively on its strength of being preontologically evident. He has to take duly into account the fact that the essence of 'education' was the subject matter of the 'allegory' and openly so declared by Plato. No doubt the 'allegory' can deliver both 'education' and 'truth' as they 'crystallize into an essential unity' (ibid.). Heidegger tried to show this unity by way of ontological relationship between the founding and the founded layers. Mere compatibility of these two things is a far cry from their 'necessary inner unity', unless a common thread, issuing forth from a centre, runs through them. The obvious difficulty in establishing such a unity was that Heidegger had to carry his argument on the force of what is *unsaid*, in order to produce even a semblance of Plato's having glimpsed 'truth' as 'unhiddenness'. This was an awkward and probably unnecessary conjecture once we recognize that simply having no fear of conflict between the 'two things' is a rather palliative solution of the problem. For we could actually make a stronger case for the theory of *paideia* by staying within the bounds of Plato's philosophy.

To reinstate the centrality of *paideia*, however, does not mean to abandon Heidegger's exposition of the 'allegory' in favour of the foundational role of *alētheia*. In a different context, his reading of Plato belongs to the broader tradition of inquiry that asks the question of *quid juris*. For the awareness of what lies underneath, which Heidegger named 'the hidden law', regardless of whether the original author was conscious of it or not, has since Kant become the backbone of the so-called 'transcendental' pursuit of knowledge. It does not seek knowledge of 'objects' as such. Rather, by clarifying the 'conditions for the possibility of objective knowledge', such knowledge of objects may be given a greater safeguard against the charge of standing on unexamined premises.

To be sure, Heidegger's is not a transcendental philosophy in the usual sense of the word reserved for the critical epistemology of Kant and Neo-Kantians. In his book on Kant, he even declared that it was considered 'progress' in his time to reaffirm 'metaphysics' over epistemology. By 'metaphysics' he meant the classical question of 'being', which, as *Being and Time* has shown, can be reinaugurated with style in our modern age. For several decades, therefore, 'ontology' was deemed to be the proper title for Heidegger's undertaking in general, but soon he was clearly distancing himself from this and other conventional labels, settling eventually on the simple parole, 'Thought of Being'. With respect to the method and philosophical 'stance' (*Einstellung*), he was deeply committed to 'phenomenology'. Yet he would sharply separate himself from Husserl and underscore the 'hermeneutic' provenance of his thinking, though even this epithet was dropped in later years.

It is in essence this 'hermeneutic bent' of inquiry, for which he owes perhaps as much to Aristotle as to Dilthey,[8] that lay at the heart of Heidegger's reading of historical texts. He would read them in such a way as to make a major issue of what remains 'unsaid' or at best only vaguely hinted at. In the broadest possible outline, for Heidegger, the unsaid but central question of Western philosophy is Being. The famous passage from Plato's *Sophist* (244a) quoted at the beginning of *Being and Time*, may not be a direct index of what is 'unsaid', but it certainly highlights the 'oblivion' that has clouded the issue of Being throughout history.

Though Heidegger's philosophy claims to address the question of Being pure and simple, the complex turns its path had to take were due to this 'hermeneutic' approach which looks at the totality of *history* as the text par excellence. Thus when the 'fundamental ontology', originally only meant to be a propaedeutic to the real issue, namely, the thought of Being, upstaged it for decades, it necessitated the so-called 'turn' (*Kehre*) to restore the primary question of Being. Heidegger's actual unfolding of the question of Being may have begun with a phenomenological method, but he traced its living historical origin back to Greek antiquity rather than to the Husserlian source of transcendental consciousness. Therefore it is only fair for his type of phenomenology so steeped in historical consciousness to be called by another name. For some time, 'hermeneutic' has remained as the appropriate epithet to qualify the basically phenomenological thrust of Heidegger's thought, but it, too, gave way to Heidegger's increased tendency to resort to simple, archaic and pictorial images tapped from ancient sources, including those of the Eastern world.

In a formal sense, hermeneutic philosophy prioritizes the questioning to the extent that any word understood is considered 'understood' in principle as an *answer* to a preceding question (*Jedes Wort ist eine Antwort*).[9] To divine what preceding question it was to which the word that I understand now is related as an answer becomes therefore a highly visible trademark of hermeneutic philosophy. Conversely, to know how to correctly formulate the question means to know how to correctly answer it, at least half way. Thus in Heidegger's hermeneutic thinking there is a shared tendency with the transcendental philosophy to go beyond or behind the obvious in search of its hidden ground. But a major difference between them with regard to the nature of this grounding should not be overlooked: transcendental inquiry seeks to justify certain a priori concepts that are presupposed in every experience, such as time and space. While these concepts may serve as the 'ground' upon which physical and geometrical sciences are built, the very mode of *being* of such time or space remains unquestioned. For Kant, the *fact* of reason itself was an indubitable ground, beyond which no meaningful question could possibly be raised.

On the other hand, the ground for Heidegger is none other than Being (*Sein*) itself, which, as has been shown above in conjunction with the question of 'truth', has the fundamentally 'bipolar' tendency of revealing and concealing itself at the same time. As such, Being is the ground that challenges thought, not so much to justify the possibility of its 'self-showing' as to make us ponder the possible aspect of its absence and self-withdrawal. An example of this line of thinking can be Heidegger's argument that 'nature' made accessible by modern natural science and technology may more likely conceal its essence than reveal it. He would point out that '*technē*' in its original Greek sense used to have a fuller and richer meaning and shared the domain of *poiēsis* ('art'). If anything perceptibly worthy and uplifting can fill the vacuum generated by the 'withdrawal of being' in the wake of the total ascendancy of the technical, it should be, according to Heidegger, the revival of the function of art as *poiēsis*. The primary function of such creative art is indeed to bring 'truth' into the open. Art for the sake of beauty or aesthetic appreciation is a derivative form of *technē* to which erstwhile *poiēsis* stood close, until *technē* started asserting its hegemony[10] over *physis*.

We know poetry has long played a 'kindred role' for philosophy in Heidegger's thought. Now painting, too, has entered its 'partnership' with philosophy, as Merleau-Ponty embarked on a search for 'unbridled' truth about nature.[11] For the structure imposed on philosophy by the ingrained 'representational' thinking was leaving little room to say anything new and meaningful about the essence of nature. 'Representational' (*vorstellend*) is a term used by Heidegger to describe the basic tendency of conventional Western philosophy to bring everything as object before the magisterial control of the thinking subject. Representation sidesteps 'things themselves' and replaces them with *ideas*. Ideas are thoroughly transparent mental constructs of subjectivity. In significant variations, the thesis of the convertibility between the subjective and the objective has been repeatedly stressed by modern philosophers and scientists alike.[12] For representational thinking, 'objective' means *idealized* reality, that is, a construct of subjectivity. Thus man sees in whatever he encounters his own mirror image. Only nature accessed through creative art would now hold the promise of revealing its many different faces. Creative art can and must contradict nature's 'domesticated' image. It is *fixated* through the time-worn Cartesian dioptric. For Cartesianism arranges the universe with man ensconced at its centre, as an unmoving axis around which everything else turns.

The contrast between 'domesticated' and 'brute' nature derives from Cézanne's paradigm. According to this, the painter's eye does not just face over against things, but rather looks out 'from within the things'. Only in this manner is the artist able to catch, if fleetingly, the brute nature untouched by domestication. This recent development in phenomenological aesthetics illustrates in a nutshell how hermeneutic consciousness is picking up what has eluded representational thinking and explores an alternative possibility of the way things are. Such alternative possibility as a matter of fact was the way of life in the early period of ancient Greece. Man was not at the centre of the world as an unchallenged, unmoving axis. Instead, nature and things of nature, with their uncanny but effortless ways to create, foster and regulate life, took the centre stage. The true subject of action was, in Heidegger's language, *Being*. Man's relation to Being is best illustrated in Heidegger's translation of the *Fragment* (5 and 8, v.34) of Parmenides. Instead of the conventional reading that 'Thought and Being are one and the same', Heidegger stresses their mutually interdependent aspect and shows the two sides of man's relationship, 'to belong to and to be appropriated by' Being. The meaning of this 'physis-centredness' is forgotten and misunderstood, since our knowledge of the way Greeks have actually thought has become largely filtered through the semantic grill of representational thinking. Not only that, our overdependence on great systematizers like Plato and Aristotle poses another problem. Since they were already at the beginning of the process of system building, their thought was affected by this 'logicized' mode of world view which loses contact with the real life process. Philosophy for Socrates still meant a living dialogue growing out of any given contingent situation. As philosophy turned with Aristotle into 'school', the gridiron of *Organon* was introduced. His logic has become the one-sized straitjacket every student of philosophy has to wear for 'correct' thinking.

The measure of Heidegger's critical slant on Plato could be hardly missed in these and similar broad sweeps of negative comments made on representational thinking. His labelling of the tradition of Western metaphysics as a singular history of 'forgetfulness of Being' is the more widely known side of his hermeneutic pre-understanding. But the fact that Heidegger's Being has a great proximity to the Greek notion of *physis* has not been recognized as early or as widely as it should have been.[13] For the 'co-primary' presence of the attributes of self-showing and self-concealing as the most salient feature of the ontological truth was already discussed in a section entitled 'Truth as Disclosedness' of *Being and Time* (para. 44). Thus 'truth' as 'disclosedness' is not a definition specially tailored to accommodate the unusual experience of subterranean cave dwellers.

Just as consistently as ever, therefore, Heidegger is guided by the same Thought of Being when he sets out to analyse Plato's 'allegory'. Only this time he can fall back on a wider range of historical attestations to the essence of 'truth'. In his 1929/30 lecture, 'The basic concepts of metaphysics',[14] Heidegger quoted the following passage from *Fragment* 123 of Heraclitus: 'Physis ... kryptesthai philei' ('It is in the nature of things to hide themselves'). Another Heraclitean epigram (*Frgm.* 54) reveals even more elegantly the bipolar, cryptic character of Being: '*harmoniē aphanēs phanerēs kreittōn*' ('Higher and mightier than what is openly showing is the harmony that does not show itself'). To a certain extent, Aristotle, too, acknowledged the primacy of the 'concealed' aspect of things.[15] If we put together his expositions in *Being and Time* and these quotations from early Greek thinkers, it is apparent that for Heidegger indeed *physis* and Being have long become a pair of mutually convertible concepts. Regrettably, however, this original sense of convertibility had to suffer a loss as soon as *physis* was replaced by its Latinized version *natura*, from which, of course, the current English word 'nature' is derived. But the significance of these fragments for Heidegger's interpretation of the 'allegory', as they certainly must have reinforced his belief in the centrality of *physis* rather than *idea* in relation to *paideia*, can hardly be overemphasized.

If, then, truth as unconcealment harks back so manifestly to the presocratic experience of Being (*on, physis*), would not the charge that Heidegger was imposing a contextually alien thesis on Plato (who, after all, bears some family resemblance to such Pre-Socratics as Parmenides) come to stand on a much weakened foothold? Of course, historical contexts have more or less open-ended contours regardless of how rigidly their core structure can be defined. Confining the context to the horizon as Plato himself knew it may not necessarily square with what Heidegger knew about it from second-hand reading. Nevertheless, if their differences could be moderated in the name of relativity of perspectives, then certainly Heidegger would be justified in offering his alternative reading of Plato's 'allegory'.

Much less do we need to make a hasty judgement on the 'historical authenticity' of Heidegger's interpretation of 'truth'. For have we not heard from him that 'a dialogue between thinkers is bound by other laws ...which are more easily violated'? What such a dialogue is about is not so much the verbal meaning of a particular text as the contextual comprehension of main issues on which the understanding of parts depends. Needless to say, the larger comprehension itself has to be referred back every so often to particular words and passages for the stabilization of its own meaning. If hiddenness of 'truth' is the original situation from which unhiddenness of 'truth' has to be salvaged, it appears that our modern world is grown so comfortable with all answers and few questions that only the bland exchange of textual criticism has survived from the ancient *hybris* of questioning gods. Nowadays we rather remote-control the aesthetic model of play heroes than expend ourselves on reality.

Against this development, Heidegger holds to a much more rough and tumble side of the struggle for the essence of Being. 'Since for the Greeks ... hiddenness reigns throughout the essence of Being as a quality that hides itself ... the unhidden must be torn away from a hiddenness' (*E* 260). Thus violence was declared to be the order of the day. The words 'unhidden' and 'hiddenness' in this sentence are locked in a deadly power struggle. It is a struggle between the force trying to find the right 'word' for the occasion (*logos*) and the force resisting it by remaining hidden (*physis*). With this reference to the Greek world view, one might point out that Heidegger has practically exonerated himself from a breach of philological accuracy. Such accuracy must have seemed to him an 'expendable' virtue, as long as he was 'expending' *himself* on the momentous question of Being.

Now applied to the actual dialogue situation surrounding the 'allegory', the prevailing 'hiddenness' may be taken to imply the absence of any direct reference by Plato to 'truth' as *alētheia*. This obliges Heidegger pro forma to admit the correctness of straightforwardly reading the 'allegory' as a document on *paideia* ('education'). However, such admission of a correct reading does not obviate the necessity to inquire into the 'foundation' of the essence of 'education'. True to the hermeneutic formula for searching for the hidden question, Heidegger suspends the 'theory' of Plato and chooses to find a better-fitting question to which the complex setting of the cave is an answer. After a thoroughgoing description of the structure of the cave, Heidegger shrewdly notes that its layout is too uncanny, or, as we might put it, it is 'overdesigned' to be utilized merely for the demonstration of Plato's theory of 'education'. The much larger purpose which the underground cave is meant to serve can only be the lesson directly drawn from the experience of dwelling in and around the cave itself. The lesson is this: to the *self-showing* of reality, *seeing* of this reality by man necessarily belongs. It is a lesson stark and forceful enough to shape the whole man for his lifetime. Other than the Being that presences itself, no further flight of imagination, no extraneous theoretical construction or physical buttressing is needed.

For the sake of education, we often project a certain exemplary image or model of man and expect that such a pattern can be generally emulated. However, the idea of man standing on his own, with his individualistic will and belief in the faculty of self-realization, is a modern prejudice. That was the widespread belief which set off, for example, the educational movement in nineteenth-century Germany under the slogan of *Bildung*. But it would be short-circuiting Plato's philosophy in general, and his view on *paideia* in particular, if we took him primarily as an 'educational reformer' who strove to mould man according to some preconceived idea of humanity. Heidegger is critical of this modern, human-centred bias. 'We certainly have to give the word [*paideia*] back the strength of its original meaning and forget the misunderstanding it fell into during the late nineteenth century' (*E* 256). Often we project into the past an ideal, 'classical' image of humanity in our modern sense. Just because Plato's 'allegory' reads prima facie like a text intoning a theory of 'education', it should not blind us to the larger picture that Plato presents here as a metaphysical theme. Inversion of soul occurs when man is brought before the reality at its 'most real', not before a grand plan, a great man, nor before himself. It is certainly not before the 'inwardness of self', as might be the case with the Augustinian precept for man's conversion. But just at this point, when Heidegger is pleading for the essence of 'truth' to override anthropological notions of 'education', have not the two philosophers in dialogue asymptotically converged to speak of the importance of seeing?

Seeing is the only issue for man who is constrained by the exigency of dwelling in a place like the cave in the 'allegory'. We should have asked much sooner: can the theory of 'education', which is ostensibly the central theme of the 'allegory' for Plato, forgo any direct link to and support from the theory of Idea, the ubiquitous principal theme of the Platonic philosophy? Assuredly such an inner connection must be presupposed as necessary and pervasive.[16] Otherwise, without the experience of direct seeing that gives the 'education' theory a stable phenomenal underpinning, the 'allegory' would be fair game for a variety of interpretive excursions. Scholars of education would offer to define the 'content', 'method' and 'ideal' tinged with all sorts of humanistic and human-centred values, when changing the very soul of man is the task at hand. Understandably, Heidegger presents the connection between Plato's *paideia* and the theory of Idea itself indirectly as the connection between *paideia* and *alētheia*, which is his theory of seeing rather than Plato's.

> The unhidden and its unhiddenness refer persistently to what is always openly present in the region in which man abides. ...The variation of the abodes and stages of the transitions are based on the difference of what persists in being standardly *alēthes*, the kind of 'truth' that prevails every time. Therefore, *alēthes*, the unhidden, must one way or another be considered and named at every stage. (*E* 257)

Whereas Heidegger's notion of seeing is focused from the beginning on what has in itself the dual aspects of showing and not showing, Plato's theory of Idea is to be understood primarily not for such an inherently ambivalent quality, but in its relation to its 'lesser' forms of manifestations, which we may compare to the relationship of the original to copies. The comparative forms of expression such as 'more real', 'the most real' and so on that are used at every stage of the movement in the cave are none other than the varying degrees of closeness or farness of the copies to the original. Since the story of the 'allegory' is in the final analysis about completing the transition from blindness to the highest state of seeing the 'most real', it is evident that the Idea represents the final destination and fulfilment of the transition. This ultimate Idea-centredness could easily be misinterpreted as if for Plato the highest reality is existing in itself, somewhere in 'the heavenly sphere' (*topos ouraniōs*). However, the name Idea (*eidos*) or the 'form that is seen' contradicts this: 'How are the things themselves, as the "highest" reality, revealed? Situated in their "outward appearance", beings themselves display themselves. In Greek, "outward appearance" is *eidos* or *idea*' (*E* 254).

Idealism, taken literally, is the 'representational' theory of seeing which shifts the centre of the 'subject–object' relation to the seeing activity. At the basis of Heidegger's criticism of the representational thinking lies, on the other hand, the mutually belonging relationship between that which shows itself (Being) and seeing. If anything, it is the primacy of Being as the ground of this connectedness that always asserts itself.

But man's seeing, important as it is, 'sees the visible only in so far as the eye is "sunlike"' (*hēlioeides*, *E* 262). This is for Heidegger an especially crucial distinction because the 'sunlikeness' of the eye implies that man's faculty to see is not wholly within himself. In a way, man is allowed to see things only because 'the eye itself "gleams" and submits to this shining, and can therefore receive and apprehend the phenomenal' (ibid.). In this description, the two aspects, namely, the 'seeing' and 'being allowed to see', are characteristically held in balance. But already in this apparent state of balance Heidegger detects Plato's subsequent interpretation that shifts away from the 'ambivalence' attached to the initial relation between Being and Thinking. What Heidegger discerns is the separation of Thinking as the 'subjective' activity of man from its state of belonging together with Being. Eventually, Thinking takes the upper hand over Being, which now becomes identified only as 'object'. Whereas heretofore the balance between 'reality showing itself' and man's 'act of seeing reality' has been preserved with an overtone of the primacy of the former, there appeared with Plato the first indication of the shifting emphasis in favour of the latter.

He who takes this shift of emphasis as seriously as Heidegger does must recognize in Plato's theme of 'education', even as a subtheme of his theory of Idea, the alarming tendency of the subjectivity asserting itself. For Plato's Allegory of the Cave, stripped to its foundation, is in a very special sense a 'Doctrine of Truth'. As 'Doctrine of Truth' subordinated to the theory of Idea, it heralded the 'fateful' change of the locus of truth from Being to seeing, and indeed, to 'correctness' of seeing and thus saying how and what is seen. Truth will no longer be concerned with Being. As 'propositional' truth, it takes over the whole business of 'truth', bypassing the question of Being. In this changeover, Heidegger saw Plato as the mastermind of the representational theory of truth who was just one step away from declaring the bankruptcy of ancient ontology.

Though no concept of 'truth' in whatever other tradition or language comes near the experience of 'unhiddenness', it was incumbent on Heidegger to explore the origin of the 'standard' truth known as 'correctness in saying'. It was as a corollary to the question of *paideia* that Heidegger went to the lengths of clarifying the essence of this 'other' kind of truth. In the process, he became something of a muted witness, if not accuser, of the sea change that took place in the early history of Western philosophy. Heidegger is certainly critical of this process, calling it 'technical thinking' that has perpetuated the formal disjunction of philosophy in logic, ethics and physics. He was reviled for this 'fateful distrust of universal concepts (e.g., truth, morality, good), which are emblematic of a Western metaphysical tradition with which he hoped to break'.[17] There are certainly passages in Heidegger's writing that show his distrust and affective reaction against some 'universal concepts' that have gained ascendancy in Western metaphysics. But he also knows that idle opposition to what has gained power and legitimacy in history may not even begin to have a viable recipe until it realizes how far its opposition, and therefore its own existence, has become dependent on that adversarial force. His genuine concern is therefore to carve a niche in his thinking in which he feels at home, freed from both antipathy and blind submission to the ethos of technological domination. It still requires a measure of 'reversal' in thinking. This is a mode of thinking with 'decentralized' selfhood and comes close to the model we discussed above in terms of mutual belongingness of Thought and Being. Reality, nature and even impersonal 'objects' must assume or partake in the role that used to be reserved for subjectivity. The 'middle voice'[18] in Greek grammar speaks volumes about this now faded legacy of an ancient world view.

From a metaphysical perspective, Heidegger's interpretation of the 'allegory' can be seen as reconfirming the awareness of the finiteness of man. It is the self-knowledge the Greeks have displayed even with their hybrid challenge to the power of Being. It is the knowledge that it is *in the nature of things* to reveal themselves only by withholding something of themselves at the same time. Nature intimates, even when it is conceptually determined, what has eluded the conceptual grasp. For the Greeks, the thought of *alterity* was the inseparable companion of the *quiddity* of Being. When Heidegger advanced the sweeping thesis that Western history is a history of 'errant' ontological journey, having forgotten the all-important question of Being, we may see in it a 'historicized' version of the Heraclitean view of the cryptic draft of nature. In other words, the self-revealing and self-concealing features of *physis* were extended on the domain of history.

Some critics would want to dismiss all of this as a hypothetical montage of history by a 'tender-minded' recluse ill at ease with the reality of the world. But, in this case, what lends a special sense of urgency to the old question whether the course of history could have possibly taken a different turn is Plato's towering stature and the gravity of the issue of 'truth' at hand. Plato stood, as Heidegger sees it, at the crossroad of moral and spiritual decision of the Greeks. What was still in a state of equilibrium at the time of Parmenides, namely, the mutually belonging relationship between Thought and Being, was tipped towards one side when Plato gave a momentous push to let *Idea* slide over and above things. This occurred when Plato stated (517c, 4/5) that 'whoever cares to act with insight ... he must have this (the idea which is called the possibility of the Idea of the Good) before his eyes'. We could paraphrase the word 'to act' in the sense of educational reform Plato had in mind. That would have meant that a man had to be moulded according to a preconceived 'ideal' of humanity. However, if 'reality' still had some residual 'bruteness' of force that Cézanne wanted to bring to his painting, then, by the same token, the Being of man should never be subjugated to whatever highest Idea of humanity we aspire to, lest the still untapped, still unruly, faces of the pluralistic human race should be glossed over by the rule of a closed system. The following words of Heidegger may well capture the sense of the magnitude of what was accomplished by Plato's 'allegory':

> Whoever is supposed to act in a world defined through the Idea – and wants to – needs before everything else the glimpse of the Idea ... whereby the *idea* became the master of *alētheia* ... (idea) is itself master, dispensing both unhiddenness (to what emerges) and the ability to perceive (the unhidden). *Alētheia* comes under the yoke of *idea*. (*E* 264–5, italics mine)

It should surprise no one that, as a thinker standing at a crossroad, Plato had his measure of ambiguity. 'In a certain manner Plato still has to adhere to "truth" as a characteristic of beings ... But at the same time the inquiry into unhiddenness is shifted to the way outward appearance manifests itself and with that *to the associated ability to see*: *to what is right and the correctness of seeing*. Therefore there is necessarily an ambiguity in Plato's doctrine. ... The ambiguity is clearly obvious in the fact that *alētheia* is mentioned and treated while at the same time *orthotēs* is meant and set as a standard – and all in the same train of thought' (*E* 265–6, italics mine). The same exposition of Being as *Idea*, which owes its precedence to a change in the essence of *alētheia*, demands that a label of the glance be placed upon the ideas. The role of *paideia*, of the 'education' of man, corresponds to this label. Concern for human beings and for the position of man in the midst of beings dominates throughout metaphysics. The beginning of metaphysics in Plato's thinking is at the same time the beginning of 'Humanism' (*E* 268–9).

Heidegger himself is unambiguous in stating that, as a result of Plato's interpretation of the 'allegory', 'the essence of truth relinquishes the basic feature of unhiddenness' (ibid.). We moderns who move knowingly or unknowingly on the logicized path first prepared by Plato may have not even a faint idea of the distressing situation of 'twofold confusions occurring for twofold reasons'. But we have more than a historical interest in finding out how such a shift in the essence of truth has actually affected the essence (being) of man.

What gives rise to the thought of otherness is rooted in the living, acting experience and encounter with *things*. If, however, a mere 'mental concept' (representation) of a thing is presented before us, then for the first time the question of its 'agreement with the thing' must arise. In the standardization of truth (*veritas*) as *adaequatio intellectus et rei* (*E* 257), Heidegger traces the long shadow Plato cast as he stood tall at the crossroad of ancient philosophy. He was the first to note that 'catching sight of outward appearance' is what we are concerned with in our every attitude towards being. In plain language, this means that we always see individual objects through the Forms or Ideas of which these objects are copies. Standing at the end of the road largely prepared by Plato, we feel rather insecure about the 'reversal' Heidegger is suggesting. For might not this return to the two-pronged, hidden and unhidden state of 'truth' cause us even more painful 'twofold' confusions?

Notes

1. Plato, *Republic* VII, 514a, 2–517a, 7. In translating various Greek and German words related to 'being', 'be' or 'entity' into English, the following rules are generally observed: (1) Being = *Sein* in Heidegger's own usage, also when he translates the Greek word *physis* (nature) as *Sein*; (2) being and beings = the Greek word '*on*' is rendered as a rule as 'being'. However, when '*on*' clearly refers to entities (objects) and Heidegger translates it as *Seiendes*, the plural form 'beings' is used; (3) an exception to the above is that, when Heidegger is talking about the being of man (*Sein des Menschen* or *menschliches Sein*) or of any other entities, the English word 'being' was used without initial capital.
2. E 256 indicates the page in English translation by John Barlow, 'Martin Heidegger: Plato's doctrine of truth', in William Barrett and Henry Aiken (ed.), *Philosophy in the Twentieth Century* (New York: Random House, 1962). H 23 refers to the page in the original German text: Martin Heidegger, *Platons Lehre von der Wahrheit* (Berne: Francke, 1947). Quotations hereafter are mostly based on the English translation.
3. Heidegger plays on the root meaning of 'dwelling' (*Wohnen*). 'Dwelling' recurs in such cognate verbs as 'forming of habit' (*gewöhnen, Gewohnheit*), 'changing of habit' (*Umgewöhnen*), 'getting accustomed to' (*Eingewöhnen*), 'breaking with habit' (*Abgewöhnen*) and similar words. They have an essential relation to forming a lasting posture of soul. The task of education is not merely to teach what is good, but to ensure that practising good becomes a habit in the character of a child. In a practical context, it is necessary first to bring a child into an environment optimally suited for gaining essential knowledge of reality. Then a sustained exposure to such a milieu over a length of time is required for consolidating his character.

To what extent the selection of a right environment has become a pedagogical obsession in the tradition of Confucianism, is illustrated by the legend of Mencius (372–289 BC), whose mother moved her home three times during her son's early childhood. Generation after generation of Chinese inspired by the Confucian spirit of learning would do anything to give their children the best possible opportunity for education. But even by that standard, what the mother of Mencius did for her young son was extraordinary. She saw her child diligently mimicking, from morning till evening, people's behaviour in the neighbourhood. First it was the funeral rites when living near a cemetery, then it was selling and haggling near a market. She moved for the third time, and she could not be happier when she saw Mencius modelling himself upon teachers, as they now lived close by a school. Even so, an educationally favourable environment can exercise its influence on a child only up to a point. In the Chinese tradition, the source and content of learning were dictated by the rigid authority of the canonized classical writings. What this authority encouraged was not the quest for 'essential reality' in Plato's sense, which presupposes the spirit of free philosophical inquiry.

Instead, its purpose was thoroughly to regulate the details of practical moral and social conduct of man after the pattern of accomplished sages.

4 We should not forget the fact that the script we are reading is not entirely Plato's own. We are reading through him the message contained in the 'allegory'. It is as if the anonymous authorship of the 'allegory' – thinking out of the depth of the Greek soul – conceived the entire process of 'education' in terms of collective responsibility. The 'inversion' of soul has nothing to do with, for example, what the language of the Christian Middle Ages would call 'finding of self'. This takes place only in the inwardness of an individual soul. The Greek mind is speaking a different language which, if anything, intones the collective aspect of 'liberation' from uneducatedness. It comes surprisingly close to the modern idea of 'freedom' as a 'species consciousness'. It implies that man is not free until all men are free.

5 The analogy of 'visual confusion' has certainly a very wide implication beyond the impediment of physical eyesight which may have been subsequently removed. The traumatic experience of loss and recovery of vision impinges on the whole person and his or her life for ever. Thus what Plato's 'allegory' offers is a poignant commentary to the state of 'educatedness', which must remain ineluctably bound with the opposite, 'uneducated' state. But even as purely ophthalmological symptoms, confusions resulting from the restored vision, after a lengthy period of blindness, can be so serious that one could doubt whether this so-called 'gift' of vision is really a blessing and not a curse.

In his *Sight Restoration after Long-Term Blindness*, the ophthalmologist Alberto Valvo reports that, to his knowledge, among the people born blind in the last ten centuries, fewer than twenty have regained their sight. Cf. Oliver Sachs, *An Anthropologist on Mars* (New York: Alfred A. Knopf, 1995), p.109. Marius von Senden reviewed every published case over a three hundred-year period in his *Space and Sight* (1932) and concluded that every newly sighted adult sooner or later undergoes a 'motivational crisis'. Initial exhilaration gives way to devastating and even lethal depression. The newly gained sense of sight comes into conflict with the fully integrated tactile sensation on which a blind man used to depend heavily. Von Senden cites cases where a patient felt so disoriented that he threatened to tear his eyes out, or others who continue to 'behave blind' or 'refuse to see' after an operation.

As an additional note, a passage from Diderot's ironically titled book, *Letter on the Blind: For the Use of Those Who Can See* (1749), may be cited. Diderot maintains that the blind may, in their own way, construct a complete and sufficient world, have a complete 'blind identity and no sense of disability or inadequacy'. The 'problem' of their blindness and the desire to cure this is therefore ours, not theirs (ibid., p.139). But what he does not discuss is the real problem that this very 'blind identity' is disrupted when the blind man regains his sight through an operation.

Philosophers in the great era of Empiricism did not pass up the opportunity to comment first hand on this specialized problem of restored visual perception. For the case could be built up against the Rationalists or Gestaltists who maintain that perceptual organization is physiologically inborn, that is, it is inherent in the innate aspects of brain functioning. William Molyneux submitted to his fellow philosopher John Locke the question whether a blind man, who has known how to tell a cube from a sphere only by his touch, could distinguish them by his sight when he was made to see. Locke considered the problem in his 1670 *Essay Concerning Human Understanding*, and his answer was 'no'. Also George Berkeley concluded, in *A New Theory of Vision*, that there was no necessary connection between a tactile world and a sight world. Thus both Molyneux and Berkeley endorsed the empiricist view that perceptual organization depends on a synthesizing process of learning to combine simpler elements into more complex, integrated wholes. In other words, it is only after a long and painstaking period of learning through experience that such seemingly primitive visual performances as discriminating a square from a triangle – both two-dimensional objects for the sight – come about.

As a passing comment on the composition of the 'allegory', it is important to note that, quite apart from physiological aspects of impaired vision, it is the peculiar setting, namely, the extreme contrast between light and darkness inherent in the structure of the cave that puts such a great demand on man's eye. The first time, he was blinded by the sun as he emerged from darkness. The second time, as he came back to the cave, his eye was again put under strain because of the darkness. In both cases, the confusion of the eye threatens to make the 'educatedness' remain a precarious, hard to adjust, 'transitional' state.

6 Over the initial outrage among Neo-Kantians (Cassirer *et al.*), Heidegger's interpretation of Kant has gradually become an accepted legacy of Kant scholarship in Europe. A notable American voice echoing this trend was that of L.W. Beck, who said that 'the student of Kant can profit by a careful study of what Heidegger has to say about pure intuition, the three-fold synthesis, and schematism' (see *Philosophical Review*, 72 (1963): 398). In another review several years later, Beck classified Heidegger's interpretation of Kant as a metaphysical treatise, acknowledging that it is 'important in its own right'. But he played down its 'informative' value on Kant. See L.W. Beck, *Early German Philosophy* (Cambridge, MA: Harvard University Press, 1969), p.537.

7 'The extent to which I have gone astray in the present endeavor and the shortcomings thereof have become so clear to me in the period of time since its first publication that I refrain from making it a patchwork through the addition of supplements and postscripts' (Author's Preface to the Second Edition, *Kant and the Problem of Metaphysics*, trans. James Churchill (Bloomington, IN: Indiana University Press, 1962), p.XXV).

8 The young Heidegger was led to his question of Being through the lecture of Brentano's *On the Manifold Meaning of Being According to Aristotle* (*Von der mannigfachen Bedeutung des Seienden nach Aristoteles*, Freiburg: Herder, 1862). Typically, Heidegger was already looking past the question of plural meanings of Being for their implicit 'unity', an issue with which he wrestled throughout his life.

9 'Thus a person who wants to understand must question what lies behind what is said. He must understand it as an answer to a question. If we go back *behind* what is said, then we inevitably ask questions *beyond* what is said. We understand the sense of the text only by acquiring the horizon of the question – a horizon that, as such, necessarily includes other possible answers.' See H.G. Gadamer, *Truth and Method*, trans. Joel Weinsheimer and Donald Marshall (New York: Continuum, 1997), p.370. There is in this totally historicized horizon no closure. Thus one may be immediately struck by the relativism implied by the scope of Gadamer's 'horizon'. Somewhere, in what is said, lines have to be drawn to curb the speculation with regard to what is unsaid. Gadamer does recognize that the 'task of understanding is concerned above all with the meaning of the text itself', but he is also keenly aware of the difference between 'the question which the text is intended to answer and the question to which it really is an answer' (ibid., p.372).

10 Plato's role in introducing the 'technological' way of thinking into philosophy is often critically commented upon by Heidegger. What Socrates used to pick up from living circumstances of daily life became a concern of 'academic discipline'. The pursuit of specialized knowledge called *epistēmē* led to the three part division of logic, ethics and

physics for the first time in Plato's school. Cf. Heidegger, *Grundbegriffe der Metaphysik* (Frankfurt: Vittorio Klostermaun, 1983), pp.54 f.

11 M. Merleau-Ponty, 'Eye and mind', trans. Charles Dallery, in James Edie (ed.), *Primacy of Perception* (Evanston, IL: North Western University, 1964), pp.159–90.

12 Whitehead speaks of Kant as 'the great philosopher who first, fully and explicitly, introduced ... the conception of an act of experience as a constructive functioning, transforming subjectivity into objectivity, or objectivity into subjectivity' (A.N. Whitehead, *Process and Reality* (New York: Macmillan, 1929), p.236).

13 In a study of Heidegger's later philosophy, I pointed out the close relationship between Heidegger's Being and *Physis*, as well as its implications for modern ecological consciousness. Included in the discussion was the dual meaning of *technē* as 'technology' (craft) and 'art'. Cf. Kah Kyung Cho, 'Ökologische Suggestibilität in der Spätphilosophie Heideggers', in *Allgemeine Zeitschrift für Philosophie* 11:3 (1986): 53–77.

14 Heidegger, *Grundbegriffe der Metaphysik*, p.41. The second quotation on 'harmony' (*Fragment* 54) is from p.44.

15 Heidegger points out that Aristotle was referring to these 'natural philosophers' (*physiologoi*) as his 'ancestors'. This 'self-concealing' nature of *physis* was presupposed when the function of *logos*, so important for Aristotle, was defined by him as one of 'bringing to self-showing (*apophainesthai*) that which is not showing' (*Basic Concepts of Metaphysics* (*Grundbegriffe der Metaphysik*, pp.42–4).

16 Plato could not have wagered his theory of *idea* on a better custom-built stage setting than the 'allegory of the cave'. The reason is that the ascent and descent within the subterranean cave is uniquely fitted to demonstrate the inner unity of the *idea* with *paideia*. Furthermore, let there be no misunderstanding that *paideia*, the arduous process of guiding and leading man away from his habit, the radical 'inversion', was designed to turn man's eye towards the higher reality. Educational guidance is needed for the sake of seeing and glancing at true reality. *Idea*, on the other hand, is defined as 'the outward appearance which gives a perspective upon what is present'. To clarify the meaning of this sentence, let us turn to Heidegger's further description (*E* 262):

> The essence of *idea* lies in the qualities of being apparent and visible. The idea achieves presence, namely the presence of every being as what it is. ...What the *idea* brings into sight and offers to be seen is, for the glance directed upon it, the thing unhidden making its appearance as what it is. ...the idea does not just let something else (behind it) 'make an appearance', it itself is what appears. And it depends upon itself alone for its appearing.

17 Richard Wolin, *Heidegger's Children: Hannah Arendt, Karl Löwith, Hans Jonas, and Herbert Marcuse* (Princeton, NJ: Princeton University Press, 2001), p.175.

18 The 'reflexive' verb in modern German and French still retains some vestige of this self-abatement of the grammatical subject. Schelling, Heidegger and Gadamer all display a philosophical writing style commensurate with their knowledge of Greek thought. Among the few in America who explored the philosophical significance of the middle voice, Charles Scott deserves special mention. Cf. 'The middle voice in *Being and Time*', in John Sallis (ed.), *The Collegium Phaenomenologicum* (Dordrecht: Kluwer, 1988), pp.159–73; also, 'The middle voice of metaphysics', *Review of Metaphysics* 42 (1998): 743–64.

Chapter 8

Maimonides on Aristotle: Judaism and Science Reconsidered

Tamar M. Rudavsky

In a recent critique of Ian Barbour's celebrated discussion of the 'religion and science' problem, Cantor and Kenny argue that all too often the term 'religion', when used in the 'religion/science' debate, is nothing but a synonym for Christianity.[1] As Cantor and Kenny acutely claim, 'since Barbour's discussion is directed to Christianity, it may not be applicable to other religious traditions ... Christianity is perhaps atypical in that it places so much emphasis on both theology and belief. Many other religions, including Buddhism and Judaism, do not share these characteristics ... Barbour's scheme, therefore, lacks broad applicability.'[2]

While I am sympathetic to Cantor's critique of Barbour, we must nevertheless keep in mind that the problem of reconciling secularism and Judaism has been a prevailing motif throughout the history of Jewish thought. Whenever Jews have lived surrounded by another culture, they have had to assess the cosmology represented by that culture. Even a cursory survey of the mediaeval period reveals a striking congruence among Jewish, Christian and Islamic thinkers, to the extent that all three are engaged in a critical attempt to analyse their own religious tradition in accordance with the ontological and metaphysical constraints of what we may call secular philosophy. At every stage in Jewish thought, Jews have tried to accommodate 'secular' elements with their Judaism. These elements have included not only moral theories, such as the Doctrine of the Mean laid out in Aristotle's *Nicomachean Ethics*, not only metaphysical and ontological schemes ranging from Neoplatonic emanationism to Aristotelian functionalist teleology; but also scientific paradigms, drawn from Plato, Ptolemy, Aristotle or Copernicus.

Cantor has reminded us, however, that Jewish examinations of the religion/ science debate are (for the most part) elaborated in counterposition to a not unrelated issue, namely the impact of secular Christian culture upon Judaism. On the contrary, Jewish philosophers, both mediaeval and modern, have had to wrestle with the project of reconciling 'outside' sources and influences with their understanding of Scriptural dicta. Hence, whereas for the Christian theologian the question is unifold, namely how to accommodate Christianity and modern scientific outlooks, for the Jew the question becomes more complex: how to accommodate Judaism to secularism, which itself has been infiltrated by Christian influences. Is it the case, then, that the very scientific world view, that the Christian sees as 'godless' and void of religious content, for the Jew is already tinged with classical 'Christian' elements? And if so, does not the enterprise of accommodation become even more complex for the Jew than for the Christian? It is here, I suggest, that the Jew and the Muslim may have more in common, for both have become heirs to a largely Christian culture.

I am not so concerned in this chapter with the specific solutions that Jewish thinkers have proposed to resolve the supposed conflict arising between Judaism and science; rather, I wish to explore the underpinnings of the *articulation* of this debate against the backdrop of increased interest in religion and science. To this end I shall concentrate upon the way Maimonides explores the relation between Judaism and science, as reflected in his selective appropriation of Aristotle's conception of science. Why Maimonides? As is well known, the philosophical works of Maimonides (1125–1204), most notably *The Guide of the Perplexed*, represent one of the most celebrated attempts in the history of Jewish thought to harmonize two worlds: the world of science and rational method, as epitomized by Aristotle and his commentators, and the world of Rabbinic thought, reflected both in the written and oral law. As Chief Rabbi of the North African community, Maimonides devoted himself not only to medicine and philosophy, but to tending to the psychic and spiritual needs of Jews throughout the Mediterranean. Kraemer warns us that Maimonides did not set out actually to harmonize science and religion; such synthesis language, he argues, is 'misleading'.[3] The proper term according to Kraemer is the accommodation 'of philosophy to religion and of the philosophers to the society in which they lived'.[4] In light of these comments, let us look carefully at Maimonides' own words in the Introduction to the *Guide*:

> For the purpose of this treatise and of all those like it is the science of Law in its true sense. Or rather its purpose is to give indications to a religious man for whom the validity of our Law has become established in his soul and has become actual in his belief – such a man being perfect in his religion and character, and having studied the sciences of the philosophers and coming to know what they signify. ... Hence he would remain in a state of perplexity and confusion as to whether he should follow his intellect, renounce what he knew concerning the terms in question, and consequently consider that he has renounced the foundations of the Law. Or he should hold fast to his understanding of these terms and let himself be drawn on together with his intellect.[5]

What Maimonides tells us is that the work itself is addressed to the individual who feels caught between Athens and Jerusalem, who has read both Genesis and the *De caelo* and who is attempting to reconcile a religious and scientific framework. The work is addressed 'to one who has philosophized and has knowledge of the true sciences, but believes at the same time in the matters pertaining to the Law and is perplexed as to their meaning because of the uncertain terms and the parables'.[6]

This purpose is reiterated in Maimonides' very characterization of the main themes of the *Guide*, themes that pertain to both Jewish belief and science. Maimonides is the first Jewish philosopher to identify the 'Account of the Beginning [*ma'aseh bereshith*]' with natural science and the 'Account of the Chariot [*ma'aseh merkabah*]', with divine science; after Maimonides, this distinction becomes commonplace.[7] But it is not clear from the work whether it is Maimonides' purpose to treat these two issues explicitly and in their entirety.[8] Harvey in fact suggests that the 'Account of the Beginning' represents that part of natural science that has not been and cannot be demonstrated, whereas the 'Account of the Chariot' represents a part of divine science that has not been and cannot be demonstrated.[9] The former applies to the question of the origin of the world, whereas the latter concerns God's governance of the world.

In what follows, I focus upon three areas. First, I explore briefly Maimonides' use of Aristotelian method. Then I turn to his cosmological speculation that highlights the tensions between Genesis, Aristotle and Ptolemy. Finally, I discuss the implications of a hylomorphic ontology with respect to human perfection. In all three areas I concentrate upon Maimonides' interpretative challenges in accommodating Judaism to the texts of Aristotle.

Methodological Concerns: the Aristotelian Challenge

Scholars readily agree that Maimonides clearly esteemed Aristotle and had high regard for his teachings in logic and scientific method; this esteem determines significant aspects of Maimonides' own conception of scientific theory.[10] That Maimonides held Aristotle in the highest esteem is evidenced in the following passages from his letter to Samuel ibn Tibbon, translator of the *Guide* from Arabic into Hebrew:

> I.1 The writings [words] of Aristotle's teacher Plato are in parables and hard to understand. One can dispense with them, for the writings of Aristotle suffice, and we need not occupy [our attention] with the writings of earlier [philosophers]. Aristotle's intellect [represents] the extreme of human intellect, if we except those who have received divine inspiration.
> I.2 The works of Aristotle are the roots and foundations of all works on the sciences. But they cannot be understood except with the help of commentaries, those of Alexander of Aphrodisias, those of Themistius, and those of Averroes.[11]

Other passages in the *Guide* attest as well to Aristotle's eminence. In *Guide*, I.5, Maimonides describes Aristotle as 'the chief of the philosophers'.[12] In *Guide*, II.14, Maimonides says he will only pay attention to Aristotle 'for it is his opinion that ought to be considered'.[13] Maimonides calls attention to the 'depth of Aristotle's penetration and to his extraordinary apprehension'.[14] And in *Guide*, I.5, Maimonides emphasizes Aristotle's willingness to investigate 'very obscure matters', noting that in the case of such obscure matters (such as celestial mechanics), one must be tentative.[15]

It is important to note Altmann's restriction, however, that Maimonides makes a determined effort to portray Aristotle as a thinker in search of the truth, rather than claiming to own it. Altmann emphasizes that Maimonides recognized that Aristotle's dialectical (aporetic) method remained ultimately open to other solutions.[16] Nevertheless, Maimonides is very much influenced by Aristotle's paradigm of scientific knowledge as developed in three works: *Posterior Analytics*, devoted to demonstration, *Topics*, to dialectic and *On Sophistical Refutations*, to sophistic argument. Of these three, Aristotle argues that demonstration is the most important, since it alone leads to scientific knowledge: 'By demonstration (*apodeixis*) I mean a syllogism productive of scientific knowledge (*syllogismos epistemonikos*), a syllogism, that is, the grasp of which is *eo ipso* such knowledge.'[17] Demonstration differs from other forms of knowledge on the basis of its premises, which must be true, primary and indemonstrable, immediate, better known than the conclusions following them, and causes of the conclusions.[18] In *Posterior Analytics*, Aristotle specifies the kind of 'showing' that would qualify as 'science', or knowledge in the fullest sense of *episteme*. He weaves together the three meanings of 'showing' (*apodeixis*), which include proving, explaining and teaching, into an account of demonstration. According to Aristotle, in order for knowledge to qualify as fully scientific, it must satisfy all three goals.[19]

Dialectic is related to demonstration, but is less certain; it is important in establishing the basic premises of demonstration. It is also important in the refutation of false claims to knowledge, and for establishing correct opinions on questions for which no demonstrative knowledge exists. Thus, according to Aristotle, for a scientific thesis to be accepted, it must be either an evident first principle or else demonstrable from these principles. Reasoning is demonstrative when it proceeds from premises that are true and primary. A demonstrative argument rests on principles that are true, necessary and universal. A demonstrative science, therefore, is an axiomatized, deductive system comprising a finite set of demonstrations.[20]

It is against the backdrop of these Aristotelian works that Maimonides worked. Maimonides' early work *Treatise on the Art of Logic* is very much indebted to Aristotle.[21] Maimonides describes there the three kinds of Aristotelian arguments mentioned above, adding to them both the rhetorical and poetic arguments accepted in the Middle Ages. In chapter 8 he enumerates the four kinds of premises upon which arguments are based: sense percepts (*ha-muhashim*), first intelligibles (*ha-muskalot*), generally agreed upon opinions (*ha-mefursamot*) and opinions received through tradition (*ha-mequbalot*). He then goes on to argue that only demonstrative arguments or syllogisms (*ha-heqqesh ha-mofti*) based on 'first intelligibles' are productive of scientific knowledge; these must rest on premises that are true and available to everybody. Maimonides there defines a demonstrative syllogism as one whose premises are certain.[22]

There are a number of contexts in the *Guide* in which the notion of demonstration plays a prominent role. Maimonides agrees with Aristotle that demonstrative arguments are not subject to disagreement: 'For in all things whose true reality is known through demonstration (*burhân, mofet*) there is no tug of war [disagreement] and no refusal to accept a thing proven.'[23] In cases where demonstration is not possible, Maimonides is careful to maintain that 'the two contrary opinions with regard to the matter in question should be posited as hypotheses and it should be seen what doubts attach to each of them: the one to which fewer doubts attach should be believed'.[24] There are numerous examples in the *Guide* of what can be demonstrated: the existence, unity and incorporeality of God;[25] that God has no magnitude and hence no motion;[26] that transparency is not a colour;[27] that the moral virtues are required as prerequisites for the intellectual virtues;[28] that affirmative attributes cannot be ascribed to God;[29] that natural things do not come about by chance;[30] and that a vacuum does not exist.[31] With these general methodological guidelines in mind, let me now turn to several specific examples of Maimonides' interpretative challenges when confronting Aristotle.

Cosmological Challenges: Maimonides on Genesis and Aristotle

By the twelfth century, the influence of Aristotle had taken hold among Jewish philosophers. The crisis between Aristotelian celestial physics and Ptolemaic astronomy reached its apogee during the time of Maimonides and Gersonides. This crisis was reflected in a number of ways, perhaps none of which has been as challenging or as divisive as determining whether the universe is created or eternal. No Jewish philosopher denied the centrality of the doctrine of creation to Jewish belief. Jews were enormously affected by Scripture and in particular by the creation account found in Genesis I–II. But, like their Christian and Moslem counterparts, Jewish thinkers did not always agree upon what qualifies as an acceptable model of creation. In the context of this topic, perhaps the most important phrase of Scripture is *b'reishit*, 'in the beginning'. The very term *b'reishit* designates the fact that there was a beginning, that is, temporality has been introduced if only in the weakest sense that this creative act occupies a period of time. But mediaeval Jewish philosophers thinking about creation were influenced as well by Aristotle's model of an eternally existing world. When trying to prove that the world was created by God in time, philosophers who wanted to support a Biblical theory of creation in time had to reject Aristotle's position that time is infinite.

As is well known, Aristotle posits an eternal universe in which time is potentially, if not actually, infinite.[32] That is, Aristotle argues that, since there can be no 'before' to time, neither time nor the universe was created. Jewish philosophers, however, almost without exception, are committed to the belief that God created the universe. At the same time they want to accept certain aspects of Aristotle's theory of time and the universe. For if, as Aristotle claimed, time is the measure of motion, and motion is of material stuff, then infinite time implies the eternity of the universe. But inasmuch as accepting the eternity of the universe qualifies the role God plays in determining the act and materials of creation, Jewish thinkers were motivated to reject the Aristotelian characterization of time while at the same time continuing to accept his overall philosophical authority.

Like other Jewish philosophers, Maimonides must interpret Aristotle in light of the first verses of Genesis. For him, the issue is whether this universe was created simultaneous with or subsequent to the creation of time. Furthermore, he must analyse the significance of the term *b'reishit* in the context of an Aristotelian theory of time. In *Guide*, II.13, Maimonides describes three opinions on creation, and then, in II.32, he describes three opinions on prophecy, stating that 'the opinions of people concerning prophecy are like their opinions concerning the eternity of the world or its creation in time'.[33] Is the word 'like' supposed to posit a one-to-one correspondence between the two sets of opinions? If so, can Maimonides' own position be linked with any one set of correspondences, or is his allegiance split? In answer to these questions, interpreters have suggested every possible combination of opinions, and have offered every possible strategy for determining which is Maimonides' own view.[34]

I cannot in this short chapter enter into the details of the Maimonidean taxonomy controversy per se. In other contexts I have argued that Maimonides' doctrine of creation of the world incorporates important elements of the Aristotelian eternity model.[35] In arguing thus, I clearly align myself with the minority of scholars who see in the *Guide* an esoteric subtext addressed to an intellectual elite. My own interpretation is that Maimonides recognized internal difficulties with the view of Scripture having to do with issues of time, but that, in the absence of definitive demonstrative argument in support of Aristotle, he was forced to a position of epistemological scepticism. This scepticism, however, represents a tacit rejection of the unwavering faith in the Scriptural account of creation.

This reading is strengthened when we turn to Maimonides' discussion of astronomy. Scholars have been careful to distinguish philosophical cosmology from astronomy. Largely like the work of natural philosophers and physicists, that of cosmologists followed Aristotle rather than Ptolemy in the quest to offer a theory of the universe as an ordered whole.[36] The formative classical texts included Aristotle's *De caelo*, supplemented by relevant passages from *Metaphysics, Physics*, and *De generatione et corruptione*. Plato's *Timaeus* and commentaries upon Genesis presented an additional dimension of this corpus.

Maimonides tended to compartmentalize physics and astronomy, a major implication being that the astronomer is free to use any mathematical model that best suits his theoretical purposes.[37] This cosmological picture is amplified in *Guide*, II:19–24. Following Aristotle, Maimonides argues that both the matter and the form of the spheres differ from those of the four elements, as reflected in the different types of motion exhibited by them. Pointing to several problems with Aristotle's attempts to explain why spheres move from the East and not from the West, and why some move faster than others, Maimonides rejects Aristotle's explanations on the grounds that 'the science of astronomy was not in his [Aristotle's] time what it is today'.[38]

Having rejected Aristotle's analysis, Maimonides presents his own solution in *Guide*, II.24. His main thesis is that the underlying premise of Ptolemy's *Almagest*, namely that 'everything depends on two principles; either that of the epicycles or that of the eccentric spheres or on both of them',[39] is untenable. Maimonides' own contention is that these two principles are 'entirely outside the bounds of reasoning and opposed to all that has been made clear in natural science'.[40] In other words, Maimonides rejects Ptolemaic astronomy on the grounds that it conflicts with Aristotelian physics. The first principle is rejected because the existence of epicycles implies that the 'epicycle rolls and changes its place completely', hence undermining the Aristotelian dictum that things in the heavens are immovable.[41] He then offers other considerations, in the name of Abu Bakr, against accepting the doctrine of epicycles.[42]

Following this analysis, Maimonides presents the following theoretical perplexity:

> II. If what Aristotle has stated with regard to natural science is true, there are no epicycles or eccentric circles and everything revolves round the center of the earth. But in that case how can the various motions of the stars come about? Is it in any way possible that motion should be on the one hand circular, uniform, and perfect, and that on the other hand the things that are observable should be observed in consequence of it, unless this be accounted for by making use of one of the two principles, or of both of them? This consideration is all the stronger because of the fact that if one accepts everything stated by Ptolemy concerning the epicycle of the moon and its deviation toward a point outside the center of the world and also outside the center of the eccentric circle, it will be found that what is calculated on the hypothesis of the two principles is not at fault by even a minute ... This is the true perplexity.[43]

That Maimonides characterizes an astronomical conundrum as the 'true perplexity' in a work devoted to defusing religious perplexities has not escaped scholars.[44] In effect, Maimonides is claiming that the heavens are 'too far away', and ultimately unknowable to humans (but not to God). The very recognition that the heavens are knowable to God suggests that it is only owing to human limitation that we do not have full knowledge of the heavens. It is only because of the accidental features of some knowers that the heavens are not fully known and comprehended. There is nothing in the nature of heavenly configurations per se that precludes their being known. Hence there is nothing in the science of astronomy that is per se beyond human grasp.

'Unseemly' Kisses: Matter, Soul and Human Perfection

This last point, namely the limits of human knowledge, leads to yet a further concern, the epistemological and spiritual limits, if any, in the attainment of human perfection. As in the case of cosmology, the issue of human perfection reflects the intersection of Aristotelian motifs and Jewish beliefs; it appears primarily within the context of problems associated with the immortality of the soul. Interestingly enough, Maimonides devotes very little space in the *Guide* to the issue of immortality itself. In *Guide*, I:41, he distinguishes three meanings to the term *nefesh*, or soul, and suggests that only in the third sense, that is, as a rational intellect, can the soul be considered immortal. However, the soul that survives after death is not the very 'same' soul that a person has when alive, for the former enjoys a separate existence after death and thus represents a distinct ontological reality. Reflecting Aristotle's celebrated passage in *De anima*, III.5, Maimonides claims,

> For that which comes into being at the time a man is generated is merely the faculty consisting in preparedness, whereas the thing that after death is separate from matter is the thing that has become actual and not the soul that also comes into being; the latter is identical with the spirit that comes into being.[45]

In this passage Maimonides seems to be suggesting that, when separated from the body, the immortal soul enjoys a special sort of existence akin to that of the Active Intellect. Like the Active Intellect, this soul has no personal features.

But this leads us to another important theme, namely the attainment of spiritual perfection. It is here that we see Maimonides grappling with the implications of Aristotelian hylomorphism. Describing at the very end of the *Guide* the ultimate goal of human existence, Maimonides provides us with the following statement about the attainment of ultimate bliss achievable by a mortal:

> III.1 The philosophers have already explained that the bodily faculties impede in youth the attainment of most of the moral virtues, and all the more that of pure thought which is achieved through the perfection of the intelligibles that lead to passionate love of Him, may He be exalted ... when a perfect man is stricken with years and approaches death, this apprehension increases very powerfully, joy over this apprehension and great love for the object of apprehension become stronger, until the soul is separated from the body at that moment in this state of pleasure ...
>
> III.2 Because of this the Sages have indicated with reference to the deaths of Moses, Aaron and Miriam that *the three of them died by a kiss* ... And they said of Miriam in the same way: She also died by a kiss. But with regard to her it is not said, *by the mouth of the Lord; because she was a woman, the use of the figurative expression was not suitable with regard to her*. [My emphasis, beginning with 'because'] Their purpose was to indicate that the three of them died in the pleasure of this apprehension due to the intensity of passionate love.[46]

In III.1, Maimonides describes the state of perfection of one who has achieved the fullness of philosophical study encouraged in this work. Reflecting the Aristotelian and Neoplatonic motif that corporeal bodies hinder immaterial perfection, III.1 emphasizes the separation from corporeality as a necessary condition for spiritual perfection. It is important to note that, according to Maimonides, a young person is never capable of achieving this level of perfection. The instant of ultimate perfection is manifested by the divesting of corporeality, a state that is presumably not possible for a youth still subject to passions. In fact, Maimonides tells us that only three individuals have ever reached this level.

III.2 is a truly remarkable passage, for here Maimonides acknowledges that even a woman (Miriam) can in theory achieve the kind of perfection described in III.1. Moses, Aaron and Miriam all die 'in the pleasure of this apprehension'. Presumably Miriam, as well as Moses and Aaron, has achieved the final separation of soul from body described in III.1. This separation is consummated by a kiss. But Maimonides is reluctant to admit that God kisses Miriam directly, presumably because to kiss a female is unseemly for the Deity. This reluctance reflects the sentiments of the following rabbinic passage:

> III.3 Our Rabbis taught: there are six [persons] over whom the Angel of Death had no dominion – Abraham, Isaac, and Jacob, Moses, Aaron, and Miriam. With respect to Moses, Aaron, and Miriam, they 'died by the mouth of the Lord' [Numbers 33:38 and Deut. 34:5]. But 'by the mouth of the Lord' is not stated in the case of Miriam ... And how

come Scripture does not say 'by the mouth of the Lord' as in the case of Moses? Because saying such a thing would be inappropriate [in the case of a woman].[47]

Why is it inappropriate to have God kiss Miriam directly if she too has shed her corporeality? Reactions to III.2 and III.3 have been surprisingly minimal in the literature. Fishbane has argued that the deaths of Moses, Aaron and Miriam are 'anthropomorphically transfigured in this midrash ... the very moment of death is itself infused with an erotic element'.[48] In these passages the kiss of God represents the culmination of a spiritual quest, a poetical way of talking about the 'consummation of spiritual eros as the death of the earthly self'.[49] But if, as Maimonides believes, matter represents the manifestation of corporeality and evil, and this matter is identified with the female principle, then in an important sense one might expect that the female in such an ontology can never fully rid herself of the mark of sexuality. And if the female is *by nature* material, then she cannot engage in the same sort of 'God-talk' as somebody who can divest himself of corporeality.

Idit Dobbs-Weinstein has pointed to the ambivalence inherent in Maimonides' thinking about the relationship between matter and evil and suggests that this ambivalence results in part from Maimonides' attempt to accept both an Aristotelian and a Neoplatonic ontology.[50] She emphasizes Maimonides' insistence upon likening matter to the female principle. This insistence is evidenced in the following passage from the *Guide*, in which Maimonides clearly identifies matter with sexual licence:

> III.4 All bodies subject to generation and corruption are attained by corruption only because of their matter ... The nature and true reality of matter are such that it never ceases to be joined to privation; hence no form remains constantly in it, for it perpetually puts off one form and puts on another. How extraordinary is what Solomon said in his wisdom when likening matter to a married harlot (Prov. 6.26), for matter is in no way found without form and is consequently always like a married woman who is never separated from a man, and is never free. However, notwithstanding her being a married woman, she never ceases to seek for another man to substitute for her husband, and she deceives and draws him on in every way until he obtains from her what her husband used to obtain. This is the state of matter.[51]

The implications of this parable are striking when juxtaposed against Maimonides' statement that it is matter that stands in the way of human perfection. Matter acts as a veil, a barrier, to human knowledge of God.[52]

> III.5 Matter is a strong veil preventing the apprehension of that which is separate from matter as it truly is. It does this even if it is the noblest and purest matter, I mean to say even if it is the matter of the heavenly spheres. All the more is this true for the dark and turbid matter that is ours. Hence whenever our intellect aspires to apprehend the deity or one of the intellects, there subsists this great veil interposed between the two. This is alluded to in all the books of the prophets; namely that we are separated by a veil from God and that He is hidden from us by a heavy cloud, or by darkness or by a mist or by an enveloping cloud, and similar allusions to our incapacity to apprehend Him because of

matter ... And though that great assembly was greater than any vision of prophecy and beyond any analogy, it also indicated a notion; I refer to His manifestation ... in a thick cloud. For it draws attention to the fact that the apprehension of His true reality is impossible for us because of the dark matter that encompasses us and not Him ... for He ... is not a body.[53]

Not only does the female, *qua* matter, stand in the way of male perfection and actualization, but she herself can never rid herself of the matter which constitutes her very essence: the female *qua* personification of matter veils herself. These texts reflect the many passages in Aristotle that associate the material principle with corporeality, grossness, imperfection and femaleness, as contrasted with the formal principle that is allied to incorporeality, perfection and maleness.[54] If we assume that Miriam is at least enough like other women to have a body, and that her body is no less identifiable with matter and with deficiency than that of other women, then it is not surprising that, following the rabbis, Maimonides would be reluctant to have God endow a 'full kiss' upon a person whose very essence is equated with corporeality and evil.

The imputation of unseemliness to God's kissing Miriam thus introduces the motif of corporeality into Maimonides' analysis. The question before us, then, is whether there exists an essential difference between Miriam, on the one hand, and Moses and Aaron on the other, a difference rooted in ontology that affects the nature of their respective unions with God. If Maimonides does in fact impute an ontological difference to Miriam, then we must ask whether women are all like Miriam in that they cannot ever transcend their materiality, or whether women are enough like Moses and Aaron that they are able in theory fully to actualize their potentiality and transcend their corporeal nature.[55]

I suggest that a key to understanding *Guide*, III.51, lies in what Langermann has recently described as 'philosophical spirituality'.[56] On this model of 'non-denominational philosophical spirituality', the philosopher achieves perfection by pursuing a rigorous path of scientific knowledge. The model followed by Ibn Gabirol in *Mekor Hayyim*, in which the spiritual leader does not evince to his disciple any hint of his Jewishness (nor did later readers even suspect that the author of this work was a Jew), is a case in point: spiritual perfection can be achieved without regard to religious particularism. In *Guide*, I.68, Maimonides claims both that God is to be identified with intellect, and second, that it is the function of humans to unite with this intellect. More specifically, in I.68, Maimonides describes God as 'the intellect as well as the subject and object of intellection'. He then describes the intellectual union of God as follows:

> When, however, you are alone with yourself and no one else is there, and while you lie awake upon your bed, you should take great care during these precious times not to set your thought to work on anything other than that intellectual worship consisting in nearness to God and being in his presence in that true reality that I have made known to you, and not by way of affections of the imagination.[57]

This meditative strand is compared with external speech (such as prayer), which type of worship 'ought only to be engaged in after intellectual conception has been achieved'. It is this intellectualist strand, reflected in the final chapters of the *Guide*, that underlies Maimonides' celebrated theory of negative predication (elucidated in Part I of the *Guide*).

Conclusion

I started this chapter with the question, 'What, then, is the relevance of science to Judaism?' In even posing this question, I reflect a set of issues found in a work by Menachem Fisch.[58] In this work, Fisch sets out to respond to the challenge of Jacob Neusner, who argued that, because the rabbinic mind was simply incapable of scientific thinking, scientific advances were conspicuously absent in Jewish intellectual development. Neusner claims that the reason observant Jews did not contribute to the scientific revolution in the sixteenth and seventeenth centuries lies in the fact that the very methods used in thinking about and elaborating Talmudic texts preclude philosophical and scientific thinking: 'The very means by which these [Talmudic] modes of thought were transmitted and held together, the extraordinary power of analysis and argument characteristic of the normative documents – these explain also the incapacity of those same modes of thought to frame philosophy, including natural philosophy.'[59] What Fisch tries to do in his own study is to demonstrate that both science and torah study represent rational endeavours which share a common *modus operandi*.

This common *modus operandi* is apparent, I have argued, in Maimonides' appropriation of Aristotle. Maimonides adopts an accommodationist strategy in trying to reconcile the two paradigms: 'Judaism and science'. But this statement is in itself problematic once we try to disentangle more carefully what we mean by the two terms 'science' and 'Judaism'. As Cantor has pointed out, 'historians of science have not succeeded in framing a universal definition of science, and it is now recognized that any such attempt is futile. Likewise, within the history of religions ... the problem of providing a definition of religion has proved notoriously difficult.'[60]

What science and philosophy have traditionally had in common, hearkening back to Aristotle's theory of demonstration, is a search for objectivity and truth. The term 'objective' has been used in many ways, including referring to material which is detached, unbiased, impersonal, publicly observable; existing independently of the knower; or reflective of what is 'really real' or 'the way things are'. Many Jewish philosophers, however, both medieval and modern, have questioned the efficacy of objectivity as a method for achieving religious truth, arguing that religious truth derives its veridical nature from divine revelation. This is not to say that all Jewish philosophers have rejected the ultimate grounding of reason. But, as we peruse the pages of both medieval and modern Jewish texts, we find among many Jewish philosophers a tendency to gravitate towards a religious form of truth based on faith rather than cognitive content. I refer in particular to the traditional Jewish notion of faith associated with a non-cognitivist 'trust in God' rather than as a propositional affirmation or denial. In fact it is Maimonides who introduced into Judaism a propositional or cognitivist notion of belief by defining heresy as the questioning of any of the thirteen principles of faith articulated in his introduction to the tenth chapter of *Tractate Sanhedrin* (*Perek Helek*). In this work Maimonides argued that anybody who questions any one of these thirteen principles excludes himself from the community of Israel, and hence forfeits his share in the world to come.[61] According to Maimonides, adherence to these propositional belief states is a necessary condition for assuring immortality of the soul.

Thus, according to Maimonides, intellectual apprehension of God represents the truest form of worship; this apprehension is modelled on the Aristotelian paradigm of divine knowledge. On the one hand, Maimonides tells us that love of God can only be achieved through intellectual and scientific pursuit: love of God 'becomes valid only through the apprehension of the whole of Being as it is'.[62] On what comes to be identified in later centuries as a Spinozistic model, it is the study of nature as a whole (the facts of the matter; or more literally, the facts of '*materia*') that yields knowledge of the divine. As we have seen above, Maimonides argues that scientific knowledge cannot be applied to God or to the supralunar sphere in general.

On the other hand, however, the very possibility of divine knowledge, of meditative reflection, is itself limited by the corporeality of humans. Spiritual perfection, which is a sine qua non for intellectual apprehension of an incorporeal entity, is by definition limited by the veil of matter. We have noted above that, according to Maimonides, scientific knowledge cannot be applied to the supralunar sphere. Both men and women are limited by this veil, inasmuch as their very human natures are ontologically rooted to their material essences. The image of Miriam, therefore, functions as a hermeneutic device that unites divine predication, intellectual union and spiritual perfection. The 'unseemliness' of God's kissing Miriam reinforces the fact that she is ontologically unable to transcend her material being. By acquiescing to midrashic interpretations of Miriam's kiss, Maimonides supports an *exoteric* reading of intellectual perfection according to which the female is ontologically imperfect to the male. However, on an *esoteric* reading, the very fact that she receives God's 'kiss' suggests that, like her male compatriots, Miriam has penetrated the divine *mysterium*. Science, as epitomized by Aristotelian method, becomes the way to transcend the superlunar sphere and achieve knowledge of God.

Notes

1. See Geoffrey Cantor and Chris Kenny, 'Barbour's fourfold way: Problems with his taxonomy of science–religion relationships', *Zygon* 36, 4 (2001): 765–82. Barbour's thesis is developed in a number of works, most notably in Ian Barbour, *Religion and Science: Historical and Contemporary Issues* (San Francisco, CA: Harper Books, 1997).
2. Cantor and Kenny, 'Barbour's fourfold way', p.799.

3   Joel L. Kraemer, 'Maimonides' use of (Aristotelian) dialectic', in *Maimonides and the Sciences*, ed. Robert S. Cohen and Hillel Levine (Dordrecht: Kluwer, 2000), p.117.
4   Ibid.
5   Maimonides, *Guide*, Intro, p.7. All quotations will be taken from Moses Maimonides, *The Guide of the Perplexed*, trans. Shlomo Pines (Chicago: University of Chicago Press, 1963).
6   Maimonides, *Guide*, Intro, p.10.
7   Steven Harvey, 'Maimonides in the sultan's palace', in *Perspectives on Maimonides: Philosophical and Historical Studies*, ed. Joel L. Kraemer (Oxford: Oxford University Press, 1991), p.55.
8   Harvey, 'Maimonides in the sultan's palace', p.56.
9   Ibid., p.60.
10 Joel L. Kraemer, 'Maimonides on Aristotle and scientific method', in *Moses Maimonides and His Time*, ed. Eric L. Ormsby (Washington, DC: The Catholic University of America Press, 1989), p.54.
11 Alexander Marx, *Jewish Quarterly Review* 25: 374ff, quoted by Pines in his introduction to Maimonides, *Guide*, p. lix.
12 Maimonides, *Guide*, I.5.
13 Ibid., II.14.
14 Ibid., II.19.
15 Ibid., I.5
16 Alexander Altmann, 'Defining Maimonides' Aristotelianism', in *Maimonides and the Sciences*, ed. Robert S. Cohen and Hillel Levine (Dordrecht: Kluwer Academic Publishers, 2000).
17 Aristotle, *Posterior Analytics* I.2.71b 17–19.
18 Aristotle, *Topics*, I.1.100a 27–29.
19 Ernan McMullin, 'The conception of science in Galileo's work', in *New Perspectives on Galileo*, ed. Robert E. Butts and Joseph C. Pitt (Dordrecht: Reidel, 1978), p.213.
20 Kraemer, 'Maimonides' use of Aristotelian dialectic'; see also Aristotle, *Topics*, 100a18ff.
21 Kraemer, *Dialetic*.
22 Ibid., p. 116.
23 Maimonides, *Guide*, I.31.
24 Ibid., II.22.
25 See Ibid., I.1: 'with respect to that which ought to be said in order to refute the doctrine of the corporeality of God and to establish His real unity ... you shall know the demonstration (*burhân, mofet*) of all of this from this Treatise'. Also *Guide*, I.18; *Guide* II.1: 'All these are demonstrative methods of proving the existence of one deity, who is neither a body nor a force in a body.'
26 Maimonides, *Guide*, I.26.
27 Ibid., I.28.
28 Ibid., I.34.
29 Ibid., I.59.
30 Ibid., II.20; III.17.
31 Ibid., II.24.
32 Aristotle's discussion of the eternity of the universe is contained in several places, most notably *De caelo*, 1, *Physics*, 8.1 and *Metaphysics*, 12.6. For a recent discussion of these and other relevant passages, see R. Sorabji, *Time, Creation and the Continuum* (Ithaca, NY: Cornell University Press, 1983), pp.276ff.

33 Maimonides, *Guide*, II.31, p.360.
34 Representative interpretations can be found in Sara-Klein Braslavy, 'The creation of the world and Maimonides' interpretation of Gen. I–V', in *Maimonides and Philosophy*, ed. S. Pines and Y. Yovel (Dordrecht: Martinus Nijhoff, 1986), pp.65–78; Herbert Davidson, 'Maimonides' secret position on creation', *Studies in Medieval Jewish History and Literature*, ed. I. Twersky (Cambridge, MA: Harvard University Press, 1979), pp.16–40; Warren Zev Harvey, 'A third approach to Maimonides' cosmogony-prophetology puzzle', *Harvard Theological Review* 74 (1981): 287–301; Arthur Hyman, 'Maimonides on creation and emanation', in *Studies in Medieval Philosophy*, ed. J.F. Wippel (Washington, DC: The Catholic University of America Press, 1987), pp.45–61; Alfred L. Ivry, 'Maimonides on possibility', in *Mystics, Philosophers, and Politicians: Essays in Jewish Intellectual History in Honor of Alexander Altmann*, ed. Jehuda Reinhartz and Daniel Swetschinski (Durham, NC: Duke University Press, 1982), pp.67–84; Lawrence Kaplan, 'Maimonides on the miraculous element in prophecy', *Harvard Theological Review* 70 (1977): 233–56.
35 See T.M. Rudavsky, *Time Matters: Time, Creation and Cosmology in Medieval Jewish Philosophy* (Albany, NY: State University of New York Press, 2000).
36 Edward Grant, 'Cosmology', in *Science in the Middle Ages*, ed. David Lindberg (Chicago: University of Chicago Press, 1978), p.266.
37 See Rudavsky, *Time Matters*, ch.2.
38 Maimonides, *Guide*, II.19, p.308. See also the comment in *Guide*, II.24, to the effect that in Aristotle's time 'mathematics had not been brought to perfection'.
39 Maimonides, *Guide*, II.24, p.322.
40 Ibid.
41 Ibid., pp.322–3.
42 See Joel L. Kraemer, 'Maimonides on Aristotle and scientific method'. Langermann points out that it is not clear whether Maimonides himself subscribes to all these arguments. See Y. Tzvi Langermann, 'The true perplexity: *The Guide of the Perplexed* Part II, ch.24', in *Perspectives on Maimonides*, ed. Joel L. Kraemer (Oxford: Oxford University Press, 1991). Maimonides does, however, lay claim to an original point in *Guide*, II.24, p.323.
43 Maimonides, *Guide*, II.24, pp.326–7.
44 Surely that is one of the bases of Langermann's point in his article, 'The true perplexity'. The intriguing question, of course, is whether Maimonides thought that all the issues in the *Guide of the Perplexed* could ultimately be traced back to this basic perplexity. As Kraemer points out, *Perspectives*, p.80, 'perplexity is not a permanent condition'.
45 Maimonides, *Guide*, I.70, p.174.
46 Ibid., III.51.
47 *Baba Bathra*, 17a.
48 Michael Fishbane, *The Kiss of God* (Seattle, WA: University of Washington Press, 1994), p.18.
49 The original eros is transfigured, and 'the male–female love of the Song is now read as God (spiritually) kissing men but not women, for that would be a consummate breach of propriety'. See Fishbane, *The Kiss of God*, p.26.
50 See Idit Dobbs-Weinstein, *Maimonides and St. Thomas on the Limits of Reason* (Albany, NY: State University of New York Press, 1995), pp.89ff.
51 Maimonides, *Guide*, III.8. For her trenchant discussion of this passage, see Susan Shapiro, 'A matter of discipline: reading for gender in Jewish philosophy', in *Judaism*

Since Gender, ed. Miriam Peskowitz and Laura Levitt (New York: Routledge, 1997), pp.158–73.
52 Maimonides, *Guide*, III.9, p.436.
53 Ibid., pp.436–7.
54 For a discussion of the implications of the female principle in religious thought, see Judith Plaskow, 'Jewish theology in feminist perspective', in *Feminist Perspectives on Jewish Studies*, ed. L. Davidman and S. Tenenbaum (New Haven, CI: Yale University Press, 1994), pp. 62–84; Susan Shapiro, 'A matter of discipline'.
55 For additional discussion of these passages, see Menachem Kellner, 'Philosophical misogyny in medieval Jewish philosophy – Gersonides vs. Maimonides', *Jerusalem Studies in Jewish Thought (Sermoneta Jubilee Volume)* (Jerusalem, 1998), pp.113–28; Abraham Melamed, 'Maimonides on women: Formless matter or potential prophet?' in *Perspectives on Jewish Thought and Mysticism*, ed. A. Ivry, E. Wolfson and A. Arkush (Amsterdam: Harwood Academic Publishers, 1998), pp.99–134.
56 See Y. Tzvi Langermann, 'Science and the Kuzari', *Science in Context* 10 (1997): 495–519.
57 Maimonides, *Guide*, III.51, p.623.
58 Menachem Fisch, *Rational Rabbis: Science and Talmudic Culture* (Bloomington, IN: Indiana University Press, 1997).
59 Jacob Neusner, *The Making of the Mind of Judaism*, quoted in Fisch, *Rational Rabbis*, p.xiv.
60 Cantor and Kenny, 'Barbour's fourfold way', p.771.
61 Maimonides' text can be found in Menachem Kellner, *Dogma in Medieval Jewish Thought* (Oxford: Oxford University Press, 1986), p.16.
62 Maimonides, *Guide*, III.28.

Chapter 9

Averroës on Aristotle

Alfred Ivry

Abû al-Walîd Muhammad ibn Ahmad Ibn Rushd (1126–98), known to the West as Averroës, is also known, following Dante, as 'The Commentator'. Asked by the Almohad Caliph, Abû Ya`qûb Yûsuf, to explain Aristotle's work to him – an offer Averroës could hardly refuse – the sage of Cordova produced some thirty-eight philosophical commentaries.[1] They covered all of Aristotle's corpus apart from his *Politics*, for which Averroës substituted Plato's *Republic*, plus Porphyry's *Eisagoge*, considered the appropriate introduction to the Organon.

This tremendous outpouring of philosophical commentary was undoubtedly more than Abû Ya`qûb Yûsuf, Caliph and 'Prince of the Believers', had in mind when commissioning the project, and it is clear that Averroës wrote with more than the caliph in mind.[2] The commentaries are addressed to different audiences, a distinction only partially manifested in the distinct styles of commentary adopted.

There are three types of commentary, known generally as the epitome or short commentary, the middle and the long. The 'short' commentaries are really epitomes, summaries of an Aristotelian work, restructuring it as required to bring out Aristotle's essential teachings on the particular subject, as well as Averroës' own views of it. While typically in agreement with 'the Master of those who know', as he considered Aristotle, Averroës regularly introduced the views of other philosophers into his remarks, construing the epitome to be an occasion to review the subject with which Aristotle's book deals, rather than a review of the book itself.[3]

Averroës' commentaries on Aristotle are more than just that, then, since his understanding of Aristotle was mediated for him by a number of highly respected predecessors. Foremost among them are the Hellenistic philosophers Alexander of Aphrodisias, Themistius and Galen, and the Muslim *falâsifa* Alfarabi (tenth century CE) and Avicenna (eleventh century), as well as his own Andalusian predecessor Ibn Bâjjah, known in the West as Avempace.

Averroës' commentaries attest to his struggle to disentangle Aristotle from all these interpreters of his thought, and to present him in his original fashion. This, of course, is a near hopeless task, particularly for one like Averroës who had no Greek, and who had to rely on translations the accuracy of which he could not fully gauge. His middle commentary on the *Poetics* in particular reveals the mistakes to which his ignorance of the language and culture of Aristotle's world led him.[4] Yet for all the inevitable (intertextual and subjectivistic) distortions of the Stagirite's views, Averroës' Aristotle is as close as one gets to the original Athenian in the Middle

Ages, and was so regarded for a long time thereafter. It is through Averroës' commentaries that Aristotle was introduced to the West in the thirteenth century, their names and destinies linked thereafter in European philosophy.[5]

Averroës' long commentaries, like his epitomes, present Aristotle's views on a given subject, together with the views of the commentators who preceded Averroës, followed by his own comments on the Master and his followers. In the long commentaries, though, Averroës is much more disciplined and didactic than in the epitomes, quoting and commenting on practically every line of Aristotle's text, often at inordinate length. There are five such commentaries, the *Posterior Analytics*, *Physics*, *De caelo*, *De anima* and *Metaphysics*, and all but the long *De anima* still await full translation into modern Western languages.[6]

It is not only the length of the long commentaries that has proved daunting to readers in the West (as well as in the East), the high level of philosophical speculation in them undoubtedly also intimidated many would-be scholars. Averroës' audience for these commentaries had to be a highly select, small coterie of fellow philosophers, perhaps only Averroës and his disciples, if he had any.[7] At the end of the day, Averroës may be seen as having written the long commentaries for himself, a not uncommon phenomenon.[8]

Averroës' middle commentaries, in contrast to the epitomes and long commentaries, have few digressions from Aristotle's text and comparatively little enlargement upon it. They mostly paraphrase the text, clarifying its author's meaning, usually within the original terms Aristotle set forth. It is this genre of commentary that most fulfils the charge Averroës was given, and which the caliph and members of his court would have found the most comprehensible.[9]

Averroës does not talk down to his presumed audience in the middle commentaries, but neither does he inform them of the full intricacies of the subject, as developed by Aristotle's commentators and by Averroës himself in the epitome and long commentaries of the same work (where extant). It is in the middle commentaries too that we find Averroës a shade more discreet and aware of the political and social realities in which he found himself. Without denying Aristotle's teachings, Averroës finds ways to ignore or distance himself from their more radical theological entailments.[10]

The picture of Averroës that emerges from an examination of these commentaries is of a man who was utterly devoted to the study of Aristotle, who indeed was convinced that Aristotle was the 'Master of those who know', and who was eager, indeed obsessed, with spreading the truth, as given by Aristotle. The only major problem that Averroës detected in Aristotle's teachings lay in the field of cosmology, Muslim astronomers, following Ptolemy, having shown the inadequacy of Aristotle's thesis of homocentric spheres. Averroës acknowledges this problem, particularly in his long *Metaphysics* and *De caelo* commentaries, but follows Aristotelian teachings anyway, not having greater confidence in alternative models, and not having an alternative proposal of his own to offer.[11]

In general, then, Averroës sees himself as a supporter of Aristotle's doctrines, and a defender of them against non-Aristotelian incursions. These are represented for him mainly in the persons of Avicenna and al-Ghazalî: as he sees them, the standard bearers respectively for Neoplatonic and Occasionalist challenges to Aristotelian nominalism and empiricism. Avicenna presents the more invidious challenge, since emanationist doctrines had become associated with Peripatetic teachings since late antiquity, and Averroës himself had adopted this synthesis at first. Much of his trajectory as a philosopher is the struggle to purge himself of this Neoplatonized Aristotelianism, an attempt at which he was only partially successful.

The conflict with al-Ghazalî, Islam's Aquinas, is more straightforward, laid out and layered systematically in Averroës' *Tahâfut al-Tahâfut*, translated as *The Incoherence of the Incoherence*.[12] Against a philosophically formidable opponent, Averroës insists upon the necessity for science of adopting Aristotelian premises in physics and metaphysics: the eternity of the world and its constituent physical principles; hylomorphic substantiality and intelligible species, all rendered as naturally as possible, with causal definition the key explanatory mechanism.

This embrace of Aristotle is less explicitly expressed in the commentaries, but no less present there as well. Not on the defensive as much as when responding to al-Ghazalî, Averroës allows himself, in the epitomes and long commentaries mostly, to question Aristotle's views, explore diverse interpretations of them, and in the process occasionally to modify his own position regarding them. All three genres of commentary testify, in effect, to Averroës' growth as a philosopher and as an interpreter of Aristotle.

An examination of Averroës' three commentaries on *De anima* can attest to this statement. The epitome itself contains diverse conceptualizations of the material, or 'hylic' intellect, the vacuous offspring of Aristotle's potential intellect.[13] Averroës vacillates over where to place this first potentiality for intellection in the human body, an unease compounded by his doubts as to its very nature. Initially, he follows Alexander of Aphrodisias and Ibn Bâjjah in denying the substantiality of the material intellect, seeing it as a mere disposition for exercising one's rational faculty.

With his mentors, Averroës at first believes the material intellect is in the body, that part of the imaginative faculty which is 'disposed' to receive the intelligible intentions of imaginative forms.[14] However, after laying out this view, Averroës proceeds to disown it.[15] Upon reflection, he has come to the conclusion that the material intellect must have its own substantial integrity, and that must be purely immaterial, however paradoxical it seems. This, in order that it not be affected whatsoever by the material nature – that is, the specific corporeal representation – of imaginative forms. The material intellect is now to be located outside the body, presumably adjacent to the Agent, or Active, Intellect (which was considered by everyone after Aristotle as extrinsic to the body).

This new view is explained at greater length in his long commentary on this text, Averroës tells the reader, indicating that he has gone back to his earlier writing to revise it. He has not seen fit to delete his earlier remarks, he says, since his epitome is in the public domain, that is, it has been copied often and is presumably being studied. Apparently, Averroës was not bothered by being identified with ideas that he no longer believed true; and there was of course little he could do to call in the 'first edition' of his epitome. However, it is also likely that Averroës had a soft spot for the Alexandrian view of the material intellect, and was not averse to having it studied. Though he was no longer able to affirm the Alexandrian position in full, he was not averse to having others do so; perhaps they would arrive at a better solution for this intellect than he found.

The epitome of *De anima* is not, however, overly concerned with the rational faculty, neither with its active nor passive aspects, the Agent or material intellect. Averroës treats this subject rather cursorily, as he does all of Book Three of Aristotle's text in the epitome. He is much more interested in Book Two, and not at all interested in this short commentary in the historical material of Book One. Book Two of *De anima*, however, with its detailed physiological descriptions of the external senses, is seen as rich in valid scientific information, which Averroës is eager to share. His point of departure is Aristotle's own writings on the natural sciences, both terrestial and celestial, which Averroës summarizes in place of Book One.

While Averroës quotes and approves of Aristotle's statement that the study of the soul 'makes a great contribution to truth as a whole, and especially to the study of nature',[16] in effect he consciously reverses Aristotle's priorities. For Averroës, the study of nature precedes and is a condition for the study of the soul. He declares, in his opening statement of this epitome, that he wants to establish what is 'most in conformity with what has been ascertained in natural science, as well as what is most in keeping with Aristotle's purpose'.[17]

Accordingly, Averroës first mentions Aristotle's hylomorphic assumptions, as given in his *Physics*, emphasizing the notion of potentiality, characteristic of prime matter and of all matter, and its phenomenological dependence upon form. The teachings of Aristotle's *On the Heavens* regarding the necessary involvement of matter with the four elements, and preceding that with the four humours, is next mentioned, leading to the lessons taught in Aristotle's *On Generation and Corruption* concerning the composition of complex bodies from the mixture and blending of these elements.

The role of the heavenly bodies in this process, as mentioned in Aristotle's *Meteorology*, is then adduced. The heavenly bodies are the remote cause of the heat found in uniform, or homeomerous, bodies, the proximate cause being the innate heat of these bodies. This innate heat, or rather the pneuma in which it resides, is thought to form a concoction of the four qualities/elements, producing the proper mixture for the intended body.[18]

The same natural causal principles are at work in the creation of living beings, Averroës next makes clear, referring to Aristotle's supposed *Kitâb al-Hayawân* (the *Liber animalium*), a book which comprised portions of the *Historia animalium*, *De generatione animalium* and *De partibus animalium*. The innate heat in sperm and seed is considered to be the proximate cause here, the heat produced by the motion of the heavenly bodies, particularly the sun, being the remote cause. Two other causal factors are then mentioned in the creation of living bodies, namely, the nutritive faculty and a separate agent, called simply `aql, intellect.

In mentioning just these two psychic faculties, Averroës is apparently thinking of the necessary conditions for creation of the lowest and highest species of living bodies, respectively. In the *Generation of Animals*, Aristotle refers to the role in procreation of a separate, immaterial intellect that enters from outside the body,[19] and Averroës is probably echoing his sentiments here in the *De anima* epitome. The intellect in question is not referred to further at this point, but, given its active role in procreation, Averroës probably identified it with the Agent, or Active, Intellect.[20] Mention of the Agent Intellect in this context, as a formal cause of living bodies, is not present, however, in the middle or long *De anima* commentaries, reflective of his later view. Averroës restricts its causal role there to the field of cognition, as Herbert Davidson has noted.

In the epitome, this intellect is called by its name, *al-`aql al-fa`āl* (the Arabic of *nous poiêtikos* in Greek, though not what Aristotle had in mind, necessarily), in the ensuing discussion Averroës has of the relation of the separate forms or intelligences of the spheres to their celestial bodies. This relation is termed 'incidental', or 'accidental', *bi'l-`ard*: the immaterial, always actual, unchanging celestial intelligence regarded as unable to be in an essential relation with anything representing matter and potentiality, however unique the matter of the heavenly bodies is. While this type of relation occurs between the intelligence of each sphere and its heavenly body, only the first mover of the heavens, the agent responsible for the motion of the outermost sphere (that is, God, as Averroës came to believe) and the Agent Intellect are specifically cited. Despite its non-essential, incidental quality, the relation is called one of 'conjunction' (*ittisâl* in Arabic), adumbrating Averroës' later description of the mechanics and goal of human cognition.

This topic rightfully belongs to metaphysics, Averroës concludes, which science, together with the physical and natural sciences mentioned, is regarded as providing the background and assumptions on which the science of the soul is constructed. The reader is left with the firm impression that metaphysics is to be construed as naturally as the others, without any extraneous theological or traditionally religious assumptions. There is a first mover, but it is that mover first recognized by Aristotle, not Muhammad. Averroës makes no attempt to pretend otherwise here, and offers precious little attempt to do so elsewhere in his commentaries.[21]

This extensive introductory background in the physical and biological sciences (and the inversion it represents of Aristotle's epistemological priorities) is missing in Averroës' other two commentaries on *De anima*; though it informs each commentary's understanding and orientation to Book Two's discussion of the external senses, and has an impact as well upon Averroës' understanding of the internal senses in Book Three. However, despite this naturalistic orientation, Averroës asserts already in the epitome that the ultimate pursuit in this discipline is to know whether the soul can be separate from the body.[22]

In declaring this as the ultimate purpose of the science of the soul, Averroës has a rich tradition on which to depend, one that could be traced back to Themistius, and ultimately to Plato. The intellect for the former, the soul for the latter, is considered a separate substance essentially independent of the body and able to reclaim its separate independence, via acts of cognition.[23] Aristotle, of course, was opposed to Plato's theory of separate forms, *De anima* being largely an attempt to posit an alternative ontology and epistemology. Thus the question 'Whether the soul can be separate from the body' is not the ultimate purpose of this science for Aristotle, even if one substitutes 'intellect' for 'soul'.

Aristotle, it is true, asks in Book Three of *De anima*, 'whether it is possible for (the intellect), while not existing separate from spatial conditions [or "not unextended", *mê kechôrismenon megethous*], to think anything that is separate [or "unextended"]'; but defers this question for later consideration, and never returns to it.[24] As this question follows the statement that 'in every case [*holôs de*] the mind which is actively thinking is the objects which it thinks' (as good a definition of conjunction as there is) a positive response to Aristotle's question would have him affirming conjunction with an eternal separate substance, thereby endorsing the possibility of an individual intellect achieving immortality.

Aristotle does, of course, refer earlier in Book Three of *De anima* to the intellect which, 'when separated [*chôristheis*] is alone just what it is, and this alone is immortal and eternal'.[25] Aristotle concludes this sentence, however, by telling us that intellect in this state of total actuality is beyond the grasp of our intermittently actual, perishable intellects. This reinforces the impression received elsewhere in *De anima* and *Metaphysics*[26] that that intellect in persons which is occasionally (and mostly in passing) posited as eternal is similar in function and universality to the intelligences of the spheres. Human beings may have an active intellect that derives from that realm, but it is compromised, even as it is individuated, by the imaginative and sensory faculties.

Aristotle, accordingly, has no doctrine of individual immortality, and Averroës knows it. He remarks in his commentaries that he could not find Aristotle's subsequent discussion of the possibility of an embodied intellect thinking separate forms (that is, a discussion of immortality) anywhere.[27]

In his *De anima* commentaries, Averroës, as a faithful disciple of Aristotle, follows him in not dwelling upon the notion of conjunction, and certainly not upon its possible entailment of immortality. He does expand upon the theme in separate, smaller treatises, in which he speaks more independently of Aristotle. There the full complexity of the relation between the Agent Intellect and an individual 'material' intellect is described, the latter's progress from pure potentiality to full actualization charted. In the last stage, an 'acquired intellect' is regarded as placing the individual on an equal footing with the universal Agent Intellect. That substance is there understood as the formal principle of material objects, constituting the essential immaterial nature of all terrestial forms. The acquired intellect at the end thus matches, or comes close to matching, the nature of the Agent Intellect, and the two are thought to merge in that union of subject and object that is the hallmark of Aristotelian *noêsis*. The person who has achieved this distinction is considered to have mastered all the sciences, to know all there is to know. He/she has acquired knowledge of universal truths, eternally true propositions, is privy to eternal truth, and thus participates in it.[28]

This person can get a taste of eternity through intellectual perfection, but no more than a taste, brief and tenuously personal.[29] The entire thrust of cognition is towards abstraction and universalization of the particular data of experience. For Averroës, the very intellect at our disposal, the 'material intellect', is not ours essentially, rather it is the expression of a universal separate substance, be it the Agent Intellect in an 'incidental' relation to a human being (the *middle commentary* view), or its own celestially based material intelligence (the *long commentary* position).[30]

Thus, achieving intellectual perfection, conjunction in this sense, is for Averroës a loss of individuality, the key players – the material and Agent Intellects – only accidentally related to a given individual, affording the person no opportunity to retain after death his or her particular collection of universal truths, however impressive it may be. Rhetorical expressions aside, for Averroës the only immortality available is a collective one, and he makes no attempt to argue for an enduring conscious awareness or individual soul in the hereafter.

Conjunction of this sort, with the entailments described, is not discussed in the commentaries. The concept – *ittisâl* in Arabic – is discussed but once and somewhat obliquely in the middle commentary.[31] The real connection is between the Agent and material intellects, the former acting upon both the individual intellect and its intended objects, actualizing their potential intelligence and intelligibility, respectively. The 'objects' of intellection are found in the forms that the imaginative faculty presents to the material intellect, representations that have an intelligible 'intention' which the Agent Intellect brings to the fore, or actualizes.

This intelligible dimension of imaginative forms is not, of course, a creation of the imaginative faculty; that faculty receives it from the sensible forms with which it works, and the sensible forms, in turn, from the external objects of sensation themselves. The intelligibility of everything thus is a function of its formal composition, an inherent part of its nature. In a sense, then, the Agent Intellect is connected to everything that exists here on earth. Indeed, Averroës was at first inclined, following Avicenna's Neoplatonic orientation, to see the Agent Intellect as endowing all material objects with their forms.[32] This concept was attractive in part for having the Agent Intellect act parallel to the role of the separate intelligences vis-à-vis the celestial spheres.

In the *De anima* commentaries, however, the Agent Intellect's role is restricted to the cognitive process. The formal constitution of substances is assumed to be intrinsic to their nature, their intelligibility significant only to that species in which it can be known, which itself possesses an intellect. The actualizing reach of the Agent Intellect is limited to the material intellect and its immediate objects, the intelligible intentions of imaginative forms.

The relation here is normative, however, and the Agent Intellect should be seen as actively engaged with a person each time he/she thinks. Conjunction, expressed mostly in the Latin long commentary of *De anima* in the verbal forms of *continuare* and *copulare*, appears there as the Agent Intellect's enabling the material intellect to do its job, being an efficient cause primarily.[33] Averroës may speak of the Agent Intellect as 'creating' and 'generating' intelligibles,[34] but this should be taken more in the sense that it makes the formal, essential being of a given object intelligible than that it creates its form.

And yet, for all his attempt to return the Agent Intellect to its Aristotelian origins, Averroës cannot fully relinquish its ultimately Neoplatonic additions. He may not treat the Agent Intellect as a repository of forms explicitly, but this is implicit both in its activity and in the activity of the individual intellect to join with it. The Agent Intellect makes forms intelligible because it possesses these forms in their essential nature, as immaterial, that is, intelligible beings. The formal structure of our world is thus reflected, and refined, in the Agent Intellect, where the essential unity of being is fully realized. That is why the individual material intellect moves towards conjunction with the Agent Intellect, it being not only an efficient cause of cognition, but a final cause as well.

The goal of intellection for Averroës thus remains conjunction on a grand scale, the activity of thinking and thus knowing all things, an activity identified as divine, which God does by himself, and man does with the aid of (that is, in conjunction with) the Agent Intellect.[35] However, such a conjunction obliterates the individual component within it, an action facilitated by the essential unity of the individual intellect with its universal agent. It is not only after death that one loses individuality, the more universal one's knowledge, the less particular to you, and you to it, it is, even while one is alive.

Averroës' dedication to this ideal, despite its denial of individual salvation, has not always been appreciated. He offers no apologia for his position in the *De anima* commentaries, nor need he, not having addressed the issue directly there in the first place. We may, however, discern his commitment to what is an essentially Aristotelian perspective on intellection through his middle commentary on the *Nicomachean Ethics*.

In his commentary to Book Ten of this work, Averroës follows Aristotle faithfully in extolling theoretical reason and the life of contemplation as the happiest and most pure of human activities (as it is unmixed with corporeality). It is that activity in which human beings most resemble God.[36] The intellect is that 'something divine' within us, Aristotle says, *theon ti*, and Averroës concurs, *davar elohii*. We ought accordingly to cultivate this divine element, to turn our attention from mortal to immortal things, that is, to think of the eternal verities, not of practical, prudential matters. As Aristotle puts it, we ought as far as possible to 'make ourselves immortal'.[37]

Averroës here paraphrases Aristotle in an interesting, and revealing manner. He writes: '[Aristotle] said: It is appropriate that man's thoughts not be of a human sort (*enoshiyyot*), though he is but man, as those who mention this indicate (i.e., wish). Nor should his thoughts be those of a mortal being, though he is mortal. Rather, it is fitting that he absents death from his thoughts,[38] to the degree that is possible to do so.' Here Averroës seems to be going out of his way to avoid an apotheosis of the intellect, spurning thereby an invitation to accommodation with popular religion.

Averroës' fidelity to Aristotle is apparent again in his concurring with Aristotle's image of God in X.8 of this *Ethics*. No other activity is seemly for the gods (which Averroës reads as God and the angels) but contemplation. Any practical activity, including acts of justice and charity, is regarded as unworthy (that is, incoherent with the idea of God that Aristotle and Averroës share).[39] While this may have been a daring statement for Aristotle to make in his time, it was positively audacious of Averroës to repeat it, updating it only to refer to the one God of his religious tradition.

How Averroës managed to maintain himself within this tradition, how he managed to reconcile this tradition with his philosophical commitments, is another story, belonging to Averroës' use and abuse of Islam. But that is a story for another day.

Notes

1. An inventory of Averroës' commentaries was prepared by H.A. Wolfson, 'Plan for the publication of a *Corpus commentariorum Averrois in Aristotelem*', *Speculum* 38 (1963): 88–104; republished in Wolfson, *Studies in the History of Philosophy and Religion*, I, ed. I. Twersky and G.H. Williams (Cambridge, MA: Harvard University Press, 1973), pp.433–40. An account of the published commentaries is given by J. Puig in his translation, *Averroës: Epítome de Física* (Madrid: Consejo Superior de Investigaciones Cientifas, Instituto Hispano-Arabe de Cultura, 1987), pp.20–24.
2. The encounter between the caliph and the philosopher is given by G. Hourani, *Averroes: On the Harmony of Religion and Philosophy* (London: Luzac, 1967), pp.12–14.
3. Th.-A. Druart, 'Averroes: The Commentator and the commentators', in *Aristotle in Late Antiquity*, ed. L.P. Schrenk (Washington, DC: The Catholic University of America Press, 1994), pp.187–96.
4. Ch. Butterworth, trans, *Averroes' Middle Commentary on Averroes' Poetics* (Princeton, NJ: Princeton University Press, 1986), pp.59–142. See too Butterworth's discussion there, pp.11–49.
5. A.L. Ivry, 'Averroes and the West: the first encounter/nonencounter', in *A Straight Path*, ed. R.L. Salinger, J. Hackett, M.S. Hyman, R.J. Long, C.H. Manekin (Washington, DC: The Catholic University of America Press, 1988), pp.142–53.
6. A translation of the long *De anima* by Richard Taylor (Yale University Press) is forthcoming.
7. No record exists of Muslim philosophers of an Averroian cast; Islamic philosophy turned theosophical after him, following and going beyond Avicenna's direction. See M. Fakhry, *A History of Islamic Philosophy* (New York: Columbia University Press, 1970), pp.326–46.
8. A.L. Ivry, 'Averroës' middle and long commentaries on the *De anima*', *Arabic Sciences and Philosophy* 5 (1995): 75–92.
9. The very name of the middle commentary in Arabic, *talkhîs*, reflects the caliph's request to *talakhkhasa* Aristotle's books; though whether the sovereign's original intention was for Averroës to abridge or summarize them, as the verb is usually taken to mean, is moot, given the more extended, paraphrastic nature of the middle commentaries. Perhaps Abu Ya'qûb Yusûf only wanted epitomes, which Averroës did write first. Once he started writing epitomes, however, he found himself straying too far from the Aristotelian text, as remarked above; a digression that the middle commentaries may have been meant to redress.
10. These generalizations about the nature of the middle commentary genre and its relation to the short and long commentary forms are based on my study of Averroës' three *De anima* commentaries. Cf. my edition and translation of Averroës' *Middle Commentary on Aristotle's De anima* (Provo, UT: Brigham Young University Press, 2002), pp.xiii–xxviii, and see particularly p.xxvi.
11. A.I. Sabra, 'The Andalusian revolt against Ptolemaic astronomy', *Transformation and Tradition in the Sciences*, ed. E. Mendelssohn (Cambridge: Cambridge University Press, 1984), pp.138–44; G. Endress, 'Averroes' *De caelo:* Ibn Rushd's cosmology in

his commentaries on Aristotle's *On the Heavens'*, *Arabic Sciences and Philosophy* 5 (1995): 37–46.

12 So called because it is a detailed response to al-Ghazalî's *Tahâfut al-Falâsifah*, the *Incoherence of the Philosophers*. Avicenna's views are those that most influenced al-Ghazalî, so that Averroës' response to the latter is often a critique of Avicenna's philosophical orientation. See Averroës' *Tahafut al-Tahafut (The Incoherence of the Incoherence)*, trans. S. Van Den Bergh (London: Luzac, 1969), pp.253, 294 and *passim*.

13 *De anima* III.4, 429a10–430a9. Alexander of Aphrodisias is credited with the new terminology, even as he is the source for much of the subsequent articulation of the diverse stages in the development of the intellect. See A.P. Fotinis, trans., *The De anima of Alexander of Aphrodisias* (Washington, DC: University Press of America, 1979), pp.105–22. Fotinis also translated the treatise 'On the Intellect' attributed to Alexander: ibid., pp.137–53. Herbert Davidson has looked closely at Averroës' various treatments of the material intellect, in all his compositions. See H. Davidson, *Alfarabi, Avicenna, and Averroës, on Intellect* (New York: Oxford University Press, 1992), pp.258–98.

14 S. Gómez Nogales, trans., *La psicología de Averroës: Commentario al libro sobre el alma de Aristóteles* (Madrid: Instituto Miguel Asin, 1987), p.209.

15 Ibid., p.211. See too A.L. Ivry, 'Averroes' short commentary on Aristotle's *De anima*' *Documenti e studi sulla tradizione filosofica medievale* 8 (1997): 544–47.

16 *De anima*, I.1, 402a26; given by Averroës in the epitome, Spanish trans. Gómez Nogales, p.102.

17 Gómez Nogales, trans., p. 99. Cf. Ivry, 'Averroes' short commentary', p.520.

18 Ivry, 'Averroes' short commentary', pp.520–22.

19 *De generatione animalium*, II 3.736b28; 737a7–11; Davidson, *Alfarabi*, p.233.

20 This is the intellect associated with reproduction also in Averroës' epitome of the *Parva naturalia*, and cf. Davidson, *Alfarabi*, pp.234–5.

21 This is in contrast to Averroës' strenuous attempts of an apologetic nature in both his *Incoherence of the Incoherence* (pp.311–63), and his *Harmony* (1967, pp.46–57).

22 This question can be taken as asking whether it is possible for an embodied intellect to think pure immaterial thoughts, to grasp the meaning of universal truth prescinded from any specific corporeal presentation; or it could be thought to ask if it is possible for a given intellect to separate itself from its corporeal embodiment, and via the process of intellection conjoin with the object of its cognition. Then again, these two questions are not mutually exclusive.

23 Davidson, *Alfarabi*, p.41.

24 Following J.A. Smith's translation of *De anima*, III.7, 431b18–19, as found in J. Barnes (ed.), *The Complete Works of Aristotle*, I (Princeton, NJ: Princeton University Press, 1984), p.686; alternative translation by W.S. Hett, *Aristotle On the Soul, Parva naturalia, On Breath* (Cambridge, MA: Harvard University Press, 1957), p.178.

25 *De anima*, III.5, 430a 23–5.

26 Cf. *De anima* I.4.408b18–19; II.1.413a4–7; *Met*. XII.3.10070a24–6. Davidson, *Alfarabi*, p.35.

27 Averroës' *Middle Commentary on Aristotle's De anima*, ed. Ivry, p.122.

28 *Averroès: La béatitude de l'âme*, ed. and trans. M. Geoffroy and C. Steel (Paris: J. Vrin, 2001), pp.198–246; *The Epistle on the Possibility of Conjunction with the Active Intellect by Ibn Rushd with the Commentary of Moses Narboni*, ed. and trans. K. Bland (New York: The Jewish Theological Seminary of America, 1961), pp.52, 68, 103.

29 A.L. Ivry, 'Averroes on intellection and conjunction', *Journal of the American Oriental Society* 86 (1966): 76–85.

30 *Middle Commentary*, p.112; *Commentarium Magnum in Aristotelis De anima libros*, ed. F.S. Crawford (Cambridge, MA: Medieval Academy of America, 1953), pp.406, 439; A.L. Ivry, 'Averroes' three commentaries on *De anima*', in *Averroes and the Aristotelian Tradition*, ed. G. Endress and J.A. Aertsen (Leiden: Brill, 1999), pp.205–14.
31 *Middle Commentary*, p.111.
32 Davidson, *Alfarabi*, pp.232–57.
33 *Commentarium Magnum*, ed. Crawford, pp.390, 404, 411.
34 Ibid., p.390.
35 Ibid., pp.500–501; cf. Davidson, *Alfarabi*, p.335.
36 *N.E.* X.7 1177b19–1178a8; *Averroës' Middle Commentary on Aristotle's Nicomachean Ethics in the Hebrew Version of Samuel Ben Judah*, ed. L.V. Berman (Jerusalem: The Israel Academy of Sciences and Humanities, 1999), pp.339, 340 lines 440–457.
37 Following W.D. Ross and J.O. Urmson's translation of *endexetai athanatizein* at *Nicomachean Ethics* 1177b34 (in Barnes, *Complete Works*, vol. II, p.1861).
38 Paraphrasing the Hebrew *aval ra'ui sheyisimah ne'ederet min hamavet* (Berman, *Averroes' Middle Commentary*, 340:459), literally, 'but it is fitting that he render it (sc., thought) void of death'.
39 *Nicomachean Ethics* X.8 1178b7–23; Berman, *Averroes' Middle Commentary*, 342: 12–343: 522.

Chapter 10

Thomas Aquinas' Commentary on Aristotle's *Metaphysics*

John F. Wippel

Thomas Aquinas spent a considerable amount of time and effort during the final years of his career writing detailed commentaries on twelve works by Aristotle as well as on the *Liber de causis*. Indeed, the latter work had also been mistakenly regarded by some thirteenth-century thinkers as written by Aristotle, although others had attributed it to al-Farabi or to some other unknown Arabic author. But with the translation in 1268 of Proclus' *Elementatio theologica* from the Greek, Aquinas quickly recognized that the *Liber de causis* had been excerpted from this work.[1]

The question has often been raised why Thomas devoted so much time and attention to writing these commentaries, especially those on Aristotle. This is especially puzzling for those who would emphasize the point that he was a theologian and who would minimize his role as a philosopher. In these commentaries he gives evidence of a profound mastery of philosophy, especially of the philosophy of Aristotle, as well as of considerable interest in philosophical thinking for its own sake.

Some of the more theologizing interpreters of Aquinas, such as R.-A. Gauthier and somewhat more tentatively, Joseph Owens, have argued that Aquinas' composition of his commentaries was simply part of his work as a theologian,[2] hence we should read them as theological writings. According to Gauthier, Aquinas composed his commentaries on the *De anima* and the *Ethics* in support of his writing of the related parts of his *Summa theologiae* (henceforth ST). Thus his *Commentary on the 'De anima'* would have been written to prepare him to compose the 'Treatise on man' in ST I, qq.75–89. And he would have composed his *Commentary on the 'Ethics'* as part of his writing of the moral part of the *Summa*. The accepted dates for the composition of these respective works do support Gauthier's claim, at least up to a point[3] (*In De anima*, and ST I, qq.75–89, date from 1267–8; and *In Ethicorum*, and ST Ia-IIae, IIa-IIae, date from 1271–2). But it does not necessarily follow from this that Thomas' only reason for writing these two commentaries was to assist him in developing the related parts of the *Summa*. There may have been a personal interest on Thomas' part in penetrating even more deeply into Aristotle's thought, even though he had been using it throughout his career. And such an explanation cannot account for Thomas' composition of the other Aristotelian commentaries or, for that matter, for his *Commentary on the 'De causis'*. This is especially true of the work on which I propose to concentrate here, his *Commentary on the 'Metaphysics'*.

And so the question remains: why did Thomas write commentaries such as these? Or, to focus on his *Commentary on the 'Metaphysics'*, why did he write this particular commentary? Scholarly opinion has long been divided on this issue. First of all, more general explanations for his writing these commentaries have been offered by the two best and most recent biographers of Aquinas, James Weisheipl and Jean-Pierre Torrell. According to Weisheipl, when Thomas returned from Italy to Paris in late 1268 or early 1269 to resume his professorship in the theology faculty at the University there, he found serious doctrinal controversies under way. These centred upon particular interpretations of Aristotle and of philosophy being offered by certain young masters from the Faculty of Arts, especially Siger of Brabant and Boethius of Dacia, who were heavily influenced by Averroës and, I would add, by other non-Christian sources, in their reading of Aristotle. In December 1270, the Bishop of Paris, Stephen Tempier, condemned thirteen propositions including, I would note, four which appear in works penned by Siger before 1270, and a fifth which does so by implication.[4] And so, according to Weisheipl, masters and students in arts, while trying to understand Aristotle, were falling into heresy and incurring excommunication. Therefore Aquinas 'commented on Aristotle because he felt an apostolic need to help young masters in arts to understand Aristotelian philosophy correctly in harmony with the actual text and the guideline of faith, where necessary'.[5]

Writing some years later, Torrell had the advantage of being able to incorporate more recent findings concerning the events reported by Weisheipl and more precise datings for some of the Aristotelian commentaries.[6] As for Thomas' commentaries on Aristotle, Torrell notes that the *Commentary on the 'Ethics'* is really a *sententia*, that is, a summary and 'rather doctrinal explication, and not an *expositio*, an in-depth commentary with textual discussions. And, regarding its purpose, he quotes Gauthier to this effect:

> So that Aristotle's ethics, which hardly speaks of anything other than man, can speak of God, Saint Thomas, without wishing it, without his even noticing it, had to transform it profoundly. If he had wanted to perform the work of a historian or critic, a historian or critic would have been right to judge his work and to find it wanting. But Thomas only wanted to compose a work of wisdom.[7]

However, Torrell also seems to recognize that this explanation cannot account for Thomas' writing of many of the other commentaries. For instance, when he turns to the commentaries on the *Physics* and *Metaphysics*, Torrell remarks: 'Thomas's motives for these labors are certainly to be found in the interest of Aristotle's work in itself.'[8]

Finally, Torrell returns to our question: what was Thomas' intention in writing these commentaries? He notes that, to use a formula Thomas himself frequently employs, in his commentaries Thomas wants to uncover the *intentio auctoris*, or as we would put it, the mind of the author. This is in accord with the tradition of *expositio reverentialis* used by medieval hermeneutics, and its purpose is to determine what an author really 'wanted to say'.

This means that, in his commentaries, Thomas wants to grasp the overall movement of Aristotle's thought and to recall the truth he is seeking, even if at certain points Aristotle himself expressed this only more or less clumsily or even incompletely. At such points Thomas feels justified in substituting his own thinking for that of Aristotle so as to extend his thought and even to make him say certain things Aristotle did not and perhaps could not have even conceived. Moreover, concludes Torrell, to appreciate Thomas' work in his commentaries more equitably, we should remember that 'he understood these texts in an apostolic perspective in order better to carry out his job as a theologian, and better to accomplish his labor of wisdom such as he would understand it in the double school of saint Paul and Aristotle'.[9] And so if in the end Torrell seems to return to a position close to the theological reading of Gauthier, he does not thereby exclude philosophical interest on Thomas' part.

As for Thomas' *Commentary on the 'Metaphysics'*, I would first note that it is not a mere summary (*sententia*), as Torrell finds the *Commentary on the 'Ethics'* to be, but an in-depth commentary with detailed textual discussion. But this is not of itself enough for us to conclude that it is merely that. And so different twentieth-century scholars have approached it in quite different ways.

According to one approach, Thomas' purpose was simply to offer an objective presentation of Aristotle's authentic thought. In other words, he really was only the *expositor* in writing it. And so we should not look to this commentary in seeking Aquinas' personal metaphysical thought. In my judgement, by far the best known example of this approach is Étienne Gilson. For instance, in his *The Philosopher and Theology*, Gilson writes:

> In his commentaries on the writings of the Philosopher, Saint Thomas is not principally concerned with his own philosophy but with Aristotle's. ... Saint Thomas is only a commentator in his writing on Aristotle. For his personal thinking one must look at the two *Summae* and similar writings, in which he shows himself an author in the proper sense of the word.[10]

Now this Gilsonian position is part of his broader view that the philosophy of Aquinas is a Christian philosophy or, as he later developed his thinking on this, that Thomas was not a philosopher but a theologian. Hence one can largely ignore the commentaries on Aristotle, including the *Commentary on the 'Metaphysics'*, in studying Aquinas' personal thought.

At the opposite end of the spectrum is another approach. Aquinas' commentaries, including his *Commentary on the 'Metaphysics'*, do indeed express his personal thought. And so we can assume that anything he says in the *Commentary* is his personal position unless he states otherwise. This seemed to be the approach of a number of mid-twentieth century interpreters of Aquinas, including members of the North American River Forest School, who would frequently cite from the commentaries without qualification in presenting their interpretations of Aquinas' personal philosophical thought.[11]

A third approach would argue that there is an objective fidelity to Aristotle's texts in his commentary, but that Thomas also expresses his personal views therein. In a somewhat controversial book of 1972, devoted to Aquinas' *Commentary on the 'Metaphysics'*, James Doig defended his own version of this approach. If one asks 'why' Thomas' *Commentary* was written, Doig finds that this third approach is correct. But if we ask 'how' Thomas wrote it, Doig would combine the first and second approaches. In other words, Thomas wanted to set forth the thought of Aristotle objectively, but he also wanted to express his personal views. Doig maintains, however, that in fact Thomas did not achieve this. Indeed, he could not achieve this, because they are not the same. And so he read into Aristotle's text important metaphysical positions that are not in fact present there, especially his own metaphysics of essence and *esse*.[12]

Before offering some personal reflections on this, I would like to consider a few test cases from Thomas' *Commentary on the 'Metaphysics'* to illustrate different ways in which he deals with certain important metaphysical issues.

Case I

The first particular topic has to do with Thomas' solution to the dilemma left for subsequent Aristotelians by Aristotle himself concerning the unity of the science of being as being that he develops in *Metaphysics*, Bk IV, cc.1–2 and in the opening part of Bk VI, c.1, and what he calls a divine science or theology as he presents it in the rest of Bk VI, c.1. To put it very briefly, can the science of being as being, the science that, unlike particular sciences, does not restrict itself to any particular part or kind of being but studies being as being, be identified with the science of separate entity or of the divine? As is well known, the success of Aristotle's effort to identify these two in the final sentences of Bk VI, c.1 continues to be disputed by present-day specialists in Aristotle. For that matter, before the time of Aquinas it had already been addressed in opposing ways by the Latin Avicenna in the *Metaphysics* or *First Philosophy* of his *Shifa*, and then by the Latin Averroës in his long commentaries on both the *Physics* and the *Metaphysics*. In brief, Avicenna argued that, because no science can establish the existence of its subject, and because God's existence is proved in metaphysics and only in metaphysics, God cannot be the subject of metaphysics. Its subject is being as being.[13] Against this Averroës countered that God's existence can only be established in physics as the First Mover and concluded that separate entity, meaning God, is the subject of metaphysics. And so, when Aristotle refers to it as the science of being, he really means the science of substance and by implication the science of the ultimate final cause of all other substance, that is, God.[14]

In Aquinas' case we are fortunate to have in the Introduction or *Prooemium* to his *Commentary on the 'Metaphysics'* his personal solution to this issue, and one which coincides with the solution he had offered in his much earlier *Commentary on the 'De Trinitate' of Boethius*, q.5, a.4.[15] Thomas begins his *Prooemium* by recalling a text from Aristotle's *Politics* to the effect that, when many things are ordered to one thing, one of those must be the director or ruler of the others, and the others directed or ruled by it. But all of the sciences and arts are directed to one end, the perfection of man which is beatitude. Therefore, one of these should be the director of the others, and it deserves the name 'wisdom'. For it belongs to the wise person to direct others.[16]

In seeking to determine which science this is, he reasons that it should be that science which is supremely (maximally) intellectual, that is, the science that studies what is most intelligible. But one can understand things as supremely intelligible from different perspectives. First of all, one may do so by taking into account the order of understanding, that is, by concentrating on those things from which the intellect derives certainty. Because certainty is reached in a science by knowledge based on causes, a knowledge of causes seems to be supremely intellectual. Therefore the science that considers the first causes seems best qualified to direct the others and, therefore, to be called wisdom.

In a second way one may identify that which is most intelligible by comparing intellectual knowledge with sense perception. Whereas the senses afford a knowledge of individuals, the intellect can grasp universals. And so that science will be most intellectual which deals with the most universal principles. But these are being (*ens*) and those things that follow upon being, such as the one and the many, potency and act, and so on. Things of this kind should not remain undetermined but should be considered in one universal science which, because it directs the others, is supremely intellectual.

Things may be regarded as most intelligible in a third way, by taking into account the nature of intellectual knowledge itself. A thing enjoys intellectual power to the extent that it is free from matter. And so those things are most intelligible which are most separate from matter. But such things are not merely separate in the sense that they are abstracted from designated matter, that is, from individuating matter, as are natural forms when they are grasped universally and studied by physics. Nor are such things merely abstracted from matter in the order of thought as are mathematicals. Rather these most intelligible things must be separate from matter in the order of being (*esse*), as is true of God and intelligences. And so it now seems that the science which deals with God and the intelligences is most intellectual and therefore mistress of the others.

Thomas realizes that he now has three candidates for the most intellectual science: the science that studies the first causes, the science that studies that which is most universal, that is, being, and the science that studies the divine, that is, God and intelligences. He immediately comments that this threefold consideration should not be assigned to three different sciences, but only to one. And so he quickly introduces a two-step reduction. First he comments that the above mentioned separate substances – God and the intelligences – are in fact identical with the first and universal causes of being (*causae essendi*). And so now he seems to have only two candidates, the science of being, and the science of the divine, meaning God and intelligences.

Here Thomas introduces a second reduction. It belongs to one and the same science to consider the proper causes of a given (subject)-genus and that genus itself. Thus the natural philosopher considers the principles of natural body as well as natural body itself (or *ens mobile*). Therefore it belongs to one and the same science to consider separate substances and *ens commune* (universal being=being in general) which, Thomas explains, is the 'genus' of which the aforementioned substances are the general and universal causes. And so, if this science does consider the three kinds of intelligible objects he has singled out, it does not consider each of them as its subject. Only *ens commune* is its subject.[17]

In developing this point Thomas writes that in a science one seeks after the causes and properties of the subject of that science. But, he warns, the causes themselves are not the subject of the science. Rather, knowledge of the causes is the end at which knowledge of a given subject genus ultimately aims. And so if the subject of this science is *ens commune*, the whole science deals with things that are separate from matter both in being and in thought.[18]

Here he introduces an important distinction he had already developed in his *Commentary on the 'De Trinitate'*, q.5, a.4.[19] Things may be separate from matter in being (*esse*) and in definition in two ways: either in the sense that they are never present in matter, as is true of God and intelligences; or in the sense that they can be without matter, as is true of *ens commune*. But things would not be separate in this second sense if they necessarily depended on matter in order to be. Hence things that are separate in the second sense constitute the subject of metaphysics – being in general – whereas what is separate in the first sense can be studied by metaphysics only indirectly, as the cause of that which does fall under its subject.[20]

It is interesting to compare Aquinas' personal solution to this problem with his commentary on the relevant passages in Aristotle's *Metaphysics*.[21] In commenting on Bk IV, c.1, he finds Aristotle presenting the science of being as being as a universal science. With Aristotle he distinguishes it from any particular science precisely because it does not cut off a part of being and study the attributes of that part. Rather, says Thomas, it considers universal being insofar as it is being (*ens universale inquantum huiusmodi* [n.532]). In commenting on Aristotle's concluding remark at the end of IV, c.1 ('That it is necessary for us too to grasp the first causes of being as being'), Thomas adds this comment: 'Therefore being is the subject of this science, because every science seeks after the proper causes of its subject' (n.533).[22]

In commenting on Bk IV, c.2 Thomas finds Aristotle addressing some of the aporiai he had raised in Bk III. Thomas divides Aristotle's discussion of these into three parts. Aristotle determines (1) whether it belongs to this science to consider both substances and accidents, and all substances as well; (2) whether it pertains to it to consider certain *communia*,[23] that is, certain things that follow upon being as such such as the one and the many, the same and the other, opposites, contrariety, and so on; and (3) whether it belongs to it to consider the first principles of demonstration (n.534).

Regarding the first, Thomas finds Aristotle giving an affirmative answer. It belongs to one science to consider both substances and accidents, but it is concerned first and foremost with substances and indeed with all substances (nn.534, 546–7). Following Aristotle's text, Thomas notes that, whereas being (*quod est*)[24] is said in different ways, this is not by pure equivocation but rather by reference to something that is one and first, and which he identifies as substance. Moreover, he adds, all substances, insofar as they are beings or substances, fall under the consideration of this science (n.547).

In Lesson II, Thomas notes with Aristotle that the one and being do not signify different natures, but one and the same thing, even though they differ conceptually. Hence they are ontologically convertible. This is part of Aristotle's effort (and of Thomas') to show that the science that studies being will also study the one (n.549). Moreover, following Aristotle, he points out that there are different parts of the one just as there are different parts of being (n.561). And so, if the parts of being are substance, quantity, quality, and so on, so the parts of the one are the same, the equal, the like, and so forth. And just as it belongs to one science, philosophy, to study all the parts of being, so does it belong to it to study all the parts of the one (n.563).

In Lesson III, Thomas follows Aristotle in continuing to defend the unity and universality of the science of being by showing that it belongs to one and the same science to consider a thing and its opposite (n.564). And multiplicity, or many, is the opposite of unity or the one, and hence will be studied by the same science that studies the one. It will also study other opposites such as the opposite of the like (the unlike), the opposite of the equal (the unequal), and all other things that can be reduced to these or to the one and the many (n.567). And so it belongs to one science to consider all of these *communia* or attributes of substance as well as substance itself (n.569).

In Lesson IV, Thomas continues to follow Aristotle as he defends the universality of the science of being and shows how the contraries are to be reduced to the one and hence to being (nn.578–83). Thomas concludes his commentary on c.2 by summing up Aristotle's thought:

> It belongs to one science to consider being insofar as it is being, and those things which pertain to it per se. And from this it is evident that this science considers not only substances but also accidents, since being is predicated of both. It considers those things which have been mentioned – the same and the other, the like and the unlike, the equal and the unequal, negation and privation and contraries, which we have said above are *per se entis accidentia* (n. 587).[25]

In commenting on Bk VI, c.1, Thomas finds Aristotle drawing upon the point he had already established in Bk IV, namely, that being as being is the subject of this science. Because every science should investigate the principles and causes of its subject, in this science one must seek after the principles and causes of beings insofar as they are beings. If every intellectual science should deal with principles and causes, the other particular sciences deal only with some particular kind of being such as number, or magnitude, or something like this. None of them considers being in general (*ens in communi*) or being insofar as it is being. This is reserved for the metaphysician, that is, to consider every being insofar as it is being (n.1147, end).[26]

After distinguishing with Aristotle natural science from the practical and productive sciences and concluding that it is theoretical, Thomas develops the point that it deals with a determined kind of being, that which can be moved. Therefore its subject is *ens mobile*, and so it has a determined way of defining things, namely, insofar as they are not separable from matter (nn.1152–5). But the things studied by mathematics are like the concave and defined without a reference to sensible matter. And so it investigates certain things *as* immobile and *as* separate from sensible matter, even though they are not such in reality (n.1161).

Next, following Aristotle, Thomas turns to the method or mode proper to this science, that is, to metaphysics, by noting that, if there is something immobile in its being and therefore sempiternal and separable from matter in *esse*, some theoretical science must study it. Since neither physics nor mathematics can do so, the study of it pertains to a science that is prior to both (n.1162). And so this first science deals with things that are separable in terms of their being and completely immobile (n.1163). Continuing to paraphrase Aristotle here, Thomas comments that these immaterial and immobile causes are the causes of the sensible things that are evident to us, meaning, presumably, the heavenly bodies. And so it is clear that the science which studies beings of this kind is first among all the sciences, and that it considers the universal causes of all beings (n.1164).

At this point the reader of Aristotle's text and of Thomas' *Commentary* may begin to wonder about the universality of this science which now seems to be defined as the science of a particular kind of being, that is, separate entity. Thomas seems to anticipate this concern by interjecting a warning. It must be noted that (*'Advertendum est autem'*) it belongs to first philosophy not only to study things that are separate from matter and motion in terms of their being and their definition; it also must consider sensible things insofar as they are beings. In other words, Thomas is concerned about safeguarding the universality of this science. Or, he adds, unless we should say with Avicenna that general things of this type (*communia*) with which this science is concerned are separate from matter in terms of *esse*, not in the sense that they always exist without matter, but in the sense that it is not necessary for them to be present in matter (n.1165). So here he introduces the distinction he had employed in the *Prooemium* (and in his *Commentary on the 'De Trinitate'*) between two kinds of things that are separable from matter and motion, that is, those that are never found therein, and those that may or may not be. While this distinction is central to Thomas' personal resolution of the unity of the science of being as being and the science of the divine, it is telling that he does not attribute it to Aristotle. But it does offer another way of defending the universality of this science.

Thomas then concludes with Aristotle that there are three parts of theoretical philosophy: mathematics, physics and theology which, Thomas specifies, is first philosophy. Thomas now cites literally the passage wherein Aristotle himself recognizes the difficulty he has created (see 1026a 23–25). Someone might wonder whether first philosophy is universal (because it considers being universally, adds Thomas), or whether it considers one determined genus and nature (n.1169). After noting reasons that might be offered for each alternative, Thomas simply repeats Aristotle's answer to this question: if there is not some other substance apart from those that exist according to nature, with which physics is concerned (Thomas adds), physics will be the first science. But if there is some immobile substance, this will be prior to natural substance. And so the philosophy that considers a substance of this kind will be (1) first philosophy, and it will be (2) universal because it is first, and (3) it will belong to it to study being insofar as it is being, both what it is and those things which pertain to being insofar as it is being (n.1170). Then he adds one remark to the text from Aristotle which he has just paraphrased: 'for the science of the first being and the science of *ens commune* are one and the same, as was stated at the beginning of Bk IV' (n.1170).[27]

The difficulty with Aristotle's text and with Thomas' paraphrase is to determine how one can justify the transition from a science that is first because it studies the first or highest being(s) to the science that is universal. Since Thomas has added only one sentence to account for this, it is important to note that the order which he, following Aristotle, suggests here is different from the order Aristotle (and Thomas) follow at the beginning of *Metaphysics* IV, and which Thomas follows in the *Prooemium* as well as in his *In De Trinitate*, q.5, a.4. In those other contexts Thomas notes that because it belongs to one and the same science to study its subject and the principles of its subject, it will belong to the science that has being as being as its subject to study the principles and causes of that subject. But here the reasoning goes in the opposite direction. Because one is studying the highest being(s), and because the science of the first being is the same as the science of being in general, this divine science also studies being taken universally, or as being.

Neither Thomas nor Aristotle fully explain the justification for the reasoning in *Metaphysics* VI. Perhaps Thomas thinks that, because of the earlier reasoning in *Metaphysics* IV, Aristotle can now take it as granted that the two sciences are one and the same. Or perhaps this is the best sense he can make out of what is admittedly a problematic passage in Aristotle. But if one were to take this text alone as representing Thomas's personal thinking, one would badly misinterpret his thought. One would conclude that for Thomas metaphysics is first and foremost the science of divine being. And so Thomas would have adopted Averroës' solution to Aristotle's problem. And then, because of some not fully explained reason, because it is the study of the first being, Thomas would conclude that it is also the study of all other being. And so while Thomas' *Commentary* on this passage is his best effort to interpret Aristotle's text, it would be a mistake to identify this as his personal view.[28]

When Thomas comments on the parallel discussion of this in Bk XI, c.7, he again repeats the question raised by Aristotle's text: is the science that deals with separable beings to be regarded as the universal science of being as being? (Thomas, of course, had no reason to question the authenticity of Kappa). He finds Aristotle replying in the affirmative by using a process of elimination (n.2266). After eliminating the practical sciences and mathematics as the universal science of all being, he comments, following Aristotle's text closely: 'If natural substances which are sensible and mobile substances are the first substances among beings, natural science must be first among the sciences.' Then Thomas adds to Aristotle's text: 'for the order of the sciences corresponds to the order of the subjects (of the sciences)'. He then basically repeats Aristotle's text: 'If there is some other nature and substance apart from natural substances, which is separable and immobile, there must be another science for this being, which science is prior to natural science. And from the fact that it is first, it must be universal.'[29] Again, the reader wonders why. Thomas this time adds two sentences of explanation. 'The science which deals with first beings is the same as the science which is universal.' This is the same as the addition he had introduced in his commentary on Bk VI, c.1. But now he adds another remark: 'For the first beings are the principles of the others' (n.2267).

One may again object, of course: how does it follow from the fact that one studies the first being that one studies all others? If Aristotle's Unmoved Mover in the *Metaphysics* is the final cause of the movers of the heavenly spheres, it does not follow that by studying the Unmoved Mover one will arrive at a direct and universal knowledge of all other things or at the science of being as being. Even if, as will be discussed below, Thomas maintains that Aristotle's God is a cause of being as well as a cause of motion, it will still not follow that in knowing this being one arrives at any direct knowledge of all other being or of being as being. Thomas leaves this largely unexplained. Again, I would suggest, he is puzzled by the reversed order in Aristotle's text. Instead of moving from the subject of metaphysics, being as being, and reasoning from this to knowledge of God as its principle and cause, here one would reason from one's knowledge of God to a universal science of being as being. This is not the order proposed by Thomas in his *Commentary on the 'De Trinitate'*, q.5, a.4 and in the *Prooemium* to his *Commentary on the 'Metaphysics'*. Hence this is not Thomas' personal position. But rather than impose his personal view on Aristotle's text here, as in his commentary on Bk VI, c.1, Thomas is again content simply to explain the text before him as best he can.

Case II

It has been suggested by some that, perhaps without intending to do so, in his *Commentary* Thomas has seriously changed Aristotle's metaphysics by reading into it his own metaphysics of essence and *esse*.[30] Yet I myself have found very few, if any instances in which Thomas explicitly assigns such an understanding to Aristotle himself. It is true that occasionally Thomas refers to being as 'that which is' or as 'what is'. For instance, at the beginning of his commentary on BK IV, Thomas quotes from the James of Venice translation of the *Metaphysics* IV, c.2, where Aristotle writes that being is said in many ways. According to this translation, which Thomas reproduces in his own commentary, 'what is' (*quod est*) is said in many ways.[31] And a little later (n.535) Thomas refers to *ens* or *quod est*.[32] This might be read as implying Thomas' view that all finite beings are composed of essence and *esse*, but it does not have to be so understood. As James' translation of Aristotle does, one can understand being as 'that which is' without having ever thought of any real composition and distinction of essence and *esse* therein.

I would say the same of certain texts that have been cited by Doig to support his claim that Thomas has read his metaphysics of essence–*esse* into Aristotle's metaphysics. Thus in commenting on Bk XII, c.1, Thomas writes: 'For being (*ens*) is expressed, as it were, as "that which has esse" (*quasi esse habens*).' And Thomas notes that this applies only to substance that subsists, in contrast to accidents, which are not called beings in the unqualified sense, but rather beings of being (n.2419). While Thomas' language here is certainly compatible with his metaphysics of essence and *esse*, it does not presuppose it. Again, in commenting on Bk VI, c. 4, Thomas refers to those things that are beings strictly speaking, each of which is either a *quod quid est* or substance, or of a certain kind, or a quantity and so on (n.1241). Here the expression *quod quid est* simply refers to a thing's quiddity and, far from implying Thomas' doctrine of essence–*esse* composition, repeats verbatim the Moerbeke translation of Aristotle.[33]

However, farther on in his commentary on Bk IV, c.2, while explaining Aristotle's effort to show that the one and being are ontologically the same, Thomas introduces an important addition. As he interprets Aristotle, the Philosopher here offers two arguments to establish this. According to the first, if two things, when added to one thing, introduce no diversity, they themselves are completely identical. But the one and being when added to a man or to anything else introduce no diversity. Therefore they are identical (n.550).

In support of the minor of this argument, Aristotle reasons that it is the same to speak of a man and of one man. Likewise it is the same to speak of an existing man and of a man. And so we do not add anything real by our repetition when we speak of an existing man, a man and one man (nn.550–51).[34] Thomas finds Aristotle reasoning in the same way about the generation of a man and the generation of one man. The addition of the terms 'one' and 'being' (*ens*) does not add any real nature to a man. So the one is not really distinct from being (n.552), even though they differ conceptually. But now he introduces a personal metaphysical observation (*Sciendum est*). The name 'man' is derived from the quiddity or nature of a man. And so the name 'thing' (*res*) is taken from a thing's quiddity, but the name 'being' (*ens*) is taken from its act of existing (*actus essendi*).[35] Now Thomas has introduced his metaphysics of essence and *esse* (here referred to as 'act of existing'). And he also adds that these three (*res, ens* and *unum*) all signify one and the same thing even though they differ conceptually.

Thomas also finds Aristotle offering a second argument to show that being and the one are the same in reality. If two things are predicated of the substance of some thing per se and not per accidens, they are identical in reality. But this is true of being and the one. The substance of each thing is one per se and not in accidental fashion. Therefore being and the one signify one and the same thing in reality (n.554).

In support Thomas introduces an argument developed by Averroes in his commentary on the same text, even though Thomas does not acknowledge his source. If being and the one were predicated of the substance of a thing by some being that was superadded, then being [and the one] would have to be predicated of that superadded thing either per se or by reason of something else superadded, and so on *ad infinitum*. Since the latter is impossible, one should grant immediately that the subtance of a thing is one and being (*ens*) by reason of itself and not by reason of something superadded (n.555).[36]

Thomas comments that Avicenna thought otherwise and held that the one and being (*ens*) do not signify the substance (essence) of a thing, but something that is superadded. Indeed, the Latin Averroës sharply criticized him for this.[37] Thomas comments that Avicenna said this about being because in everything which receives existence (*esse*) from something else, the *existence* (*esse*) of that thing differs from its substance or essence. But the name 'being' (*ens*) signifies *esse* itself. Therefore it ('being') seems to signify something superadded to essence (n.556).

Thomas notes that Avicenna held this about the one because he thought that the one that is convertible with being is identical with the one that is a principle of number. While the numerical one signifies a nature added to substance because it is based on quantity, this is not true of the one that is convertible with being, that is, of what we refer to as transcendental unity (see nn.557, 559–60). But of greater immediate interest to us is Thomas' critique of Avicenna concerning *esse*:

> Although the *esse* of a thing is other than its essence, it must not be thought that it is something superadded in the manner of an accident, but it is, as it were, constituted by the principles of the essence. And therefore the name 'being' *(ens)*, which is taken from *esse* itself, signifies the same thing as does the name ['thing'] which is taken from the essence itself.[38]

In sum, in this important but easily misunderstood text, Thomas is stating that (i) a thing's *esse* is different from that thing's essence; (ii) *esse* should not be viewed as an accident added to essence, that is, as a predicamental accident; (iii) *esse* is, as it were, constituted by the principles of a thing's essence (which I take as meaning that, according to Thomas' metaphysics, a thing's act of existing is received, limited and specified by that thing's essence principle); (iv) the name 'being' (*ens*) is derived from a thing's act of existing; (v) the name *ens* which is taken from *esse* signifies the same reality as does the name *res* which is taken from essence.[39]

In this discussion Thomas does add a great deal to Aristotle's metaphysics, yet he does not attribute his views on the essence–existence distinction and relationship to Aristotle, even though he does correctly maintain that the identity of the one and being is found in Aristotle.

Case III

Next I would like to mention some points on which Thomas' interpretation of Aristotle's text does seem to differ from the thought of Aristotle himself. In his commentary on *Metaphysics*, II, c.1, Thomas is explaining a discussion by Aristotle of truth as it is present in things (993b 23–31). Note in particular Aristotle's remark at 993b 26–31:

> So that which causes derivative truths to be true is most true. Therefore the principles of eternal things must always be most true; for they are not merely sometimes true, nor is there any cause of their being, but they themselves are the cause of the being of other things, so that as each thing is in respect of being, so is it in respect of truth.[40]

In commenting on this, Thomas observes that the name 'truth' is not restricted to any species but applies in general to all beings (n.294). In other words, he finds Aristotle dealing with truth of being or transcendental truth. And so, he continues, what causes derived things to be true is itself most true. From this he finds Aristotle concluding that the principles of those things that exist always, that is, the principles of heavenly bodies, must themselves be most true. This is so because they are not at some time true and at some time not, and therefore they surpass in truth things subject to generation. This also follows because these principles – the causes of heavenly bodies – are not themselves caused; rather they are the cause of being (*causa essendi*) for other things. And so the heavenly bodies, while incorruptible, have a cause not only for their motion, as some have claimed, but also for their very existence (*esse*), as the philosopher here expressly states, observes Thomas (n.295).[41]

In commenting on Bk VI, c.1 (Lesson I, n.1164) Thomas notes, following Aristotle, that all (with the Leonine text) causes must be sempiternal; for the first causes of generated things must be ungenerated, lest generation regress to infinity. And this is especially true of those causes that are completely immobile and immaterial. A little farther on, Thomas comments that the science which considers beings of this kind, that is, separate entities, is first among the others, and considers the universal causes of all things. Therefore these are causes of beings insofar as they are beings. And so Thomas writes: 'And from this the falsity of the view of those is clearly evident who held that Aristotle thought that God is not the cause of the substance of the heaven, but only of its motion.'[42]

And so, while most modern interpreters of Aristotle do not find him presenting the Unmoved Mover as a cause of being, and certainly not as a creator, Thomas maintains that in these two texts Aristotle really does think that the principle(s) of the heavenly bodies or God is the cause of being or of the substance of the heavenly bodies. As Van Steenberghen puts it, he exploits a certain ambiguity in these texts of Aristotle when they are read in isolation apart from his overall metaphysical thought.[43] By doing this, Thomas attributes to Aristotle a position that runs counter to the view of the Unmoved Mover Aristotle presents elsewhere, and thus seems to force upon Aristotle a position that Aquinas regards as true on both philosophical and religious grounds, but one that Aristotle did not actually hold. This is not to say that Thomas did not *think* that Aristotle defended the position in question. It is rather to suggest that in Thomas' eyes the truth of this position was so evident that Aristotle could not possibly have overlooked it.

Case IV

Next we may turn to Thomas' commentary on Aristotle's effort in Bk VII to determine the meaning of substance (*ousia*) and in particular of one of the four meanings proposed for this by Aristotle in c.3 (1028b 33–36), that is, the *quod quid erat esse* (Moerbeke's translation of the τὸ τί ἦν εἶναι), or what Thomas often renders as the quiddity or essence of a thing. In commenting on the beginning of c.4

(see lect. 2, nn.1299–1300), Thomas says that we must consider the *quid erat esse* of sensible substances, and then turn later to intelligible substances (Bk XII).

In commenting on c.10 (see Lesson 9) Thomas finds Aristotle raising the question about the relationship between a definition, taken as a formula (*ratio*), and the parts of that formula to the parts of a thing that is defined. Is the formula (*ratio*) of the parts included in the formula (*ratio*) of the whole (n.1460)? Aristotle's and Thomas's answer to this will turn on the distinction between different kinds of parts, that is, parts of the form or species, on the one hand, and parts of the composite (1035b 31–32). But before taking up this answer, which we cannot examine in detail here, Thomas introduces a major addition to Aristotle's text.

He notes that there are two different opinions concerning the definitions of things and their essences. Some say that the entire specific essence is the form so that, for example, the entire essence of a human being is the human soul. Therefore the form of the whole signified by the name 'humanity' and the form of the part signified by the name 'soul' are one and the same in reality, but differ conceptually. Insofar as the form perfects and actualizes matter, it is called the form of the part. Insofar as the composite whole is placed in its species by this same form, that form is called the form of the whole. Consequently, according to this view, no parts of matter are included in the definition that expresses the species, but only the formal principles of the species, that is to say, the form. Such, says Thomas, seems to be the view of Averroës and of some who follow him (n.1467).[44]

Thomas comments that this position seems to be opposed to the mind of Aristotle. In Bk VI, c.1 of the *Metaphysics* Aristotle holds that natural things include sensible matter in their definition and thereby differ from mathematicals (see 1025b 32–1026a 7). But, Thomas comments, it cannot be said that natural substances are defined by something that is not included in their essence, since they are not defined by addition as are accidents. Therefore sensible matter is a part of the essence of natural substances, and not only as it is realized in an individual, but also as regards the essence of the species; for definitions are not given for individuals but for species (n.1468).

And so, Thomas continues, there is another opinion, that Avicenna follows, according to which the form of the whole, which is the quiddity of the species, differs from the form of the part just as a whole differs from its part. For the quiddity of the species is composed of matter and form, although not of this form and this individual matter. This, says Thomas, is Aristotle's view, which he introduces here in order to eliminate Plato's theory of separate forms or ideas (n.1469).[45]

From this it is clear not only that Thomas wants to include matter within the essence or quiddity (and therefore the *quod quid erat esse*) of the species, but that he believes that this is Aristotle's view. As for the text Thomas has cited from *Metaphysics* VI, c.1, Maurer has pointed out that there Aristotle is not attempting to explain the meaning of substance taken as essence, but merely wants to indicate how the natural philosopher defines a natural substance, that is to say, as composite.[46] But in Bk VII he is much concerned with defining substance taken as essence. And so he excludes matter from this, as not being part of the essence. In agreement with most Aristotelian scholars, Maurer insists that for Aristotle substance taken in this sense, that is, as essence, is form alone.[47]

The view Thomas defends and attributes to Aristotle is the position Thomas himself had personally held throughout his career, as early as the *De ente et essentia* (see cc.1, 2). But in order to assign this view to Aristotle, as Maurer points out, Thomas has to force some of his texts.[48] Nonetheless, in this case it seems clear enough that he does so on strictly philosophical grounds. Since Thomas is philosophically convinced that the essence or quiddity of a natural substance includes both matter and form, he seems to have concluded that Aristotle himself must have held the same view. And so he does his best to find that position in the text of Aristotle's *Metaphysics*.

Case V

Another interesting case where Thomas goes beyond the letter of Aristotle's text is to be found in his commentary on Bk VI, cc. 2–3. In commenting on c.2, he finds Aristotle denying that there can be scientific knowledge of being *per accidens* (nn.1189–90). Nonetheless, in *Lect.* 3, Thomas also finds Aristotle rejecting the view of those who would completely eliminate being *per accidens* and who would hold that everything on earth happens out of necessity and that nothing happens by chance (nn.1192–1201). As Thomas interprets Aristotle's text, in the case of a future contingent event the tracing of that event to some cause per se and that to another will ultimately lead to a principle that cannot be reduced to another cause per se, but which will be a 'chance' cause or a cause *per accidens* of the chance event. Because being *per accidens* is not truly generated, one should not seek for a per se cause of its generation (n.1201).

At this point Thomas observes that Aristotle's position seems to eliminate certain things defended by some philosphers, namely, fate and providence. For both of these positions seem to entail that (1) nothing in the world happens *per accidens*, that is, by chance or fortune; and (2) all things here happen out of necessity, both of which claims Aristotle would reject (nn.1203–4). Thomas introduces a fairly lengthy discussion wherein he first shows that fate, understood as a certain disposition present in terrestial bodies owing to the influence of heavenly bodies, does not eliminate all chance events (nn.1212–14). Next he shows that a doctrine of divine providence does not eliminate contingency, even though he grants that this is more difficult to establish because of the universal character of God's causality (nn.1217–22). Indeed, he has here granted that, insofar as things that happen on earth are related to their first divine cause, they are found to be ordered and not to exist merely *per accidens*. And so, according to the Catholic faith, it is said that nothing happens fortuitously with respect to divine providence, since all things are subject to it (n.1216).

Thomas argues that, if one grants divine providence and therefore divine foreknowledge of future events, it still does not follow that every such event happens in necessary fashion, but only that every event must either be contingent or necessary. That it be contingent or necessary depends upon a higher cause which is the cause of being as being, and upon which the entire order of necessity and contingency itself depends (nn. 1220–22). For Thomas, of course, this cause is God. While Thomas here wants to show that Aristotle's discussion of being *per accidens* is perfectly compatible with such an understanding of divine providence, he does not here explicitly attribute to Aristotle the doctrine of providence itself. He is content to show that Aristotle's position does not exclude it.

Case VI

More forced, however, is Thomas' attribution to Aristotle's God both of knowledge of things other than himself and of will in his commentary on Bk XII. In commenting on c.6, Thomas closely follows Aristotle's text. He recognizes that Aristotle is convinced of the eternity of motion and of time, and that if motion is sempiternal one must posit a sempiternal substance that actually moves (nn.2490–2492). But Thomas comments that the arguments offered by Aristotle to prove that motion and time are sempiternal in *Physics* VIII, as well as the argument offered here in *Metaphysics* XII, are not demonstrations but probable arguments, unless perhaps they are demonstrative simply insofar as they refute the views of the ancient naturalists who claimed that motion began to be (nn.2496–8). He adds that Aristotle's argumentation for the sempiternal and immaterial nature of the first substance does follow necessarily (n.2499).

In commenting on c.7 (see *lect.* 7) Thomas finds Aristotle reasoning that the Unmoved Mover for which he has just argued moves as something that is desirable and intelligible. Only such things, things that are desirable and intelligible, can move without being moved (n.2519). While Thomas grants that among movers known to us there is a distinction between that which moves as something desired and that which moves as an intelligible good (as illustrated by an incontinent person), there can be no such diversity in the case of the first intelligible entity and the first desirable entity. They must be identical (n.2522). And just as the First Mover is a simple substance and actuality, so too is the first intelligible a simple substance and actuality (2524). Therefore, concludes Thomas, the First Mover is identical with the first intelligible entity and the first desirable entity, which is the best (n.2527).

Thomas notes that Aristotle compares the First Immobile Mover with the first mobile thing. Because the Immobile Mover moves as something that is 'loved' (a term that Thomas finds preferable to 'desired'), there must be something that is first moved by it, and by means of which it moves other things. This is the first heaven (n.2529). Thomas follows Aristotle's text in concluding that the motion of the first heaven is local and circular (nn. 2530–31). And then, writes Thomas, the first heaven depends upon this First Mover as upon its end both with respect to the perpetual nature of its substance and with respect to its perpetual motion.[49] By saying that the heaven depends upon the First Mover with respect to the perpetual nature of its substance, Thomas has again gone beyond the letter of Aristotle's text, although this addition is consistent with his earlier claim in the *Commentary* that Aristotle's God is a cause of being and not merely of motion. Moreover, there is a certain ambiguity in Aristotle's text once more. According to the Moerbeke translation of 1072b 13–14, Aristotle's text reads: 'On such a principle *depends* the heaven and nature' (italics mine).[50]

And in another significant addition, Thomas remarks that Aristotle states that the necessity of the first motion (of the first heaven) is not absolute but is based on its end (that is, on that principle that Aristotle subsequently names God), insofar as by its motion it attains to a likeness or assimilation to God. But an assimilation to that which wills and is intelligent as, says Thomas, Aristotle shows God to be, is attained according to will and intelligence, just as artifacts are assimilated to an artisan insofar as the artisan's will is realized in them. Therefore, continues Thomas, the necessity of the first motion (of the first heaven) is subject to the will of God (n.2535).[51] So here Thomas attributes intellect to Aristotle's God, for which there is a basis in Aristotle's subsequent text. But Thomas also attributes will to Aristotle's God, for which there is no such textual support.

In Lesson VIII, Thomas continues to comment on c.7 of Aristotle's text. As Aristotle compares the First Mover as an object of understanding and desire to that which actually understands and desires it, Thomas comments that the first moved thing – the first heaven – must understand and desire the First Mover. This, says Thomas, is true for Aristotle since he holds that the heaven is animated by a soul that understands and desires (n.2536). But the greatest and most perfect act of understanding is directed to the very best object and involves the greatest delight. And so in the act of understanding the First Mover consists the greatest delight (n.2538). But now, continues Thomas, Aristotle shows that within the first intelligible object, the First Mover itself, there is still more perfect understanding and delight. It is the nature of intellect that it understands itself insofar as it transumes or conceives in itself something that is intelligible; for the intellect itself becomes intelligible by reason of the fact that it attains some intelligible object. Hence the intellect and the intelligible object are one (n.2539). And insofar as the intellect attains an intelligible object, it actually understands (n.2540).

Now if one were to stop at this point, one would not yet have really shown that the First Mover itself actually understands, but only that it is actually understood by the soul of the first heaven. Thomas recalls that there is an intelligible substance that exists per se, with which Aristotle is now dealing. Therefore this First Mover must be both a substance that is intelligible and understood, and one that actually understands. In support he reasons that the relationship between the intellect of the first mobile thing and its object is similar to that which the Platonists posit between our intellect and separate forms. According to the Platonists, it is by entering into contact with such forms or ideas and by participating in them that our intellects are actualized. In like manner the intellect of the first moved thing (the first heaven) actually understands by reason of its contact with the first intelligible substance, that is, the First Mover (n.2542). Here Thomas appeals to a principle or adage he has apparently taken from *Metaphysics* II, c.1. As he formulates it here: 'That by reason of which every other thing enjoys a given perfection is that perfection to a greater degree.' Therefore it follows that whatever divine and excellent thing, such as understanding and taking delight, is present in the intellect which understands the first intelligible object must be present to a still greater degree in the first intelligible object or the First Mover itself.[52] In other words, the act of understanding and taking delight must be present to a still greater degree in the Unmoved Mover because it causes these acts to be present in the soul of the First Heaven. And so for the First Mover to consider this most intelligible object, that is, itself, is most delightful and best. And, lest there be any doubt, Thomas notes that this first intelligible object is called God (n.2543).

Here, therefore, Thomas has made a major addition to Aristotle's text, but this time in order to supply something that seems to be missing from that text itself, that is, a justification of the transition from a First Mover which is the object of intelligence and love on the part of the soul of the first heaven to a First Mover that understands and loves itself. And Thomas has done this by appealing to an apparent version of a principle which he also finds elsewhere in Aristotle, that is, in Bk II, c.1.

Here I will bypass Lessons 9 and 10, where Thomas comments on Aristotle's discussion in c.8 of the number of sempiternal movers. In Lesson 11, Thomas comments on c.9 and considers certain doubts raised by Aristotle concerning the intellect of his First Mover or God. Most interesting for our immediate purpose is the question whether the First Mover understands itself, or something else (n.2603). After presenting in some detail Aristotle's argumentation to show that it understands itself and that in it intellect and what is understood are identical (nn.2611–13), Thomas adds a personal remark. It must be noted that Aristotle here intends to show that God does not understand something other than himself but only himself in the sense that what is understood is viewed as perfecting both the one who understands and the act of understanding itself. When viewed in this way, acknowledges Thomas, it is clear that nothing other than God can be understood by him for it would then perfect his intellect. But, continues Thomas, it does not follow from this that all other things are unknown to God; for by understanding himself he understands everything else (n.2615).

In support of this Thomas reasons that because God is identical with his act of understanding and is most excellent and most powerful, his act of understanding is most perfect. Therefore he understands himself most perfectly. But insofar as a principle is more perfectly understood, so much the more is its effect understood. The things produced are contained within the power of the principle that produces them. Therefore, because the heaven and the whole of nature depend upon the first principle, which is God, it is clear that by knowing himself God knows all other things (n.2615).

This reasoning is not to be found in Aristotle's text although, it should be noted, Thomas does not explicitly state that it is. Moreover, for it to be reconciled with Aristotle's Unmoved or First Mover, one would have to assume that it is not only the final cause of the motion of other things, but also the cause of the being of those other things. And more than this, one would also have to assume that it is the efficient cause of their being. Otherwise, by knowing himself as the end of other things, God would still not know those things themselves. But Thomas himself thinks that all of these things are true of God, and that they can be discovered philosophically. He also thinks that Aristotle's God is the cause of the being or the substance of other things and not merely of their motion. And he apparently takes this as at least implying that Aristotle's God is also the efficient cause of their being, not merely their final cause. This will be confirmed by our next text.

In commenting on c.10, Thomas notes that here Aristotle inquires whether the universe has a good and a best, and hence an end that is separate from it, or whether it has a good and a best that is intrinsic to it which consists in the ordering of its parts (n.2628). Thomas finds Aristotle defending both positions. The First Mover is a separate good on which the heaven and the whole of nature depend as upon their end. And an appropriate intrinsic ordering must be present in its parts (n.2629). In developing this Thomas expands upon an analogy drawn by Aristotle between the good of an army considered in itself and in its commander. Thomas comments that the greater good is found in the commander because the end is more perfect than the means to the end, and the order of the army exists in order to fulfil the goal of the commander (n.2630). He also remarks that, because the nature of things ordered to an end is taken from their end, not only does the good of the army exist for the sake of the good of the commander; the order of the army derives from the commander (n.2631).

So too, he reasons, the separate good for the universe, that is, the First Mover, is better than the internal good or order of the universe. This is because the internal order of the universe is for the sake of the First Mover, so that what is present in its intellect and will may be realized within the ordered universe itself. Therefore the entire ordering of the universe comes from the First Mover (n.2631). In other words, Thomas here attributes the internal order of the universe to the intellect and will of the First Mover and thereby, without using the word itself, attributes something like providence to Aristotle's God or First Mover. But this is a First Mover endowed with will and with knowledge or understanding of all things, and, moreover, one which, says Thomas, instils in each thing a certain nature or inclination which orders that thing to its proper end. In other words, Thomas here assigns the efficient causation of natures or of natural inclinations to Aristotle's First Mover (n.2634).[53]

Concluding Remarks

And so Thomas' treatment of Aristotle in this *Commentary* varies considerably. Most of the time he expounds Aristotle's text as carefully as he can. Much of what he adds is intended to develop the implications of Aristotle's thought. At other times, as when he deals with the unity of the science of being as being and divine science while commenting on Bk VI, c.1, Thomas proceeds very cautiously. He does not read his full personal solution for this issue into Aristotle's text. Again, in commenting on Bk IV, c.2, even though he briefly introduces his own views on essence and *esse*, he does not attribute his position concerning this to Aristotle himself.

When dealing with Aristotle's supreme principle(s) as a cause of the being or of the substance of other things, he cites two texts from Aristotle (and eventually a third) to support his claim that this is Aristotle's position. He exploits a certain ambiguity in these texts in order to attribute to Aristotle what he takes to be the correct philosophical position; one should at least recognize the ambiguity in those texts even while granting that Thomas' interpretation is very difficult to reconcile with Aristotle's fuller discussions of the First and Unmoved Mover. In dealing with the specific essence or quiddity and the matter of composite entities, he does seem to misinterpret Aristotle and therefore finds himself constrained to force some of Aristotle's other passages. But theological motivations have nothing to do with this. It is rather that Thomas is philosophically convinced of the truth of his own position, and seems to think that Aristotle himself must also have held that position.

In finding Aristotle leaving a place for providence in his defence of being *per accidens* and contingency in *Metaphysics*, VI, cc.2–3, Thomas is careful not to attribute the doctrine of providence itself to Aristotle. However, in his discussion of Aristotle's conception of the First Mover or God in *Metaphysics*, XII, Thomas does make some significant additions to Aristotle's text. There is really no foundation in Aristotle's text for thinking that his First Mover is equipped with will, or that it knows things other than itself, or that it exercises providential care over the ordering of the created universe or, to repeat a point just made, that it is an efficient cause of the being or substance of other entities. Thomas is convinced that each of these points is true of God and that each can be established philosophically. He must have realized that most of these points are not explicitly defended by Aristotle, but he seems to have felt that they are not incompatible with Aristotle's description of his First or Unmoved Mover, and of its highest activity, thinking on its own thinking. Hence he may have thought that he was simply rendering explicit points that were only implicit in Aristotle.

In sum, in his effort to set forth Aristotle's thought as carefully and faithfully as possible, I would suggest that Thomas is largely successful, but not always. I also think that he is proceeding philosophically and not theologically in writing it. Some seem to assume that, whenever he defends a position that is compatible with Christian faith, he is proceeding theologically. There are two difficulties with this. First, as I have already mentioned, the positions he finds in Aristotle, even those we cannot justify on textual grounds, are positions that Thomas himself defends on philosophical grounds. If he finds them in Aristotle, he obviously thinks that Aristotle also defended them for philosophical reasons. Second, if Thomas is interested in showing that philosophy or, in this case, Aristotle's philosophy, is not incompatible with Christian faith with respect to the points mentioned above, this is not for him to proceed theologically. It is rather for him to be consistent with his claim as a Christian believer, not necessarily as a theologian, that divinely revealed truth and philosophically discovered truth cannot be in conflict with one another because both ultimately derive from one and the same source, God as the author of revelation and God as the creator (see his *Commentary on the 'De Trinitate'*, q.2, a.3). What is missing from the *Commentary on the 'Metaphysics'* is any effort to derive conclusions from premises based on religious belief and Scripture, in other words, the formal practice of scholastic theology.[54]

Finally, it seems to me that Thomas' *Commentary on the 'Metaphysics'* can be read with profit by students of Aquinas' personal metaphysics, by those interested in his understanding of Aristotle's metaphysics and by those interested in Aristotle's thought. This *Commentary* should not be viewed merely as an exposition of Aristotle's thought since in writing it Thomas is also clearly interested in arriving at philosophical truth. Thus at times he goes beyond the text of Aristotle and at times he even corrects Aristotle (as with respect to his alleged demonstration of the sempiternal character of the universe).

On the other hand, the *Commentary* should not be taken as a complete or even as an adequate expression of Thomas' personal metaphysics. If one were to restrict oneself to this *Commentary*, one would have a very impoverished understanding of Thomas' metaphysics. To mention just a few points, one would know nothing about his recommended way of discovering the subject of metaphysics through the negative judgement known as *separatio*. One would not realize that Thomas himself assigns considerable importance to a metaphysics of participation of beings in *esse*, since throughout the *Commentary* he constantly discusses participation in connection with Plato's theory of forms, a theory which both Thomas and Aristotle reject. One would know almost nothing about Thomas' metaphysics of essence and *esse*, nor would one have any appreciation of the philosophical argumentation he offers for their distinction, composition and correlation as potency and act. While one would have a foundation for understanding his theory of analogy of being as it applies at the predicamental level to substance and accidents, one would not understand how Thomas applies it at the level of divine being. And one would know very little about Thomas' views on what philosophical reason can establish about the divine names and attributes, his rejection of quidditative knowledge of God on our part in this life notwithstanding.

Hence, while his *Commentary on the 'Metaphysics'* can and should be taken seriously by those interested in his metaphysical thought and in his understanding of Aristotle's metaphysics, it should be read with great care and in concert with Thomas' more independent writings. There is no simple key to understanding Thomas' *Commentary* or to understanding why he wrote it. Nor is there any simple key that will apply to all of his other commentaries on Aristotle. As I have attempted to do with respect to the *Commentary on the 'Metaphysics'*, one should also pay particular attention to the prologues to the other commentaries.[55] One must read each of them with an open mind and constantly ask (1) whether Thomas at any particular point is explaining the text or at least the thought of Aristotle, (2) whether he also regards what he finds in Aristotle as true, or (3) whether he is introducing certain personal insights because he regards these as true. As for the *Commentary on the 'Metaphysics'*, in the large majority of cases he is doing the first and the second, but at times he is doing the third, or so it seems to me.

Notes

1 And so he introduces his *Commentary on the 'De causis'* by referring both to the original Greek work by Proclus and to the Arabic treatise known by the Latins as the *De causis* which, says Thomas, was translated from the Arabic and does not exist in Greek at all. Thomas concludes that it seems to have been excerpted by one of the Arab philosophers from the aforementioned writing by Proclus, especially so since the things contained in it are to be found much more fully and extensively in the Proclean work. See *Sancti Thomae de Aquino Super Librum De causis expositio*, ed. H.D. Saffrey, (Fribourg: Société Philosophique, 1954), p.3.

2 See J. Owens, 'Aquinas as Aristotelian commentator', in *St. Thomas Aquinas 1274–1974. Commemorative Studies*, vol. 1 (Toronto, ON: Pontifical Institute of Mediaeval Studies, 1974), pp.213–38. Here Owens proposes his position by asking a series of rhetorical questions. He also finds Thomas reading into Aristotle his own metaphysics of existence, especially in the *Commentary on the 'Metaphysics'* (see pp.222–29). For Gauthier see the following note. While he also strongly emphasizes the view that Aquinas was a theologian who has changed the philosophy he uses into theology, Mark Jordan views his commentaries on Aristotle as efforts to explain or set forth the thought of Aristotle himself, and not as expressions of Thomas' personal philosophy. In other words he views them as straightfoward *expositiones*. See 'Thomas Aquinas's disclaimers in the Aristotelian commentaries', in *Philosophy and the God of Abraham: Essays in Memory of James A. Weisheipl, O.P.*, ed. R. James Long (Toronto, ON: Pontifical Institute of Mediaeval Studies, 1991), pp.99–112, esp. p.104; *The Alleged Aristotelianism of Thomas Aquinas*, The Étienne Gilson Series 15 (Toronto, ON: Pontifical Institute of Mediaeval Studies, 1992); 'Theology and philosophy', in *The Cambridge Companion to Aquinas*, ed. Norman Kretzmann and Eleonore Stump, (Cambridge: Cambridge University Press, 1993), pp.232–51.

3 For the dates, see Jean-Pierre Torrell, *Saint Thomas Aquinas. Vol. I: The Person and his Work* (Washington, DC: The Catholic University of America Press, 1996), pp.341, 343. For Gauthier, see his Preface (1984) to the Leonine volume: *Sententia Libri De anima*, vol. 45.1, pp.288*–294*; also see his Appendix (1971), 'Saint Thomas et l'*Éthique à Nicomaque*', in the Leonine volume 48: *Sententia libri politicorum. Tabula libri ethicorum*, pp.xxiv–v. But in his recent *Aquinas's Philosophical Commentary on the Ethics. A Historical Perspective* (Dordrecht: Kluwer, 2001), pp.xv–xvi, n.22, James Doig points out that, after dating the *Commentary on the 'Ethics'* as written after the *Prima-Secundae*, Gauthier refers to it as written in preparation for the *Pars Secunda*. If one takes this remark as applying only to the *Secunda-Secundae*, Doig asks why Thomas needed to comment on the Ethics to write this part if he did not judge it necessary for writing the *Prima-Secundae*. For Gauthier's dating of the *Commentary* after the *Prima-Secundae* Doig cites 'La date du Commentaire sur l'*Éthique à Nicomaque*', *Recherches de théologie ancienne et médiévale* 18 (1951): 66–105; Preface (1969) to Leonine edn, *Sententia libri Ethicorum*, vol. 47.1, 178*; and 'Saint Thomas et l'Éthique a Nicomaque', p.xxiv. Doig strongly emphasizes the philosophical character of Thomas' *Commentary on the 'Ethics'*. For further references to different views on Thomas' purpose in writing the commentaries, see John Jenkins, 'Expositions of the text: Aquinas's Aristotelian commentaries', *Medieval Philosophy and Theology* 5 (1996): 39–62, esp.39, n.1.

4 *Friar Thomas d'Aquino. His Life, Thought & Works*, 2nd edn (Washington, DC: The Catholic University of America Press, 1983), p.273. Note that Weisheipl states that all

thirteen propositions are taken from Siger's writings or public teaching, but the evidence does not support this with respect to all thirteen. Weisheipl notes that much of the controversy centred upon Siger's 'Averroistic' interpretation of Aristotle's *De anima*, III, c.5, concerning the unicity of the material or possible intellect for the entire human race, and the implied denial of personal immortality of the soul. Aquinas dealt directly with this issue in his *De unitate intellectus* of 1270, and argued against the 'Averroistic' account on the grounds that it was both an incorrect interpretation of Aristotle and bad philosophy in its own right. Other contested issues condemned in 1270 and clearly aimed at Siger in addition to unicity of the possible intellect (pr. 1) included eternity of the human species (pr. 6) and hence eternity of the world (pr. 5), the denial that the separated soul suffers from corporeal fire (pr. 8) and, by implication, probably pr. 2: that it is false or improper to say that this human being understands, and perhaps pr. 7 (that the soul which is the substantial form of man as man is corrupted with the corruption of the body). For further discussion of the Condemnation of 1270 and of Siger's implication in it see Fernand Van Steenberghen, *Maître Siger de Brabant* (Louvain–Paris: Éditions de l'Institut Supérieur de Philosophie, 1977), pp.74–80; my 'The Condemnations of 1270 and 1277 at Paris', *The Journal of Medieval and Renaissance Studies* 7 (1977): esp. 169–85; 'Thomas Aquinas and the Condemnation of 1277', *The Modern Schoolman* 72 (1995): 233–7; David Piché, *La condamnation parisienne de 1277. Texte Latin, traduction, introduction et commentaire* (Paris: J. Vrin, 1999), pp.159–64.

5   Weisheipl, *Friar Thomas*, p.281. See pp.284–5: 'There was no need for Thomas to comment on Aristotle for his own amusement. He must have seen an academic apostolate demanding his best efforts. This apostolate, as we have said, was the plight of young masters in arts who needed an exegetical guide in order to understand and teach the Aristotelian books accurately without being led into heresy.'
6   Torrell, *Saint Thomas Aquinas*, pp.191–4. However, he also seems to accept Gauthier's debatable claim that the doctrine of unicity of the intellect is not to be found in Averroës' *Long Commentary on the 'De anima'*, but was rather invented by theologians such as Albert, Robert Kilwardby, Bonaventure, and then accepted by Thomas as being the view of Averroës. Against this interpretation see B.C. Bazán, 'Le Commentaire de S. Thomas d'Aquin sur le *Traité de l'âme*', *Revue des Sciences philosophiques et théologiques* 69 (1985): 529–31. Also see H. Davidson, *Alfarabi, Avicenna and Averroes, on Intellect* (New York: Oxford University Press, 1992), pp.282–98, for an excellent discussion of Averroes' development on this issue and his position in his *Long Commentary on the 'De anima'* which, while not written in direct response to Gauthier, argues strongly against Gauthier's interpretation.
7   Torrell, *Saint Thomas Aquinas*, p.228, quoting Gauthier's Appendix to Leonine edition, vol. 48, pp.xxiv–v.
8   Ibid., pp.231–2.
9   Ibid., pp.238–9; quoted text, p.239.
10 Gilson, *The Philosopher and Theology* (New York: Random House, 1962), pp.210–11. Also see his *Elements of Christian Philosophy* (Garden City, NY: Doubleday, 1960), p.282, n.6: '*Expositor* Thomas is not the author of the *Summa Theologiae*; he is the author of the commentaries on Aristotle, in which it is literally true to say that he seldom or never disagrees with the teaching of Aristotle. Now this is precisely the reason one cannot expound the philosophy of Saint Thomas out of his commentaries on Aristotle alone.' For my own presentation and critique of Gilson's views on Thomas' philosophy as a 'Christian philosophy', see my *Metaphysical Themes in Thomas Aquinas* (Washington, DC: The Catholic University of America Press, 1984), c.1.

11 For a strong statement of this position, Jenkins ('Expositions of the text', p.40, n.2), cites R. Ioannes Isaac, 'Saint Thomas interprète des œuvres d'Aristote', in *Scholastica Ratione Historico-Critica Instauranda*, Acta Congressus Scholastici Internationalis Romae anno sancto MCML celebrati, (Rome: Bibliotheca Pontificii Athenaei Antoniani, 1951), pp.353–63. For a leading representative of the River Forest School who defends this view see Benedict Ashley, 'The River Forest School and the philosophy of nature today', in R. James Long (ed.) *Philosophy and the God of Abraham: Essays in Memory of James A. Weisheipl, O.P.* (Toronto, ON: Pontifical Institute of Mediaeval Studies, 1991), pp.2–3, where he lists the principal theses of the River Forest School: 'The first is that the philosophy of Aquinas, as distinct from his theology, is best gathered not from the *Summa theologiae* (supplemented by the *Commentary on the 'Sentences'* and the *Summa contra gentiles*, etc.), as Gilson for example chose to do, but from the commentaries on Aristotle, in which the philosphical disciplines are treated according to their own principles and methods *via inventionis*. Nor can it be rightly maintained that these works are merely commentaries on Aristotle, not expressions of Aquinas' own thought.' But one finds many other interpreters of Aquinas indiscriminately citing from his commentaries on Aristotle and from his more original works in their presentations of his thought.

12 Doig, *Aquinas on Metaphysics: A Historical Doctrinal Study of the Commentary on the Metaphysics* (The Hague: Martinus Nijhoff, 1972), pp.ix–xi. Also see his Conclusion, pp.383ff.

13 *Liber de philosophia prima sive scientia divina, I–IV*, ed. S. Van Riet (Louvain–Leiden: Peeters–Brill, 1977), c.2 (vol. 1, 4–6). For secondary literature, see Wippel, *The Metaphysical Thought of Thomas Aquinas: From Finite Being to Uncreated Being* (Washington, DC: The Catholic University of America Press, 2000), p.13, n.1, and especially Albert Zimmermann, *Ontologie oder Metaphysik? Die Diskussion über den Gegenstand der Metaphysik im 13. und 14. Jahrhundert* (Leuven: Peeters, 1998), pp.144–52.

14 *In I Phys.*, in *Aristotelis opera cum Averrois commentariis* (Venice, 1562–74), vol.4, ff.47rb–48va; *In IV Met.*, vol.8, ff.64rb, 65rb–66rb; *In XII Met.*, f.293va. Cf. Zimmermann, *Ontologie oder Metaphysik?*, pp.152–4.

15 For a presentation and comparison of the two, see my *The Metaphysical Thought*, pp.15–22.

16 See *In duodecim libros Metaphysicorum Aristotelis expositio*, ed. M.-R. Cathala and R.M. Spiazzi (Turin–Rome: Marietti, 1950), pp.1–2 for the *Prooemium*. In citing from Thomas' *Commentary* itself I usually insert into my text the appropriate paragraph numbers from this (the Marietti) edition.

17 'Ex quo apparet, quod quamvis ista scientia praedicta tria consideret, non tamen considerat quodlibet eorum ut subiectum, sed ipsum solum ens commune' (2).

18 'Quamvis autem subiectum huius scientiae sit ens commune, dicitur tamen tota de his quae sunt separata a materia secundum esse et rationem' (ibid).

19 See *Super Boetium 'De Trinitate'* (Leonine Vol. 50), 154: 182–206. Thomas had already introduced this distinction in q.5, a.1 (see 138: 154–67).

20 Note that, in q.5, a.4 of his *Commentary on the 'De Trinitate'*, Thomas refers to the subject of metaphysics as 'ens in quantum est ens' (154: 161–162), whereas in the discussion in the *Prooemium* he describes it as 'ens commune'. In effect he takes these two as equivalent.

21 To anticipate a possible objection, I should note that the solution Thomas proposes in his *Commentary on the 'De Trinitate'* does not appear in the literal exposition of the text with which he introduces each section of the *Commentary*, but rather in the much fuller

part where he follows the scholastic method of disputation using questions and articles, a method he retains even in his *Summa theologiae*. This being so, one can be confident that in that part of the *Commentary on the 'De Trinitate'* he is expressing his personal views, just as he does in the *Prooemium* to the *Commentary on the 'Metaphysics'*.

22 'Ergo in hac scientia nos quaerimus principia entis inquantum est ens: ergo ens est subiectum huius scientiae, quia quaelibet scientia est quaerens causas proprias sui subiecti.'

23 Correction according to the not yet published Leonine edition of Thomas' *Commentary*, courtesy of Professor James Reilly, Jr.

24 According to Reilly, in this part of Bk IV Thomas is following the twelfth-century translation from the Greek of Aristotle's *Metaphysics* by James of Venice (*translatio Iacobi*). For Reilly's identification of the different translations from the Greek used by Thomas in composing the *Commentary*, see 'The *Alia Littera* in Thomas Aquinas' *Sententia libri Metaphysicae*', *Mediaeval Studies* 50 (1988): 559-83, especially the chart on 562. Reilly concludes that the other two principal sources used by Thomas are the *Media (Anonyma)* and the *Moerbecana*. For the critical edition of the *translatio Iacobi*, see *Aristoteles Latinus XXV 1-1a. Metaphysica, Lib. I-IV.4. Translatio Iacobi sive 'Vetustissima' cum scholiis et translatio composita sive 'Vetus'*, ed. Gudrun Vuillemin-Diem (Brussels–Paris, 1970). See 62:14: 'Quod autem est dicitur quidem multipliciter, sed ad unum et unam quandam naturam et non equivoce,' which corresponds to 1003a 33 in Aristotle's Greek text.

25 'Colligit quae sunt supra ostensa; dicens, manifestum est, quod ad unam scientiam pertinet considerare ens secundum quod est ens, et ea quae per se illi insunt. Et per hoc patet, quod illa scientia non solum est considerativa substantiarum, sed etiam accidentium, cum de utrisque ens praedicetur. Et est considerativa eorum quae dicta sunt, scilicet eiusdem et diversi, similis et dissimilis, aequalis et inaequalis, negationis et privationis, et contrariorum; quae supra diximus esse per se entis accidentia.'

26 'Nulla enim earum determinat "de ente simpliciter", idest de ente in comnmuni, nec etiam de aliquo particulari ente inquantum est ens, sicut arithmetica non determinat de numero inquantum est ens, sed inquantum est numerus. De quolibet enim ente inquantum est ens, proprium est metaphysici considerare' (n.1147).

27 Note in particular: 'Sed, si est aliqua substantia immobilis, ista erit prior substantia naturali; et per consequens philosophia considerans huiusmodi substantiam, erit philosophia prima. Et quia est prima, ideo erit universalis, et erit eius speculari de ente inquantum est ens, et de eo quod quid est, et de his quae sunt entis inquantum est ens: eadem enim est scientia primi entis et entis communis, ut in principio quarti habitum est.' Compare Thomas' *Commentary* with the Moerbeke translation of Aristotle which, according to Reilly, he is here following: 'Sed si est aliqua substantia immobilis, haec prior et philosophia prima, et universalis sic quia prima; et de ente inquantum ens huius utique erit specuari, et quae est et quae insunt in quantum ens.' See *Aristoteles Latinus XXV 3.2. Metaphysica Lib. I–XIV. Recensio et Translatio Guillelmi de Moerbeka*, ed. G. Vuillemin-Diem (Leiden: Desclée de Brouwer, 1995), 127: 64–68. However, in some respects Thomas' paraphrase here is closer to the *Media* version. Cf. *Aristoteles Latinus XXV 2. Metaphysica Lib. I–IX, XII–XIV. Translatio Anonyma sive 'Media'*, ed. G. Vuillemin-Diem (Leiden: Brill, 1976), 118: 9–13. Note at the end of the text: 'et de ente in quantum est ens eius est speculari, et quid est et quae insunt in quantum ens'.

28 For fuller discussion of Thomas' personal view concerning this in its application to the conditions of possibility for discovering being as being and hence for beginning metaphysics, see my *The Metaphysical Thought*, pp. 51–9.

29 'Si autem est alia natura et substantia praeter substantias naturales, quae sit separabilis et immobilis, necesse est alteram scientiam ipsius esse, quae sit prior naturali. Et ex eo quod est prima, oportet quod sit universalis' (*In XI Met.*, lect, 7, n.2267). Compare with the Moerbeke translation of Aristotle: 'Si autem est altera natura et substantia separabilis et immobilis, alteram necesse et scientiam ipsius esse et priorem naturali et universalem eo quod priorem' (edn cit., 233: 416–18).

30 See Doig, *Aquinas on Metaphysics*, pp.312–16; Owens, 'Aquinas as Aristotelian commentator', pp.222–8. They make this point in quite different ways, however, perhaps because they have significantly different conceptions of Aquinas' personal metaphysics.

31 Revised according to the Leonine version so as to read: 'Quod autem est dicitur multipliciter' instead of 'Ens autem multis' (Marietti, n.529), courtesy of Professor Reilly. Cf. the James of Venice translation: 'Quod autem est dicitur quidem multipliciter' (edn cit., 62: 14).

32 'Dicit ergo primo, quod ens sive quod est, dicitur multipliciter' (n.535).

33 The Moerbeke version reads: 'aut enim quod quid est aut quia quale aut quia quantum' (edn cit., 131: 176). For Doig, *Aquinas on Metaphysics*, on this text and the previous one see pp.315–16.

34 Here the Marietti edition (n.550) should be corrected so as to read with the Leonine edition: 'Minor patet: idem enim est dictu "homo" et "unus homo". Et similiter idem est dictu "ens homo" vel "quod est homo" et "homo"; et non demonstratur aliquod alterum cum secundum dictionem replicamus, dicendo "ens homo" et "homo" et "unus homo"' (courtesy of Professor Reilly).

35 'Sciendum est enim quod hoc nomen Homo, imponitur a quidditate, sive a natura hominis; et hoc nomen Res imponitur a quidditate tantum; hoc vero nomen Ens, imponitur ab actu essendi' (n.553).

36 For Averroës, see *In IV Metaphysicorum*, vol. 8, f. 67va.

37 'Avicenna autem peccavit multum in hoc, quod existimavit quod unum et ens significant dispositiones additas essentiae rei' (*In IV Met.*, f. 67ra).

38 'Esse enim rei quamvis sit aliud ab eius essentia, non tamen est intelligendum quod sit aliquod superadditum ad modum accidentis, sed quasi constituitur per principia essentiae. Et ideo hoc nomen Ens quod imponitur ab ipso esse, significat idem cum nomine quod imponitur ab ipsa essentia' (n.558).

39 Certain specialists in Arabic philosophy have argued that Thomas was misled by the mediaeval Latin translation of Avicenna's *Prima Philosophia* into thinking that he viewed existence as an accident superadded to essence. Others disagree. While I must leave this to Arabic scholars to decide, I would recall that the Latin Averroes does accuse Avicenna of making this very mistake. See *In IV Metaphysicorum*, vol. 8, fol. 67ra (cited above in n.37). For discussion and references, see my 'The Latin Avicenna as a source for Thomas Aquinas's metaphysics', *Freiburger Zeitschrift für Philosophie und Theologie* 37 (1990): 66, n.32 for references to the dispute concerning Avicenna's position, 67–71 for discussion of the relevant texts from Avicenna's *Metaphysics*, that is, Bk I, c.5 and Bk V, c.1.

40 Ross's translation in *The Complete Works of Aristotle. The Revised Oxford Translation*, ed. Jonathan Barnes (Princeton, NJ: Princeton University Press, 1984), p.1570.

41 'Secundo, quia nihil est eis causa, sed ipsa sunt causa essendi aliis. Et per hoc transcendunt in veritate et entitate corpora caelestia: quae etsi sint incorruptibilia, tamen habent causam non solum quantum ad suum moveri, ut quidam opinati sunt, sed etiam quantum ad suum esse, ut hic Philosophus expresse dicit' (*In II Metaphysicorum*, lect. 2,

n.295). On this text in Aristotle and in Thomas' commentary, see Fernand Van Steenberghen, *Le problème de l'existence de Dieu dans les écrits de s. Thomas d'Aquin*, Louvian-la-Neuve: Éditions de l'Institut Superieur de Philosophie, pp.263, 266; Jenkins, 'Expositions of the text', 46–8; Doig, *Aquinas's Philosophical Commentary on the Ethics*, pp. 153–6. On Aristotle's text also see Augustin Mansion, 'Le Dieu d'Aristote et le Dieu des chrétiens', in *La philosophie et ses problèmes. Recueil d'études de doctrine et d'histoire offert à Monseigneur R. Jolivet* (Lyon-Paris: Éditions Emmanuel Vitte, 1960), pp.23–5. These writers agree with the generally accepted view that Aristotle himself does not hold that the causes of the heavenly bodies are causes of the existence of the heavenly bodies themselves, but only of their eternal motion. Also see Mark Johnson, 'Did St. Thomas Aquinas attribute a doctrine of creation to Aristotle?', *New Scholasticism* 63 (1989): 129–55 (he offers an affirmative answer to the question posed in his title).

42 'Necesse vero est omnes causas esse sempiternas' (Leonine correction courtesy of Professor Reilly). Note from the following text: 'Unde sunt causae entium secundum quod sunt entia, quae inquiruntur in prima philosophia, ut in primo proposuit. Ex hoc autem apparet manifeste falsitas opinionis illorum, qui posuerunt Aristotelem sensisse, quod Deus non sit causa substantiae caeli, sed solum motus eius.' Here Thomas is commenting on *Met. VI*, c.1 (1026a 16–18).

43 Van Steenberghen, *Le Problème*, pp.266–8.

44 For Averroës see *In VII Metaphysicorum*, vol. 8, 184DG. Also see Armand Maurer, 'Form and essence in the philosophy of St. Thomas', in *Being and Knowing. Studies in Thomas Aquinas and Later Medieval Philosophers* (Toronto, ON: Pontifical Institute of Mediaeval Studies, 1990), pp.4–5.

45 For Avicenna, see his *Liber de philosophia prima sive scientia divina*, V–X, ed. S. Van Riet (Louvain–Paris: Peeters–Brill, 1980), Bk V, c.5, (vol. 2, p.275).

46 For Aristotle see *Metaphysics* VI, c. 1 (1025b 28ff). For Thomas' commentary on this, see nn.1155–9. For Maurer, see 'Form and essence', pp.6, 8.

47 Maurer, 'Form and essence', p.8.

48 For discussion of these see ibid., pp.11–13. He lists Thomas' *Commentary on 'Metaphysics'* VII, c.10 (1035b 31–33), n.1491, (1035b 14–16), n.1484, c.7 (1032b 14), n.1406 and c.11 (1037a 26–30), n.1530. Maurer also discusses Thomas' position in the *De ente* (see 14–16). For further discussion, see the careful and detailed study by Gabriele Galuzzo, 'Il problema dell'oggetto della definizione nel commento di Tommaso d'Aquino a *Metafisica* Z 10–11', *Documenti e studi sulla tradizione filosofica medievale* 12 (2001), 417–65, esp. 439–56.

49 'Ex hoc igitur principio, quod est primum movens sicut finis, dependet caelum, et quantum ad perpetuitatem substantiae suae, et quantum ad perpetuitatem sui motus; et per consequens dependet a tali principio tota natura, eo quod omnia naturalia dependent a caelo, et a tali motu eius' (In *XII Metaphysicorum, lect.* 7, n.2534).

50 Ed. cit., p.258.

51 'assimilatio autem ad id quod est volens, et intelligens, cuiusmodi ostendit esse Deum, attenditur secundum voluntatem et intelligentiam, sicut artificiata assimilantur artifici, inquantum in eis voluntas artificis adimpletur: sequitur quod tota necessitas primi motus subiaceat voluntati Dei' (n.2535).

52 See n.2543: 'Propter quod autem unumquodque tale, et illud magis. Et ideo sequitur quod quicquid divinum et nobile, sicut est intelligere et delectari, invenitur in intellectu attingente, multo magis invenitur in intelligibili primo quod attingitur.' This seems to be another version of the adage Thomas finds in Bk II, c.2 (993b 24–25). There Thomas

refers to this as a certain universal proposition, that is, as an adage or axiom, and paraphrases it thus: 'Unumquodque inter alia maxime dicitur, ex quo causatur in aliis aliquid univoce praedicatum de eis' (n.292). In these two texts Thomas reasons, as Aristotle himself does, from the fact that something causes a perfection to be present in something else, to the conclusion that it is present in that cause to a maximum (or to a greater) degree. However, more frequently, as in the second part of the Fourth Way in ST I, q.2, a.3, Thomas reverses this reasoning. He moves from the maximum instance of a perfection within a given class or genus to the conclusion that this causes that perfection to be present in all others within that class. For a helpful examination of this in Thomas' texts, see V. de Couesnongle, 'La causalité du maximum. L'utilisation par Saint Thomas d'un passage d'Aristote', *Revue des sciences philosophiques et théologiques* 38 (1954): 433–44; 'La causalité du maximum. Pourquoi Saint Thomas a-t-il mal cité Aristote?', ibid., 658–80.

53 On this see Van Steenberghen, *Le problème de l'existence de Dieu*, pp.271–2. On Aristotle's God see also Augustin Mansion, 'Le Dieu d'Aristote et le Dieu des Chrétiens', pp.21–44.

54 Without necessarily agreeing with every interpretation in his article, I would cite Leo Elders as another who strongly emphasizes the philosophical character of this Commentary in his 'St. Thomas Aquinas's *Commentary on the 'Metaphysics'* of Aristotle', *Divus Thomas* (Piacenza) 86 (1983): 307–26.

55 Very useful in this respect is the recent bilingual publication of the prologues to the Aristotelian commentaries (and the *Commentary on the 'Liber de causis'*) edited and introduced by Francis Chevenal and Ruedi Imbach, *Prologe zu den Aristoteleskommentaren* (Frankfurt am Main: Vittorio Klostermann, 1995). Their Introduction is also quite helpful.

Chapter 11

MacIntyre's Interpretation of Aristotle's Ethics

Jiyuan Yu

In *After Virtue* (hereafter, AV, in the notes), Alasdair MacIntyre develops a theory of virtue based on Aristotle's *Nicomachean Ethics* (hereafter, NE, in the notes) which has been quite influential. This chapter examines the way in which MacIntyre's own ethics is related to his interpretation of Aristotle. Following the theme of this volume, the focus of the discussion is more on how MacIntyre creatively uses the *Nicomachean Ethics* than on the evaluation of the content of his interpretation.

Interpretation and Revival

Let me begin by examining how MacIntyre relates his project to Aristotle. In the contemporary revival of virtue ethics, Aristotle's *Nicomachean Ethics* has been hailed as the most important classic in Western ethics. However, it has not always been the case that it has received such a warm reception. In the first half of the twentieth century, moral philosophers showed little philosophical interest in it. H.A. Prichard, for example, in his influential paper 'Does moral philosophy rest on a mistake?', states:

> The fact, if it be a fact, that virtue is no basis for morality will explain what otherwise it is difficult to account for, viz. the extreme sense of dissatisfaction produced by a close reading of Aristotle's *Ethics*. Why is the *Ethics* so disappointing?... It is, rather, because Aristotle does not do what we as Moral Philosophers want him to do, viz. to convince us that we really ought to do what in our non-reflective consciousness we have hitherto believed we ought to do, or if not, to tell us what, if any, are the other things which we really ought to do, and to prove to us that he is right.[1]

Prichard is convinced that an appropriate moral philosophy should address the issue of what one ought to do. Since Aristotle's ethics is concerned with virtue and character, an approach which does not fit Prichard's notion of moral philosophy, Prichard concludes that there is not much to learn in Aristotle's *Nicomachean Ethics*.[2]

The evaluation of Aristotle's *Nicomachean Ethics* changed after Elizabeth Anscombe published her 1958 article, 'Modern moral philosophy'.[3] Like Prichard, Anscombe is impressed with the sharp contrast between Aristotle and modern moral philosophers, but, unlike Prichard, Anscombe dismissed the concepts of 'moral obligation' or 'moral duty' which are at the core of modern moral philosophy. To do ethics appropriately, in her judgement, we must turn to the notion of virtue, and we must first of all provide a sound psychology of virtue. Anscombe's paper inaugurated the contemporary revival of virtue ethics. It is in the shift from what one ought to do to what kind of person one should be that Aristotle's *Nicomachean Ethics* becomes a model for most moral philosophers. Clearly, in Prichard and Anscombe, we see that different philosophical sensibilities lead to radically different evaluations of the same classic.

In line with Anscombe, MacIntyre claims that Aristotle is '*the* protagonist against whom I have matched the voices of liberal modernity' (AV, p.146).[4] However, different from many virtue theorists who, although using Aristotle to criticize modern moral philosophy, do not see him as a viable paradigm to develop a positive theory, MacIntyre proceeds to develop, following Aristotle's thinking, an alternative theory of virtue to replace modern morality.[5] Indeed, it is his positive and substantial Aristotelian reconstruction that makes him a worthy subject of discussion for this volume.

MacIntyre argues that our current language of morality is full of disagreements and is 'in a state of grave disorder' (AV, p.2). Different moral positions are derived from incompatible and incommensurable premises which have different historical origins. There is no rational way of securing moral agreement and terminating these disagreements. Such a situation, according to him, is the result of the failure of what he calls 'the Enlightenment project', that is, the project of discovering and providing a rational justification of morality (AV, p.39). This project fails because moral thinkers 'cannot agree among themselves either on what the character of moral rationality is or on the substance of the morality which is to be founded on that rationality' (AV, p.21). Furthermore, MacIntyre claims that the Enlightenment project itself results from the wrongful rejection of the Aristotelian tradition: 'It was because a moral tradition of which Aristotle's thought was the core was repudiated during the transitions of the fifteenth to seventeenth centuries that the Enlightenment project of discovering new rational secular foundations for morality had to be undertaken' (AV, p.117). Accordingly, it was wrong in the first place to reject Aristotle, and the Enlightenment project should never have been started. Such a diagnosis leads MacIntyre to return to Aristotle, to 'make a new start to the enquiry in order to put Aristotelianism to the question all over again' (AV, p.119). Macintyre's enquiry contains two aspects. The first is as follows:

> It will be necessary to consider Aristotle's own moral philosophy not merely as it is expressed in key texts in his own writings, but as an attempt to inherit and to sum up a good deal that had gone before and in turn as a source of stimulus to much later thought. (AV, p.119)

Two tasks are involved in this first aspect: to comment on Aristotle's own texts and to provide an exposition of the tradition in which Aristotle's thinking was developed and of which Aristotle serves as the source and representative. Clearly, the former task is the interpretation usually conducted by Aristotelian commentators who seek to transmit and explain the original meaning of Aristotle's texts, and the latter task is a job usually carried out by scholars of the history of philosophy.

The second aspect of his enquiry has to do with answering the following key question: 'Can Aristotle's ethics, or something very like it, after all be vindicated?' (AV, p.118). The goal MacIntyre envisages is to provide a positive answer to this question, showing that 'the Aristotelian tradition can be restated in a way that restores intelligibility and rationality to our moral and social attitudes and commitments'. (AV, p.259). In vindicating and reviving Aristotle's ethics and the Aristotelian tradition in contemporary ethics, MacIntyre aims to develop a new Aristotelian ethical theory.

It might be relevant and useful to introduce here two expressions from Chinese philosophy regarding the interpretation of the classics. In editing and commenting on the classics, Confucius claims: 'I transmit but do not create' (*Analects*, 7:1). By this he means that he only explains the original meaning of the classics, with no intention of adding anything of his own. Such an attitude is usually called 'I-comment-on-the-classics'. In contrast, the Neo-Confucian philosopher Lu Hsiang-Shan (1139–93) holds that to produce faithful commentaries on ancient classics is not his aim. For him, 'if in our study we know the fundamentals, then all the six classics comment on me'.[6] By 'all-the-classics-comment-on-me', he means that the classics are no longer the objects of commentary, but become resources to exploit. One should appropriate the themes and ideas of the ancient classics to develop new philosophical views. This practice leads to the production of interpretive texts that are no longer historical commentaries, but are themselves original philosophical works and may even be classics themselves. In the history of philosophy, Lu himself is not called a Confucian commentator, but a 'Neo-Confucian' philosopher.

In terms of these two approaches,[7] the first aspect of MacIntyre's enquiry can be called 'I-comment-on-Aristotle', and the second aspect 'Aristotle-comments-on-me'. In the second, Aristotle's ideas are used to criticize modern moral philosophy, and his approach is borrowed in order to grapple with current ethical issues. Aristotle's *Nicomachean Ethics* becomes a source from which MacIntyre's own theory is constructed and developed. *After Virtue* is, then, an important work in contemporary virtue ethics rather than merely a historical commentary. MacIntyre is more a 'Neo-Aristotelian' moral philosopher than an Aristotelian commentator.

'I-comment-on-the-classics' and 'the-classics-comment-on-me', however, are clearly two different and even conflicting interpretive practices. They reflect the traditional rivalry between the historian of philosophy and the philosopher. Most philosophers represented in this volume adopt the 'the-classics-comment-on-me' type of interpretation, but historians of philosophy usually dismiss this type of interpretation and favour the 'I-comment-on-the-classics' approach. For many historians of philosophy, as long as philosophers use a classic as a source to defend or develop new thinking, the faithfulness of the philosophers' interpretations of the original classics are held in doubt. Hence, for instance, few Aristotelian commentators take seriously Heidegger's interpretation of Aristotle. Indeed, it is with regard to the approach of 'the-classics-comment-on-me' that the problem of uses and abuses arises.

If this is right, the two aspects of MacIntyre's enquiry, 'I-comment-on-Aristotle' and 'Aristotle-comments-on-me', are in conflict. How, then, is it possible for MacIntyre to pursue both in his inquiry? The answer seems to be that Macintyre holds a unique conception of how moral philosophy should be carried out. For him, philosophical analysis cannot be isolated from historical inquiry, and the prevalent academic division of labour between philosophy and history should be abandoned. The present is intelligible only as a commentary on the past. Taking Vico, Hegel and Collingwood as models, MacIntyre seeks to write a philosophical history, a narrative which is a fusion of historical inquiry and philosophical analysis. It is by historical narrative, rather than by logical argument, that he justifies and defends his thesis. As he himself states:

> I hold not only that historical enquiry is required in order to establish what a particular point of view is, but also that it is in its historical encounter that any given point of view establishes or fails to establish its rational superiority relative to its particular rivals in some specific contexts. (AV, p.269)

This approach makes MacIntyre's commentary on Aristotle's *Nicomachean Ethics* an intrinsic part of his project. In the remainder of this chapter, the next section focuses on Macintyre's 'Aristotle-comments-on-me'. The third section deals with his 'I-comment-on-Aristotle' and the final section examines the implications of his combination of these two approaches.

An Aristotelian Account of Virtue

One of the fundamental features that distinguishes Aristotle from modern moral thinking, according to MacIntyre, is that Aristotle focuses on the question of 'what sort of person I am to become'. This 'is in a way an inescapable question in that an answer to it is given *in practice* in each human life' (AV, p.118). Aristotle answers it by locating virtue in the central place of ethics. Modern moral philosophy, however, ignores this question and turns, instead, to the question of 'what rules we should follow'.

This turn in modern moral philosophy, according to MacIntyre, results from the rejection of Aristotle's teleology (AV, p.119). Aristotle holds a teleological view in which human beings have a specific and essential nature that determines their proper aims and goals (*telos*). His ethics starts from human nature as it happens to be, and seeks to understand human nature as it could be if its *telos* were realized. Its central task is to show the way to fulfil this *telos*. To become a good man is to actualize or fulfil this nature, and the virtues are excellences of character that enable people to achieve their *telos* (AV, p.148). With the development of modern science, this teleological view of human nature is dismissed. As a consequence, a moral agent is simply seen in modernity as a rational agent who has no specific or identifiable purpose independent of his own choice.

If the rejection of Aristotelian virtue ethics results from the dismissal of Aristotelian teleology, what should MacIntyre do with regard to teleology in his attempt to revive virtue ethics? As with other modern philosophers, MacIntyre does not find Aristotle's version of teleology acceptable. Indeed, he sees Aristotle's teleology as the first of the major difficulties that Aristotle's ethics faces, because it 'presupposes his metaphysical biology', and that biology has been rejected.[8]

Nevertheless, MacIntyre maintains that for answering adequately the question of 'what sort of person I am to become', a general teleological scheme is necessary. 'Without an overriding conception of the *telos* of a whole human life, conceived as a unity, our conception of certain individual virtues has to remain partial and incomplete' (AV, p.202). We need a *telos* of human life to view life as a whole and to provide some general account of what human flourishing consists in; we also need a *telos* to find a rational way of discriminating and ordering different individual virtues. In short, a teleological account of a life provides a basic structure for a virtuous life.

Accordingly, MacIntyre envisages that he needs to replace Aristotle's metaphysical biology with a new version of teleology: 'Hence any adequate teleological account must provide us with some clear and defensible account of the *telos*, and any adequate generally Aristotelian account must supply a teleological account which can replace Aristotle's metaphysical biology' (AV, p.163). A contemporary attempt at developing a new teleology is, as MacIntyre is fully aware, a challenge, given that modernity has divided human life into many segments and our dominant way of thinking is atomistic analysis. Yet, for him, this is a mission that must be accomplished in order to revive virtue ethics. For to provide this alternative version of teleology amounts to providing 'the necessary background against which the concept of a virtue has to be made intelligible' (AV, p.186).

This new teleology is developed in MacIntyre's three-tiered conception of virtue which consists of a notion of a practice, an account of the narrative order of human life and an account of what constitutes a moral tradition. They form three stages of logical development in the sense that each of the earlier stages provides an essential constituent for each of the later stages, and each of the later stages presupposes and modifies each of the earlier ones. The first stage is to understand virtues in terms of 'practices'. Practice is defined not by rules but by goods. Each practice has its internal goods which refer to those objective standards of excellence appropriate to the activity itself, and external goods which refer to the goods such as money, status or reputation. Virtue at this stage is defined as the quality the possession and exercise of which enables one to achieve the internal goods of a practice.

This practice-based account of the virtues, however, is only preliminary. There are competing practices and competing goods worth pursuing. To bring specific practices into harmony with one another, we need to put practices and virtues in the larger arena of human life. For this reason, we must regard a life not merely as a sequence of individual actions and episodes, but as a unity. MacIntyre therefore proceeds to stage two of his concept of virtue 'to envisage each human life as a whole, as a unity, whose character provides the virtues with an adequate *telos*' (AV, p.204). It is at this point that the new teleology emerges.

The unity of an individual life consists in the unity of a narrative embodied in a single life. It is through narrative that human conduct can be made intelligible. A whole life is a course of living out a story that runs from one's birth to death. The unity of a life always has to be understood in a social context: 'For the story of my life is always embedded in the story of those communities from which I derive my identity' (AV, p.221). Furthermore, such a unity of life lies in 'the unity of a narrative quest' (AV, p.219). It is a quest for the human good. The good is not something fixed, not something already adequately characterized so that all other actions are moving towards it progressively. Rather, it is a process of self-understanding: 'A quest is always an education both as to the character of that which is sought and in self-knowledge' (ibid.). In this quest, one encounters and deals with various events and episodes. Through these one comes to understand the meaning of the life and the direction it should take: 'The good life for man is the life spent in seeking for the good life for man' (ibid.). At stage two, virtue is further defined as a quality which not only enables us to achieve the internal goods of a practice and to sustain us in the relevant kind of quest for the good, but also 'will furnish us with increasing self-knowledge and increasing knowledge of the good' (ibid.).

This account of virtue is complemented by a notion of tradition. It is within a tradition that practices are situated, shaped and transmitted across generations. It is the tradition that provides the resources for a narrative quest and makes intelligible one's claims of the good life. The given of one's life constitutes one's moral starting point and makes us bearers of a tradition. Virtue is embedded in a tradition. 'Hence the individual's search for his or her good is generally and characteristically conducted within a context defined by those traditions of which the individual's life is a part, and this is true both of those goods which are internal to practices and of the goods of a single life' (AV, p.222). The end is discovered and rediscovered within a living social tradition. MacIntyre's account of tradition in *After Virtue* is brief, yet tradition becomes the central theme of the two volumes subsequent to *After Virtue*: *Whose Justice? Which Rationality?*[9] and *Three Rival Versions of Moral Enquiry*.[10]

In MacIntyre's own assessment, there are three aspects in which his account of virtue is clearly Aristotelian (AV, pp.197–9). First, he defends and elaborates various ideas of Aristotle, such as voluntariness, the distinctions of different kinds of virtues, the relation between virtue and passion, the structure of practical reasoning, and so on. Second, his account 'can accommodate an Aristotelian view of pleasure and enjoyment'. Third, his account 'is Aristotelian in that it links evaluation and explanation in a characteristically Aristotelian way'. To this list, we can add that the view of the relation between virtue and practice at stage one has an Aristotelian origin.[11] The emphasis on the social embeddedness of conceptions of the good and on the social constitution of the person at stage two is derived from Aristotle's thesis that 'man is by nature a political animal'. More important, MacIntyre's insistence that an appropriate account of virtue must put it in the human life as a whole is clearly inspired by Aristotle's point that virtue must be related to the function of human life. The list can go even further, but MacIntyre's concept of virtue is impressive, not because it is full of Aristotelian elements, but because MacIntyre moulds all these and other Aristotelian elements together and works out an original theory of virtue.

What, then, is the most significant difference between MacIntyre's theory and Aristotle's? MacIntyre's own reply is that 'although this account of the virtues is teleological, it does not require any allegiance to Aristotle's metaphysical biology' (AV, p.196).[12] I mentioned earlier that the mission MacIntyre sets for himself is to replace Aristotle's version of teleology. With his notion of virtue, MacIntyre believes that he has accomplished this undertaking. Since his teleology relies heavily on the unity of life which is derived from social embededness and tradition, he calls his theory a 'socially teleological account' (AV, p.197) in contrast to Aristotle's 'biologically teleological account'. His contribution consists in removing Aristotle's general account of virtue from its original biological teleology and putting it on the foundation of MacIntyre's own social teleology. In his understanding, whereas Aristotle associates the *telos* of human life with human species, he himself locates the *telos* of human life in tradition. Despite this difference, MacIntyre claims that he remains fundamentally an Aristotelian:

> Hence if it turns out to be the case that this socially teleological account can support Aristotle's general account of the virtues as well as his own biologically teleological account, these differences from Aristotle himself may be regarded as strengthening rather than weakening the case for a generally Aristotelian standpoint. (AV, p.197)

That is to say, even where he differs from Aristotle, he maintains and strengthens Aristotle's original position.

A question arises, however. On the one hand, MacIntyre claims that Aristotle's virtue theory is deeply rooted in his teleology; on the other, he takes it that by removing Aristotle's theory of virtue from its original biologically teleological basis, he is strengthening Aristotle's standpoint. This seems to be a paradoxical situation. First, if his view that Aristotle's virtue theory is rooted in his teleology is right, then, by splitting them apart, MacIntyre must have seriously undermined the integrity of Aristotle's framework in ethics and, consequently, Aristotle's view on the place of the virtue in human life. It is then unclear that he is really strengthening Aristotle's standpoint.

Second, if in replacing the basis of Aristotle's theory of virtue MacIntyre truly strengthens rather than weakens Aristotle's standpoint, then Aristotle's theory of virtue must not really be rooted in his biological teleology and is related to that teleology only in an external way. If so, MacIntyre must have overemphasized the connection between Aristotle's virtue ethics and his teleology.

Virtue and Teleology

We are therefore driven to examine how MacIntyre interprets the relation between the theory of virtue and teleology in Aristotle. First, MacIntyre holds that a biological teleology is essential for Aristotle's view of virtue.

> Human beings, like the members of all species, have a specific nature; and that nature is such that they have certain aims and goals, such that they move by nature towards a specific *telos*. The good is defined in terms of their specific characteristics. Hence Aristotle's ethics, expounded as he expounds it, presupposes his metaphysical biology. (AV, p.148)

This view seems to have its textual basis in the function argument of *Nicomachean Ethics*, i.7. In this argument Aristotle claims that human beings have a function or characteristic activity, that is, rational activity. Accordingly, a human being has a metaphysical rational nature. Aristotle also affirms that human excellence (virtue) lies in the excellent performance of rationality. However, MacIntyre moves further to claim that the *telos* of the human species is the basis of virtue in Aristotle: 'Virtues attach not to men as inhabiting social roles, but to man as such. It is the *telos* of man as a species which determines what human qualities are virtues' (AV, p.184). Probably this is the reason MacIntyre says that Aristotle's teleology presupposes a metaphysical biology. But Aristotle himself does not clearly make such a strong claim. Furthermore, MacIntyre maintains that in Aristotle it is the metaphysical contemplation of the unchanging divinity that 'furnishes man with his specific and ultimate human *telos*' (AV, p.158).

Yet MacIntyre also recognizes that there is a different view regarding the basis of virtues in Aristotle. He says: 'It is worth remembering Aristotle's insistence that the virtues find their place not just in the life of the individual, but in the life of the city and that the individual is indeed intelligible only as a *politikon zoon*' (AV, p.150). This is of course true of Aristotle's well-known view that 'a human being is a naturally political animal'. This view, however, is not the same as the first one because, if virtue is related to a human social nature and the nature of one's society, it should not be fixed and determined because of one's membership in human species.

Thus Aristotle seems to have presented two different views about the basis of the virtues: human beings have a metaphysical nature and a political or social nature. MacIntyre is right in pointing out both of them.[13] How, then, does he think that these two views are related? His general position is that these two views form a tension: 'There is a certain tension between Aristotle's view of man as essentially political and his view of man as essentially metaphysical' (AV, p.158). And he also claims that Aristotle fails to reconcile these two positions:

> Aristotle thus sets himself the task of giving an account of the good which is at once local and particular – located in and partially defined by the characteristics of the polis – and yet also cosmic and universal. The tension between these poles is felt throughout the argument of the *Ethics*. (AV, p.148)

Although contemplation is said to be the final end to which all other virtues are supposed to be subordinate, MacIntyre recognizes, rightly, I think, that this is not always the case in *Nicomachean Ethics*:

> To become *eudaimon* material prerequisites and social prerequisites are necessary. The household and the city-state make the metaphysical human project possible; but the goods

which they provide are, although necessary, and although themselves part of that whole human life, subordinate from the metaphysical standpoint. Nonetheless in many passages where Aristotle discusses individual virtues, the notion that their possession and practice is in the end subordinate to metaphysical contemplation would seem oddly out of place. (AV, p.158)

Faced by this situation, MacIntyre does not proceed, as many Aristotelian scholars do, to reconcile these two views on Aristotle's behalf. Instead, he asserts that the *telos*-providing metaphysical contemplation does not deserve a serious treatment: 'It is nothing other than thought timelessly thinking itself and conscious of nothing but itself' (ibid.).

On this interpretation, there is a persistent and internal tension in Aristotle, and Aristotle does not really have a unified framework in his ethics. I should point out that MacIntyre's reading is not unique. Quite a number of commentators hold that there is an unresolved and unresolvable tension in Aristotle's ethics. For example, J.L. Ackrill puts it thus: 'Most of the *Ethics* implies that good action is – or is a major element in – man's best life, but eventually in Book 10 purely contemplative activity is said to be perfect *eudaimonia*; and Aristotle does not tell us how to combine or relate these two ideas.[14]

It is also a popular position among commentators that, whereas Aristotle's theory of moral virtue is illuminating, his theory of contemplation is mysterious and not significant. As Anthony Kenny remarks:

The main reason why interpreters are motivated to reject this intellectualist position is that they do not find the position credible as a piece of philosophy, and as admirers of Aristotle they are unwilling to saddle his mature ethical work with such a strange doctrine. In particular, they find the contemplative who is the hero of NE 10 a strange and repellent human being.[15]

Given this, there is no special reason to believe that MacIntyre's interpretation of Aristotle is biased by his own theory.

If this view is not biased, is it correct? To answer this question, we would need to establish a standard interpretation of Aristotle's *Nicomachean Ethics* against which MacIntyre's interpretation may be evaluated. Yet it is doubtful that such a 'standard' interpretation could be established, given the fact that Aristotle's *Nicomachean Ethics* has been open to so many different and even contradictory interpretations. Commentators are sharply divided even on Aristotle's notion of happiness and whether Aristotle has a unified project.[16] This itself raises a difficult but significant issue related to the theme of this volume, that is, whether and how the criteria of validity and legitimacy could be determined in order to judge different and conflicting accounts of the same classic.

However, as mentioned at the beginning of this chapter, it is not my main goal to judge the validity of MacIntyre's interpretation. For my current purpose, what is important is the relation between his interpretation and his own enquiry. In this regard, we notice that MacIntyre's interpretation puts him in an inconsistent position regarding his relation to Aristotle. Recalling the paradoxical situation mentioned at the end of the previous section, we can now see where MacIntyre stands. Since Aristotle has two different views regarding the basis of virtue, MacIntyre's affirmation that in Aristotle 'it is the *telos* of man as a species which determines what human qualities are virtues' (AV, p.184) is only a partial position, and since his interpretation entails that Aristotle's theory of moral virtue is not always related to or based on his metaphysical teleology, he clearly overemphasizes the relation between teleology and virtue in Aristotle. MacIntyre claims that his major work is to separate Aristotle's theory of virtue from its original biologically teleological basis and to relocate it on a new socially teleological basis. Yet, if moral virtue and metaphysical teleology are two poles in a tension, a separation between them becomes not as necessary and significant as MacIntyre claims it to be.[17]

It is worth noting that MacIntyre's socially teleological account is in line with one of Aristotle's two views regarding the basis of virtue, that is, Aristotle's insistence that the end of human life should be grasped by political science and that a human being is by nature a social animal. Hence it might be more appropriate to say that MacIntyre's work does not replace Aristotle's teleology. Rather what he is doing, in *After Virtue*, is abandoning Aristotle's metaphysical teleology, while strengthening Aristotle's standpoint with respect to the relation between virtuous agents and their societies.

Relativism, Contemplation and Interpretation

Having discussed separately MacIntyre's two approaches, 'Aristotle-comments-on-me' and his 'I-comment-on-Aristotle', now I turn to the impact of his combined approach on his own ethics. I do this by first identifying the major difficulty that MacIntyre's theory faces and then showing how that difficulty affects Aristotle.

MacIntyre's account of virtue has been subjected to innumerable, justified or unjustified, criticisms.[18] In all these criticisms, the one that is the most frequent and also most troublesome is that MacIntyre's theory falls prey to moral relativism. Although his notion of practice is defined in terms of intrinsic goods, it can be argued that even within single practices there might be different and conflicting goods. In his account of narrative unity, a question arises about how one can decide the single true narrative account of one's life. More important, since there are various tensions and conflicts within one tradition, and there are also conflicting traditions, it seems difficult to understand a good life in terms of tradition.

In response, MacIntyre has made great efforts to show that he can escape relativism. To a great extent, we can even say that fighting this charge of relativism has become one of his central preoccupations since *After Virtue* was first published. He addresses the issue in the postscript to the second edition of the book. In both *Whose Justice? Which Rationality?* and *Three Rival Versions of Moral Enquiry*, he seeks to argue in detail that the existence of incommensurable and rival traditions does not negate rational inquiry or choice. In MacIntyre's contention, although morality has to be understood socially and historically and there is no morality as such, although rationality has to be embedded in a tradition and is a concept with a history, critical reflection and rational progress can be made based on the dynamic interaction of rival traditions. Inspired by post-Kuhnian philosophy of science, MacIntyre argues that an ethical system is more advanced if it overcomes the problems and inconsistencies of previous ethical systems and transcends the limits of these systems. Since his theory allows for the progressive changes of morality, MacIntyre insists that he is not a relativist. Instead, he describes his position as 'a kind of historicism which excludes all claims to absolute knowledge' (AV, p.270).

MacIntyre's persistent and stimulating defence against relativism has occasioned a significant amount of philosophical literature, but it is difficult to say that he has convinced his critics. The charge of relativism seems to hang there and the debate goes on.[19] It is unnecessary here to get into the details of this debate. I would like to point out, however, that in the course of responding to the charge of relativism, MacIntyre has gradually departed from Aristotle and has come to embrace Aquinas. According to his position in *After Virtue*, 'The Aristotelian moral tradition is the best example we possess of a tradition whose adherents are rationally entitled to a higher measure of confidence in its epistemological and moral resources' (AV, p.277). Yet in *Whose Justice? Which Rationality?* Aquinas emerges as the centre of focus. The reason for this shift is that he thinks the Thomist tradition, as a creative synthesis of the Aristotelian and Augustinian traditions, is more promising in resolving the conflicts within and between preceding traditions and in allowing moral progress. Here we see an interesting phenomenon: it is MacIntyre's Neo-Aristotelian theory that leads him to face the accusation of relativism, yet in the struggle to dismantle this charge he shifts his focus from Aristotle to Aquinas. Relativism does seem to be an internal problem for MacIntyre's thinking.

The charge of relativism is derived from MacIntyre's historical and social understanding of morality and rationality. Such an understanding, however, is a characteristic Aristotelian standpoint. Yet, although relativism is almost a standard charge against MacIntyre, it is rarely levelled against Aristotle. Why? Aristotle classifies virtue into two kinds: moral and intellectual. He explicitly claims that moral virtues are socially conditioned. For him, moral virtue 'comes as a result of habit [*ethos*] whence also its name is one that is formed by a slight variation from the word for "habit"' (NE, 1103a16–8). The formation of moral virtue involves a process of the inculcation of *ethos*. *Ethos* refers to custom or habit that is relative to some particular society. Accordingly, moral virtue must have a dimension of social relativity. Indeed, Aristotle defines moral virtue as the mean and then claims that the mean is 'relative to us' (1107a1).

Furthermore, intellectual virtues are further divided by Aristotle into practical and theoretical (NE, 1138b35–1139a17). Of these, the practical intellectual virtue (that is, practical wisdom) is said to be inseparable from moral virtues. 'We cannot be fully good without practical wisdom, or practically wise without virtue of character' (1144b31–2; cf. 1178a15–20) One cannot be completely good without being practically wise. Yet practical wisdom is not simply the effective exercise of practical rationality; rather it is concerned with living well in general (1140a25–8), with what is good and bad for human beings (1140b5–6, 20–21).

The notion of the goal or end, that is, of living well, is derived from moral cultivation and moral virtues. 'Virtue makes the aim right' (NE, 1144a8; cf. 1144a30–34). The good end of practical wisdom is associated with the agent's moral qualities (1144a8; 20–27; a35–6; 1145a5–6; *Eudemian Ethics*, 1227b20–1228a2). Hence practical wisdom is embedded in social morality.[20] This notion of rationality, which contrasts to the tradition-independent and instrumental conception of rationality in modernity, is so deeply appreciated by MacIntyre that he declares that 'Aristotle's account of practical reasoning is in essentials surely right' (AV, p.150). In a sense, the main thesis of *Whose Justice? Which Rationality?* is a historical illustration of Aristotle's thesis of the interdependence of practical wisdom and moral virtues.

Although practical wisdom and moral virtues are socially conditioned, they are not the whole content of Aristotle's theory of virtue. In addition, there are other non-practical intellectual virtues, the supreme one of which is contemplation. Indeed, the final conclusion that Aristotle reaches is that the life of moral virtue and practical wisdom results only in secondary happiness, whereas the life of contemplation is the happiest (NE, 1178a8–10). Contemplation is related, not to moral cultivation, but to the metaphysical rational nature of human beings. It is the excellent exercise of pure intellect. Hence the relativity of moral virtues does not entail the relativity of Aristotle's theory of happiness.

If this is right, it appears that, when MacIntyre dismisses Aristotle's theory of contemplation, he is giving away the standpoint which makes Aristotle's ethics immune to relativism. The charge of relativism that MacIntyre faces seems to be rooted in his very project to reject Aristotle's teleology while retaining only his theory of moral virtue. In dismissing Aristotle's theory of contemplation, MacIntyre also removes Aristotelian primary happiness. A person, living as MacIntyre prescribes, can only have secondary happiness according to Aristotle.

Aristotle's explicit conclusion, that there is a hierarchy of happiness between contemplation and the life of practical wisdom (and moral virtue), leads one to question whether, as MacIntyre's interpretation shows, there is an internal inconsistency on Aristotle's part. It is true that Aristotle presents two different views of human nature: the metaphysical rational and the social nature. Yet these two views do not form a tension in Aristotle's ethics. On the contrary, on my reading, Aristotle's ethics is precisely about this tension. Aristotle has these two views because he believes that human nature has these two different dimensions. A correct understanding of a good human life requires revealing and understanding these different dimensions and their interrelations. This is probably why Aristotle calls his discussion in the *Nicomachean Ethics* and the *Politics* '*peri ta anthrôpina philosophia*' ('philosophy of human affairs', or 'philosophy of human nature'; NE, 1181b14). Aristotle's two kinds of happiness seem to correspond respectively to the metaphysical rational nature and to the political or social nature. The hierarchy or order between them indicates clearly that he has a unified solution to this tension.

Corresponding to this dual view of human nature, Aristotle holds a distinction between a good citizen and a good person (NE, 1130b28–9). A good citizen is relative to the constitution of which he is a member and hence lacks a unified standard of excellence, whereas a good person can be determined in terms of one single excellence (*Politics*, 1276b20–34). Relating this to Aristotle's function argument, this single excellence should refer to the excellent exercise of pure human rationality. A good citizen and a good person could be completely the same, according to Aristotle, only under the ideal and perfect constitution.

This leads us to question whether Aristotle's theory of contemplation is as insignificant as MacIntyre takes it to be. Contemplation is usually taken to be the passive meditation of eternal truth. Taken in this way, this life is, of course, hardly appealing. Yet, although not all things Aristotle says about contemplation are clear, I think the following two points are. First, contemplation is the activity of the intellect (*nous*) which is 'the best thing in us' (NE, 1177a14, a21). That this activity is primary happiness is established on the basis of the function argument (1177a11–12). Since happiness lies in the rational activity of the soul, it follows that primary happiness must be the activity in which one's rational function is most perfectly or most fully exercised. Thus it is in contemplation that human rational function is fully exercised and human rational nature is fully actualized. In contrast, the life of practical wisdom and moral wisdom is secondary happiness because of its bodily affection and its civic involvement (1178a10–22). On my reading, this means that, since practical wisdom has its goal determined by moral virtues, it must always be understood in terms of particular and historical society. This condition makes it less self-determined, and its exercise is not a fully autonomous exercise of human rationality. For Aristotle, 'It would be strange to think that the art of politics, or practical wisdom, is the best knowledge, since man is not the best thing in the world' (1141a20–1). This passage can be made to make sense only if we take it to be emphasizing the limitation of human societal nature.

The second point that is clear is that contemplation is beyond moral boundary. Although a contemplative person needs moral virtues and external goods to survive, Aristotle maintains that so far as the contemplative activity itself is concerned, moral deeds are not only not required, but are 'even hindrances (*empodia*), at all events to his contemplation' (NE, 1178b4–5). This point is further reinforced when Aristotle describes how God, whose life is nothing but contemplative activity, and who represents pure rational activity, does not possess any moral virtue or vice (1178b16–7).

Putting the first and second points together, a contemplative life appears to be a life in which one goes beyond one's social relativity and fully actualizes one's metaphysical rational nature. Aristotle is not suggesting that contemplation can establish absolute moral objectivity, since contemplation for him is concerned with eternal truth rather than with ethical affairs. However, he shows that there is a dimension in human rational nature that enables human beings to transcend moral value. MacIntyre accuses liberalism of overestimating the ability of the individual to transcend the social and cultural framework. Yet contemplation in Aristotle turns out to be precisely the point at which Aristotle claims that a human being can rise above his social relativity. Aristotle also instructs us not to listen to the advice that, because we are humans, we should only take care of human matters. Instead he encourages us to transcend ordinary human affairs, since we 'must, so far as we can, make ourselves immortal, and strain every nerve to live in accordance with the best thing in us' (1177b32–3).[21] For Aristotle, there is a unified framework to examine the human life as a whole.

The above line of interpretation of Aristotle's ethics will undoubtedly encounter opposition, in particular since it has to be presented here in such a sketchy form.[22] However, it is not my intention to introduce it to 'prove' that MacIntyre's interpretation must be 'wrong'. Rather my alternative interpretation is aimed at providing a mirror to show that MacIntyre's way of commenting on Aristotle affects his use of Aristotle, that is, the way he develops his own Aristotelian theory. Through the above comparison between MacIntyre and Aristotle with regard to the problem of relativism, what we see is this. On the one hand, MacIntyre, while abandoning Aristotle's theory of contemplation, still tries to put virtue in the context of the whole human life. He is thereby motivated to develop his theories of the narrative unity of human life and of tradition, which are by all means provocative and have a lot to offer even to those who disagree with MacIntyre's interpretation of Aristotle. It is indeed the case that, although Aristotle claims at the beginning of *Nicomachean Ethics* that the end of human life should be grasped by political science, he does not provide a full account of the end at which political science aims, and his discussion of how practical wisdom obtains the general notion of human good is very abstract.[23] MacIntyre's theory of narrative unity and his theory of tradition should be viewed as significant extensions and developments in this line of investigation. On the other hand, his rejection of Aristotle's contemplation makes him ignore the ethical significance of humans' metaphysical rational nature and focus on practical rationality only.[24] This opens him to the charge of relativism. MacIntyre's 'Aristotle-comments-on-me' approach is based on his 'I-comment-on-Aristotle' approach and is supported by a line of plausible reading of the texts. In his combination of these two approaches, it is his interpretation of Aristotle that significantly shapes the conception and development of his own moral philosophy.[25]

Notes

1 H. Prichard, 'Does moral philosophy rest on a mistake?', *Mind*, 21 (1912): 33.
2 The case of W.D. Ross, Prichard's Oxford colleague, is also suggestive in this regard. As the editor and main translator of the *Oxford Translations of Aristotle's Works*, and the author of numerous volumes of commentaries on Aristotle's major treatises, Ross is probably the greatest commentator of Aristotle in the twentieth century. Yet, although he spent most of his life translating and commenting on Aristotle, he did not appreciate the approach of virtue ethics. Ross' ethical theory of prima facie duty, although not without some Aristotelian influence, is essentially a Kantian deontological theory. Indeed, Ross' Kantian position affects, to some extent, his translation of the *NE*. A well known instance in which this happens is that he translates *orthos logos* (literally, the right reason) as 'the correct rule', a phrase with deep Kantian flavour. In J. Barnes (ed.), *The Revised Oxford Translation of the Complete Works of Aristotle* (Princeton, NJ: Princeton University Press, 1984), Ross' translation of the *NE* is revised by Urmson.

3   E. Anscombe, 'Modern moral philosophy', *Philosophy*, 33 (1958): 15–33.
4   He acknowledges his indebtedness to Anscombe regarding the diagnosis of the ills of modernity in *After Virtue* 2nd edn (Notre Dame, IN: University of Notre Dame Press, 1984), p.53.
5   For an example of those who only use Aristotle to criticize modernity, see Bernard Williams, another major advocate of virtue ethics. He comes to the conclusion that 'even if we leave the door open to a psychology that might go some way in the Aristotelian direction, it is hard to believe that an account of human nature – if it is not already an ethical theory itself – will adequately determine one kind of ethical life as against others. Aristotle saw a certain kind of ethical, cultural and indeed political life as a harmonious culmination of human potentialities, recoverable from an absolute understanding of nature. We have no reason to believe in that' (*Ethics and the Limits of Philosophy*, Cambridge, MA: Harvard University Press, 1985, p.52).
6   Lu Hsiang-Shan, *Complete Works of Lu Hsiang-Shan* (Beijing: China Book Bureau, 1980), 34:1b. The six classics originally comprised *The Book of Odes*, *The Book of History*, *The Book of Rites*, *The Book of Changes*, *The Book of Music* and *The Spring and Autumn Annals*. Later, *The Book of Music* was lost and replaced by *The Rites of Zhou*.
7   To some extent, the distinction between 'I-comment-on-the classics' and 'The-classics-comment-on-me' is close to the distinction Jorge J.E. Gracia draws between 'meaning interpretations' and 'relational interpretations'. In Gracia's view, a meaning interpretation aims 'to understand what the author of a text understood by the text', whereas a relational interpretation is 'one whose aim is to provide an understanding of the relation of a text, or its meaning, to something else'. See 'Relativism and the Interpretation of Texts', in J. Margolis and T. Rockmore (eds), *The Philosophy of Interpretation*, special issue of *Metaphilosophy*, 31, 1–2 (2000): 47–8.
8   The second problem is that Aristotle's ethics is developed on the basis of the structure of the *polis* and thus has historical specificity. And the third is that Aristotle overemphasizes unity and harmony, but ignores the importance of conflicts, in human life (AV, pp.162–3). For the third problem, see note 21. The second problem is related to Aristotle's unwelcome views on slavery and women. MacIntyre defends Aristotle on this point by contending that this is part of the general blindness of Aristotle's culture: 'Yet it remains true that these limitations in Aristotle's account of the virtues do not necessarily injure his general scheme for understanding the place of the virtues in human life, let alone deform his multitude of more popular insights' (AV, p.160).
9   A. MacIntyre, *Whose Justice? Which Rationality?* (Notre Dame, IN: University of Notre Dame Press, 1988). The book deals with four traditions: Aristotelian, Aquinas' synthesis of Aristotelianism and Augustinian Christianity, the Scottish Enlightenment and its Humean sequel, and liberal individualism.
10 A. MacIntyre, *Three Rival Versions of Moral Enquiry* (Notre Dame, IN: University of Notre Dame Press, 1990). This book discusses three traditions: Encyclopedia (that is, the liberal rationalism in the nineteenth century), the genealogists introduced by Nietzsche and the Thomist tradition.
11 'When Aristotle speaks of excellence in human activity, he sometimes, though not always, refers to some well-defined type of human practices: flute-playing, or war, or geometry. I am going to suggest that this notion of a particular type of practice as providing the arena in which the virtues are exhibited and in terms of which they are to receive their primary, if incomplete, definition is crucial to the whole enterprise of identifying a core concept of the virtues' (AV, p.187).

12 Other than the issue of teleology, another major difference which MacIntyre thinks distinguishes him from Aristotle is expressed as follows: 'Just because of the multiplicity of human practices and the consequent multiplicity of goods in the pursuit of which the virtues may be exceeded – goods which will often be contingently incompatible and which will therefore make rival claims upon our allegiance – conflict will not spring solely from flaws in individual character' (AV, pp.196–7). It is unclear why this difference has the same weight as the difference with regard to teleology.

13 Sometimes, however, he seems to confuse them. For example, he reads metaphysical biology into the opening remarks of NE (AV, p.148). Yet, when Aristotle claims there that we must search for an end, the end at which all actions aim, he explicitly suggests that the supreme end of human life is the object of political science (NE 1094a27–b12), not that of metaphysics.

14 J.L. Ackrill, 'Aristotle on *Eudaimonia*', in A.O. Rorty (ed.) *Essays on Aristotle's Ethics* (Berkeley, CA: University of California Press, 1980), p.15.

15 Anthony Kenny, *Aristotle on the Perfect Life* (Oxford: Clarendon Press, 1992), p.89.

16 Anthony Kenny assesses the situation of interpreting the *NE* in this way: 'No explanation succeeds in the three goals which most commentators have set themselves: (1) to give an interpretation of book 1 and book 10 which does justice to the texts severally; (2) to make the two books consistent with each other; (3) to make the resulting interpretation one which can be found morally acceptable by contemporary philosophy'. (*Aristotle on the Perfect Life*, p.93).

17 Furthermore, for MacIntyre, the rejection of Aristotle's theory of virtue in modern philosophy is a consequence of the dismissal of Aristotle's teleology in modern science. But, if there is a tension between virtue and metaphysical teleology in Aristotle, this claim appears to be too strong as well.

18 For a good source of these controversies and criticisms, see John Horton and Susan Mendus (eds), *After MacIntyre* (Notre Dame, IN: University of Notre Dame Press, 1994).

19 For instance, even a sympathetic commentator, such as Robert Stern, admits that MacIntyre's historicism faces some difficulties in establishing itself as a stable third option between dogmatism and scepticism (relativism). Stern remarks: 'It could be argued, MacIntyre's position remains in effect indistinguishable from skepticism, for although MacIntyre insists that an ethical outlook is to be preferred to another when it 'transcends the limitations of its predecessors', he makes clear that what one perceives these limitations to be, and how one might take them to be transcended, is relative to one's particular perspective; and when the choice is not just within *one* tradition of enquiry, but between *conflicting* traditions, then, the criterion is so vague as to be empty' (R. Stern, 'MacIntyre and historicism', in John Horton and Susan Mendus, (eds), *After MacIntyre*, p.154).

20 For Aristotle's repeated claims that practical wisdom alone cannot determine the goodness of its goal, see NE 1140b11–20, 1144a8–9, 1144a30–31, 1145a5–6, and 1151a15–9.

21 Other than teleology and historical specificity, the third major charge made against Aristotle by MacIntyre is that Aristotle embraces harmony and denies conflict (AV, p.157). He claims that 'I argued earlier that it is a merit of an account of the virtues in terms of a multiplicity of goods that it allows for the possibility of tragic conflict in a way in which Aristotle's does not' (AV, p.21). Yet, given this advice at 1177b32–3, Aristotle seems to suggest that the conflict between one's social obligations and one's pure exercise of rational nature is inherent in human life.

22 For a full defence of this interpretation of Aristotle's theory of happiness, see J. Yu, 'Aristotle on *Eudaimonia*: After Plato's *Republic*', *History of Philosophy Quarterly*, 18 (2001): 115–38.

23 There has been a debate over whether Aristotle's practical wisdom involves a 'Grand Conception' of the end. Cf. Sarah Brodie, *Ethics with Aristotle* (Oxford: Oxford University Press, 1991), pp.198ff.

24 In his most recent book, *Dependent Rational Animals – Why Human Beings Need the Virtues* (La Salle, IL: Open Court, 1999), MacIntyre admits that he went too far in his rejection of Aristotle's metaphysical biology: 'Although there is indeed good reason to repudiate important elements in Aristotle's biology, I now judge that I was in error in supposing an ethics independent of biology to be possible' (p.x). By this, however, MacIntyre means that an ethics of human life should take into account our initial animal condition and understand the importance of human vulnerability and disability.

25 Thanks to Jorge Gracia and Gerol Petruzella for their helpful comments.

Bibliography

Ackrill, J.L. (1980), 'Aristotle on *Eudaimonia*', in A.O. Rorty (ed.), *Essays on Aristotle's Ethics*, Berkeley, CA: University of California Press.

Adomenas, M. (2002), 'The fluctuating fortunes of Heraclitus in Plato', in A. Laks and C. Louguet (eds), *Qu'est-ce que la philosophie présocratique? What is Presocratic Philosophy?*, Lille: Presses Universitaires du Septentrion, pp.419–47.

Alexander of Aphrodisias (1979), *The De anima of Alexander of Aphrodisias*, trans. A.P. Fotinis, Washington, DC: University Press of America.

Altman, Alexander (2000), 'Defining Maimonides' Aristotelianism', in Robert S. Cohen and Hillel Levine (eds), *Maimonides and the Sciences*, Dordrecht: Kluwer, pp. 1–8.

Anscombe, E. (1958), 'Modern moral philosophy', *Philosophy*, 33, 15–33.

Apostle, H.G. and Lloyd P. Gerson (1991), *Aristotle: Selected Works*, 3rd edn, Grinnell, IO: The Peripatetic Press.

Aquinas, Thomas (1882–), *Sancti Thomae de Aquino Opera omnia*, Leonine edn, Rome: Typographia Polyglotta S.C. de Propaganda Fidei.

Aquinas, Thomas (1950), *In duodecim libros Metaphysicorum Aristotelis expositio*, ed. M.-R. Cathala and R. M. Spiazzi (eds.), Turin-Rome: Marietti.

Aquinas, Thomas (1954), *Sancti Thomae de Aquino Super Librum De causis expositio*, ed. H.D. Saffrey, Fribourg: Societé Philosophique.

Aristotle (1957), *Aristotle on the Soul, Parva naturalia, On Breath*, trans. W.S. Hett, Loeb Classical Library, Cambridge, MA: Harvard University Press.

Aristotle (1970), *Aristoteles latinus XXV 1–1a. Metaphysica, Lib. I–IV.4. Translatio Iacobi sive 'Vetustissima' cum scholiis et translatio composita sive 'Vetus'*, ed. G. Vuillemin-Diem, Brussels–Paris: Desclée de Brouwer.

Aristotle (1976), *Aristoteles latinus XXV 2. Metaphysica Lib. I–IX, XII–XIV. Translatio anonyma sive 'Media'*, ed. G. Vuillemin-Diem, Leiden: Brill.

Aristotle (1984), *The Complete Works of Aristotle. The Revised Oxford Translation*, ed. J. Barnes, Princeton: Princeton University Press.

Aristotle (1995), *Aristoteles latinus XXV 3.2. Metaphysica Lib. I–XIV. Recensio et Translatio Guillelmi de Moerbeka*, ed. G. Vuillemin-Diem, Leiden: Brill.

Ashley, B. (1991), 'The River Forest School and the philosophy of nature today', in R. James Long (ed.), *Philosophy and the God of Abraham: Essays in Memory of James A. Weisheipl, O.P.*, Toronto, ON: Pontifical Institute of Mediaeval Studies, pp.1–15.

Averroës (1562–74), *In Aristotelis opera cum Averrois Commentariis*, vols. 4–8, Venice: Iunctas; rep. 1962, Frankfurt-on-Main: Minerva.

Averroës (1953), *Commentarium Magnum in Aristotelis De anima libros*, ed. F.S. Crawford, Cambridge, MA: Medieval Academy of America.

Averroës (1961), *The Epistle on the Possibility of Conjunction with the Active Intellect by Ibn Rushd with the Commentary of Moses Narboni*, ed. and trans. K. Bland, New York: The Jewish Theological Seminary of America.

Averroës (1967), *Averroes: On the Harmony of Religion and Philosophy*, trans. George Hourani, London: Luzac.

Averroës (1969), *Averroes' Tahafut al-Tahafut (The Incoherence of the Incoherence)*, trans. S. Van Den Bergh, London: Luzac.
Averroës (1981), *Commentario al libro sobre el alma de Aristóteles*, in S. Gómez Nogales (trans.), *La psicología de Averroes: Commentario al libro sobre el alma de Aristóteles*, Madrid: Instituto Miguel Asin.
Averroës (1985), *Epítome 'De anima'*, ed. S. Gómez Nogales, Madrid: Instituto Miguel Asin.
Averroës (1986), *Averroes' Middle Commentary on Aristotle's Poetics*, trans. Charles Butterworth, Princeton: Princeton University Press.
Averroës (1987), *Epítome 'De física'*, trans. J. Puig, in *Averroes: Epítome de física*, Madrid: Consejo Superior de Investigaciones Científicas.
Averroës (1999), *Averroes' Middle Commentary on Aristotle's Nicomachean Ethics in the Hebrew Version of Samuel Ben Judah*, ed. L.V. Berman, Jerusalem: The Israel Academy of Sciences and Humanities.
Averroës (2001), *Averroès: La Béatitude de l'âme*, ed. and trans. M. Geoffroy and C. Steel, Paris: J. Vrin, pp. 198–246.
Averroës (2002), *Averroes' Middle Commentary on Aristotle's De anima*, ed. and trans. A.L. Ivry, Provo, UT: Brigham Young University Press.
Avicenna (1977), *Liber de philosophia prima sive scientia divina, I–IV*, ed. S. Van Riet, Louvain–Leiden: Peeters-Brill.
Avicenna (1980), *Liber de philosophia prima sive scientia divina, V–X*, ed. S. Van Riet, Louvain–Paris: Peeters-Brill.
Ayache, L. (1997), 'Est-il vraiment question d'art médical dans le *Timée?*', in L. Brisson and T. Calvo (eds), *Interpreting the Timaeus – Critias, Proceedings of the IV Symposium Platonicum. Selected Papers*, Saint Augustin: Academia Verlag, pp.55–63.
Barbour, Ian (1997), *Religion and Science: Historical and Contemporary Issues*, San Francisco, CA: Harper Books.
Bazán, Bernard C. (1985), 'Le Commentaire de St. Thomas d'Aquin sur le *Traité de l'âme*', *Revue des sciences philosophiques et théologiques*, 69, 521–47.
Beck, L.W. (1969), *Early German Philosophy*, Cambridge, MA: Harvard University Press.
Boulding, M. (trans.). (1997), *The Confessions*, Hyde Park, NY: New City Press.
Braslavy, Sara-Klein (1986), 'The creation of the world and Maimonides' interpretation of Gen. I–V', in S. Pines and Y. Yovel (eds), *Maimonides and Philosophy*, Dordrecht: Martinus Nijhoff, pp.65–78.
Brentano, F. (1862), *On the Manifold Meaning of Being According to Aristotle (Von der mannigfachen Bedeutung des Seienden nach Aristoteles)*, Freiburg: Herder.
Brodie, S. (1991), *Ethics with Aristotle*, Oxford: Oxford University Press.
Burkert, W. (1960), 'Platon oder Pythagoras?', *Hermes*, 88, 159–77.
Burkert, W. (1962), *Weisheit und Wissenschaft: Studies zu Pythagoras, Philolaos und Platon*, Nuremberg: Carl.
Calvino, Italo (1999), 'Why read the classics?' trans. Martin McLaughlin, in *Why Read the Classics?*, New York: Pantheon Books, pp.3–9.
Cantor, Geoffrey and Chris Kenny (2001), 'Barbour's fourfold way: problems with his taxonomy of science–religion relationships', *Zygon*, 36 (4), 765–82.
Chadwick, H. (trans.) (1991), *Saint Augustine: Confessions*, Oxford: Oxford University Press.
Cherniss, H. (1935), *Aristotle's Criticism of Presocratic Philosophy*, Baltimore, MD: Johns Hopkins University Press.
Cherniss, Harold (1944), *Aristotle's Criticism of Plato and the Academy*, vol. 1, Baltimore, MD: Johns Hopkins University Press.

Chevenal, Francis and Ruedi Imbach (1995), *Prologe zu den Aristoteleskommentaren*, Frankfurt am Main: Vittorio Klostermann.
Cho, K.K. (1986), 'Ökologische Suggestibilität in der Spätphilosophie Heideggers', *Allgemeine Zeitschrift für Philosophie*, 11 (3), 53–77.
Cho, K.K. (1987), *Bewusstsein und Natursein*, Freiburg: Karl Alber.
Cooper, J.M. (1984), 'Plato's theory of human motivation', *History of Philosophy Quarterly*, 1, 3–21.
Cordero, N.-L. (1991), 'L'invention de l'école éléatique: Platon, *Sophiste*, 242 D', in P. Aubenque (ed.), *Études sur le Sophiste de Platon*, Naples: Bibliopolis, pp.91–124.
Cornford, F.M. (1939), *Plato and Parmenides*, trans. with an intro. and running commentary, London: Routledge & Kegan Paul.
Curd, Patricia (1998), *The Legacy of Parmenides*, Princeton, NJ: Princeton University Press.
Davidson, Herbert A. (1979), 'Maimonides' secret position on creation', in I. Twersky (ed.), *Studies in Medieval Jewish History and Literature*, Cambridge, MA: Harvard University Press, pp.16–40.
Davidson, Herbert A. (1992), *Alfarabi, Avicenna and Averroes, on Intellect*, New York: Oxford University Press.
de Couesnongle, V. (1954), 'La causalité du maximum. L'utilisation par Saint Thomas d'un passage d'Aristote', *Revue des sciences philosophiques et théologiques*, 38, 433–44.
de Couesnongle, V. (1954), 'La causalité du maximum. Pourquoi Saint Thomas a-t-il mal cité Aristote?', *Revue des sciences philosophiques et théologiques*, 38, 658–80.
Diels, Hermann and Walther Kranz (eds) (1951), *Die Fragmente der Vorsokratiker*, 6th edn, 2 vols, Dublin: Weidmann.
Dixsaut, M. (2000), 'Platon et ses multiples dialogues', in M. Dixsaut and A. Brancacci (eds), *Platon source des présocratiques*, Paris: Vrin.
Dobbs-Weinstein, Idit (1995), *Maimonides and St. Thomas on the Limits of Reason*, Albany, NY: State University of New York Press.
Doig, James C. (1972), *Aquinas on Metaphysics: A Historical Doctrinal Study of the Commentary on the Metaphysics*, The Hague: Martinus Nijhoff.
Doig, James C. (2001), *Aquinas's Philosophical Commentary on the Ethics: A Historical Perspective*, Dordrecht: Kluwer.
Druart, Th.-A. (1994), 'Averroes: The Commentator and the commentators', in L.P. Schrenk (ed.), *Aristotle in Late Antiquity*, Washington, DC: The Catholic University of America Press, pp.187–97.
Düring, Ingemar (1966), *Aristoteles: Darstellung und Interpretation seines Denkens*, Heidelberg: Winter.
Elders, Leo (1983), 'St. Thomas Aquinas's *Commentary on the "Metaphysics"* of Aristotle', *Divus Thomas* (Piacenza), 86, 307–26.
Endress, G. (1995), 'Averroes' *De caelo*: Ibn Rushd's cosmology in his Commentaries on Aristotle's *On the Heavens'*, *Arabic Sciences and Philosophy*, 5, 9–49.
Eucken, Christoph (1983), *Isokrates*, Berlin: W. de Gruyter.
Fakhry, M. (1970), *A History of Islamic Philosophy*, New York: Columbia University Press.
Fisch, Menachem (1997), *Rational Rabbis: Science and Talamudic Culture*, Bloomington, IN: Indiana University Press.
Fishbane, Michael (1994), *The Kiss of God*, Seattle, WA: University of Washington Press.
Frede, M. (1992), 'Plato's arguments and the dialogue form', in J.C. Klagge and N.D. Smith (eds), *Methods of Interpreting Plato and His Dialogues*, Oxford Studies in Ancient Philosophy Suppl., 201–19.

Frère, J. (1991), 'Platon lecteur de Parménide dans le *Sophiste*', in *Études sur le* Sophiste *de Platon*, publiées sous la direction de P. Aubenque, Naples: Bibliopolis, pp.124–43.

Fronterotta, F. (2001), *Methexis. La teoria platonica delle idee e la partecipazione delle cose empiriche. Dai dialoghi giovanili al Parmenide*, Pisa: Scuola Normale Superiore.

Gadamer, H.G. (1997), *Truth and Method*, trans. Joel Weinsheimer and Donald Marshall, New York: Continuum.

Gallop, David (1984), *Parmenides of Elea: Fragments*, Toronto, ON: University of Toronto Press.

Galuzzo, Gabriele (2001), 'Il problema dell'oggetto della definizione nel commento di Tommaso d'Aquino a Metafisica Z 10–11', *Documenti e studi sulla tradizione filosofica medievale*, 12, 417–65.

Gauthier, René A. (1951), 'La date du Commentaire sur l'Éthique à Nicomaque', *Recherches de théologie ancienne et médiévale*, 18, 66–105.

Gauthier, René A. (1969), 'Preface', in *Sancti Thomae de Aquino Opera omnia*, vol. 47.1, *Sententia Libri Ethicorum*, Rome: Leonine Edition, pp.1–268.

Gauthier, René A. (1971), 'Appendix: Saint Thomas et l'Éthique à Nicomaque', in *Sancti Thomae de Aquino Opera omnia*, vol. 48.1, *Sententia libri politicorum*, Rome: Leonine Edition, pp. I–XXV.

Gauthier, René A. (1984), 'Preface', in *Sancti Thomae de Aquino Opera omnia*, vol. 45.1, *Sententia Libri De anima*, Rome: Leonine Edition, pp.1–294.

Gilson, Étienne (1960), *Elements of Christian Philosophy*, Garden City, NY: Doubleday.

Gilson, Étienne (1962), *The Philosopher and Theology*, New York: Random House.

González, F.J. (1995), 'Self-knowledge, practical knowledge, and insight: Plato's dialectic and the dialogue form', in F.J. González (ed.), *The Third Way. New Directions in Platonic Studies*, Lanham, MD: Rowman & Littlefield Publishers, pp.155–87.

Gracia, Jorge J.E. (1992), *Philosophy and Its History: Issues in Philosophical Historiography*, Albany, NY: State University of New York Press.

Gracia, Jorge J.E. (1995), *A Theory of Textuality: The Logic and Epistemology*, Albany, NY: State University of New York Press.

Gracia, Jorge J.E. (2000), 'Relativism and the interpretation of texts', in J. Margolis and T. Rockmore (eds), *The Philosophy of Interpretation*, special issue of *Metaphilosophy*, 31 (1–2), 43–62.

Gracia, Jorge J.E. (2001), *How Can We Know What God Means? The Interpretation of Revelation*, New York: Palgrave.

Gracia, Jorge J.E., Gregory Reichberg and Bernard Shumacher (eds) (2002), *The Classics of Western Philosophy: A Reader's Guide*, Oxford: Blackwell Publishers.

Graham, Daniel W. (1984), 'Aristotle's discovery of matter', *Archiv für Geschichte der Philosophie*, 66, 37–51.

Graham, Daniel W. (1987), *Aristotle's Two Systems*, Oxford: Clarendon Press.

Graham, Daniel W. (1989), 'The etymology of *entelecheia*', *American Journal of Philology*, 110, 73–80.

Grant, Edward (1978), 'Cosmology', in David Lindberg (ed.), *Science in the Middle Ages*, Chicago: University of Chicago Press.

Guthrie, W.K.C. (1962–78), *A History of Greek Philosophy*, 6 vols, Cambridge: Cambridge University Press.

Hare, Peter H. (ed.) (1988), *Doing Philosophy Historically*, Buffalo, NY: Prometheus Books.

Harvey, Steven (1991), 'Maimonides in the sultan's palace', in Joel L. Kraemer (ed.), *Perspectives on Maimonides: Philosophical and Historical Studies*, Oxford: Oxford University Press.

Harvey, Warren Zev (1981), 'A third approach to Maimonides' cosmogony–prophetology puzzle', *Harvard Theological Review*, 74, 287–301.
Heidegger, M. (1929), *Kant und das Problem der Metaphysik*, Bonn: Cohen; trans. Richard Taft (1990), *Kant and the Problem of Metaphysics*, Bloomington, IN: Indiana University Press.
Heidegger, M. (1962), *Being and Time*, trans. John Macquarrie and Edward Robinson, New York: Harper.
Heidegger, M. (1962), 'Martin Heidegger: Plato's doctrine of truth', trans. John Barlow, in William Barrett and Henry Aiken (eds), *Philosophy in the Twentieth Century*, New York: Random House.
Heidegger, M. (1983), *Basic Concepts of Metaphysics (Grundbegriffe der Metaphysik)*, Frankfurt: Vittorio Klostermann.
Heitsch, E. (1983), *Xenophanes: Die Fragmente*, Munich: Artemis Verlag.
Hershbell, J.P. (1974), 'Empedoclean influences on the *Timaeus*', *Phoenix*, 28, 145–66.
Hicks, R.D. (trans. and comm.) (1907), *Aristotle: De anima*, Cambridge: Cambridge University Press.
Horton, J. and Susan Mendus (eds) (1994), *After MacIntyre*, Notre Dame, IN: University of Notre Dame Press.
Hyman, Arthur (1987), 'Maimonides on creation and emanation', in J.F. Wippel (ed.), *Studies in Medieval Philosophy*, Washington, DC: The Catholic University of America Press, pp.45–61.
Irwin, T.H. (1995), *Plato's Ethics*, New York and Oxford: Oxford University Press.
Isaac, Ioannes (1951), 'Saint Thomas interprète des œuvres d'Aristote', in *Scholastica Ratione Historico-Critica Instauranda*, Acta Congressus Scholastici Internationalis Romae 1950, Rome: Bibliotheca Pontificium Atheneaum Antonianum, pp.353–63.
Ivry, A.L. (1966), 'Averroes on intellection and conjunction', *Journal of the American Oriental Society*, 86, 76–85.
Ivry, A.L. (1982), 'Maimonides on possibility', in J. Reinhartz *et al.* (eds), *Mystics, Philosophers and Politicians: Essays in Jewish Intellectual History in Honor of Alexander Altmann*, Durham, NC: Duke University Press, pp.67–84.
Ivry, A.L. (1988), 'Averroes and the West: The first encounter/nonencounter', in R.L. Salinger *et al.* (eds), *A Straight Path*, Washington, DC: The Catholic University of America Press, pp.142–58.
Ivry, A.L. (1995), 'Averroes' middle and long commentaries on the *De anima*', *Arabic Sciences and Philosophy*, 5, 75–92.
Ivry, A.L. (1997), 'Averroes' short commentary on Aristotle's *De anima*', *Documenti e studi sulla tradizione filosofica medievale*, 8, 511–49.
Ivry, A.L. (1999), 'Averroes' three commentaries on *De anima*', in G. Endress and J.A. Aertsen (eds), *Averroes and the Aristotelian Tradition*, Leiden: Brill, pp.199–216.
Jaeger, Werner (1948), *Aristotle: Fundamentals of the History of his Development*, 2nd edn, trans. Richard Robinson, Oxford: Oxford University Press.
Jenkins, John (1996), 'Expositions of the text: Aquinas's Aristotelian commentaries', *Medieval Philosophy and Theology*, 5, 39–62.
Johnson, Mark (1989), 'Did St. Thomas attribute a doctrine of creation to Aristotle?', *New Scholasticism*, 63, 129–55.
Jordan, Mark (1991), 'Thomas Aquinas's disclaimers in the Aristotelian commentaries', in R. James Long (ed.), *Philosophy and the God of Abraham: Essays in Memory of James A. Weisheipl, O.P.*, Toronto, ON: Pontifical Institute of Mediaeval Studies, pp.99–112.

Jordan, Mark (1992), *The Alleged Aristotelianism of Thomas Aquinas*, The Étienne Gilson Series 15, Toronto: Pontifical Institute of Mediaeval Studies.

Jordan, Mark (1993), 'Theology and philosophy', in Norman Kretzmann and Eleonore Stump (eds), *The Cambridge Companion to Aquinas*, Cambridge: Cambridge University Press, pp.232–51.

Jouanna, J. (1992), *Hippocrate*, Paris: Les Belles Lettres.

Kahn, C.H. (1966), 'The Greek verb "to be" and the concept of being', *Foundations of Language*, 2, 245–65.

Kahn, C.H. (1969), 'The thesis of Parmenides', *Review of Metaphysics*, 22, 700–724.

Kahn, C.H. (1973), *The verb 'be' in ancient Greek*, Dordrecht: Reidel.

Kahn, C.H. (1986), 'Restrospect on the verb "to be" and the concept of being', in S. Knuuttila and J. Hintikka (eds), *The Logic of Being*, Dordrecht: Reidel, pp.1–28.

Kaplan, Lawrence (1977), 'Maimonides on the miraculous element in prophecy', *Harvard Theological Review*, 70, 233–56.

Kellner, Menachem (1986), *Dogma in Medieval Jewish Thought*, Oxford: Oxford University Press.

Kellner, Menechem (1998), 'Philosophical misogyny in medieval Jewish philosophy – Gersonides vs. Maimonides', *Jerusalem Studies in Jewish Thought*, Sermoneta Jubilee Volume, Jerusalem, 113–28.

Kenny, Anthony (1992), *Aristotle on the Perfect Life*, Oxford: Clarendon Press.

Kerferd, G.B. (1963), 'Plato and Hippias', *Durham University Journal*, 42, 35–6.

Kerferd, G.B. (1981), *The Sophistic Movement*, Cambridge: Cambridge University Press.

Ketchum, R.J. (1992), 'Plato's "refutation" of Protagorean relativism', *Oxford Studies in Ancient Philosophy*, 10, 73–105.

Kirk, G.S., J.E. Raven and M. Schofield (1983), *The Presocratic Philosophers*, 2nd edn, Cambridge: Cambridge University Press.

Kraemer, Joel L. (1989), 'Maimonides and Aristotle on scientific method', in Eric L Ormsby (ed.) *Moses Maimonides and His Time*, Washington, DC: The Catholic University Press, pp.53–88.

Kraemer, Joel L. (2000), 'Maimonides' use of (Aristotelian) dialectic', in Robert S. Cohen and Hillel Levine (eds), *Maimonides and the Sciences*, Dordrecht: Kluwer Publishing, pp.111–30.

Laks, A. (2002), 'Philosophes présocratiques: Remarques sur la construction d'une catégorie de l'historiographie philosophique', in A. Laks and C. Louguet (eds), *Qu'est-ce que la philosophie présocratique? What is Presocratic Philosophy?*, Lille: Presses Universitaires de Septentrion, pp.17–38.

Langermann, Y. Tzvi (1991), 'The true perplexity: *The Guide of the Perplexed*, Part II, ch. 24', in Joel L. Kraemer (ed.), *Perspectives on Maimonides*, Oxford: Oxford University Press, pp.159–74.

Langermann, Y. Tzvi (1997), 'Science and the Kuzari', *Science in Context*, 10, 495–519.

Lesher, J.H. (1992), *Xenophanes of Colophon*, Toronto, ON: University of Toronto Press.

Lloyd, G.E.R. (2002), 'Le pluralisme de la vie intellectuelle avant Platon', in A. Laks and C. Louguet (eds), *Qu'est-ce que la philosophie présocratique? What is Presocratic Philosophy?*, Lille: Presses Universitaires de Septentrion, pp.39–53.

Locke, J. (1959), *An Essay Concerning Human Understanding*, ed. A.C. Fraser, New York, Dover.

Longrigg, J. (1993), *Greek Rational Medicine. Philosophy and Medicine from Alcmaeon to the Alexandrians*, London and New York: Routledge.

Lu, Hsiang-Shan (1980), *Complete Works of Lu Hsiang-Shan*, Beijing: China Bureau.

MacDonald, S. (2001), 'Divine nature', in E. Stump and N. Kretzmann (eds), *The Cambridge Companion to Augustine*, Cambridge: Cambridge University Press, pp.71–90.
MacIntyre, A. (1984), *After Virtue*, Notre Dame, IN: University of Notre Dame Press.
MacIntyre, A. (1988), *Whose Justice? Which Rationality?*, Notre Dame, IN: University of Notre Dame Press.
MacIntyre, A. (1990), *Three Rival Versions of Moral Enquiry*, Notre Dame, IN: University of Notre Dame Press.
MacIntyre, A. (1999), *Dependent Rational Animals – Why Human Beings Need the Virtues*, LaSalle, IL: Open Court.
Maimonides, Moses (1963), *The Guide of the Perplexed*, trans. Shlomo Pines, Chicago: University of Chicago Press.
Mann, Wolfgang-Reiner (2000), *The Discovery of Things*, Princeton, NJ: Princeton University Press.
Mansfeld, J. (1983), 'Cratylus 402 a–c: Plato or Hippias?', in L. Rossetti (ed.), *Atti Del Symposium Heracliteum 1981*, vol. 1, Rome: Edizioni dell'Ateneo, pp.43–55.
Mansion, Augustin (1960), 'Le Dieu d'Aristote et le Dieu des chrétiens', in *La philosophie et ses problèmes. Recueil d'études de doctrine et d'histoire offert à Monseigneur R. Jolivet*, Lyons/Paris: Éditions Emmanuel Vitte, pp.21–44.
Matthews, Gareth B. (1999), *Socratic Perplexity and the Nature of Philosophy*, Oxford: Oxford University Press.
Maurer, Armand (1990), 'Form and essence in the philosophy of St. Thomas', in Armand Maurer (ed.), *Being and Knowing. Studies in Thomas Aquinas and Later Medieval Philosophers*, Toronto, ON: Pontifical Institute of Mediaeval Studies, pp.3–18.
McCabe, Mary Margaret (1994), *Plato's Individuals*, Princeton, NJ: Princeton University Press.
McMullin, Ernan (1978), 'The conception of science in Galileo's work', in Robert E. Butts, and Joseph C. Pitt (eds), *New Perspectives on Galileo*, Dordrecht: D. Reidel, pp.209–58.
Mckeon, Richard, ed. (1941), *The Basic Works of Aristotle*, New York, NY: Random House.
Meiland, J.W. (1978), 'Interpretation as a cognitive discipline', *Philosophy and Literature*, 2, 23–45.
Melamed, Abraham (1998), 'Maimonides on women: formless matter or potential prophet?', in A. Ivry, E. Wolfson and A. Arkush (eds), *Perspectives on Jewish Thought and Mysticism*, Amsterdam: Harwood Academic Publishers, pp. 99–134.
Menn, S. (1998), *Descartes and Augustine*, Cambridge: Cambridge University Press.
Merleau-Ponty, M. (1964), 'Eye and mind', trans. Charles Dallery, in James Edie (ed.), *The Primacy of Perception*, Evanston, IL: North Western University Press, pp.159–90.
Migliori, M. (1990), *Dialettica e Verità. Commentario filosofico al 'Parmenide' di Platone*, Milan: Vita e Pensiero.
Mouraviev, S. (1994), 'Cratylos d'Athènes?', in R. Goulet (ed.), *Dictionnaire des philosophes antiques*, vol. II, Paris: Éditions du CNRS, pp.501–10.
Mouraviev, S. (1999), *Heraclitea II.A.1: Traditio (a) Ab Epicharmo usque ad Philonem*, Sankt Augustin: Academia Verlag.
Mourelatos, A.P.D. (1970), *The Route of Parmenides*, New Haven, CT: Yale University Press.
Nietzsche, Friedrich (1962), *Philosophy in the Tragic Age of the Greeks*, trans. M. Cowan, Chicago: University of Chicago Press.
Nietzsche, Friedrich (1969), *Götzen-Dämmerung, Nietzsche: Werke 6*, Abteilung, 3. Band, Berlin: Walter de Gruyter, pp.49–154.

Nietzsche, Friedrich (1988), *Also sprach Zarathustra*, Berlin: Deutscher Taschenbuch Verlag de G.
Nietzsche, Friedrich (1994), *Die Philosophie im tragischen Zeitalter der Griechen*, Stuttgart: Reclam, pp.5–76.
Nietzsche, Friedrich (1995), *Die vorplatonischen Philosophen, Nietzsche: Werke*, 2, Abteilung, 4. Band, Berlin: Walter de Gruyter, pp.207–362.
Nietzsche, Friedrich (1996), *Thus Spoke Zarathustra*, trans. W. Kaufmann, Harmondsworth: Penguin Books.
Nietzsche, Friedrich (1997), *Twilight of the Idols*, trans. R. Polt, Indianapolis, IN: Hackett.
Nietzsche, Friedrich (2001), *The Pre-Platonic Philosophers*, ed. and trans. G. Whitlock, Urbana, IL: University of Illinois Press.
O'Donnell, J.J. (ed.) (1992), *Augustine: Confessions* (Vol. 1): *Introduction and Text*, Oxford: Clarendon Press.
O'Meara, Dominic J. (2003), 'Plotinus, *Enneads* (250–270): A Philosophy for Crossing Borders', in Jorge J. E. Gracia, Gregory Reichberg and Bernard Shuumacher (eds), *The Classics of Western Philosophy*, Oxford: Blackwell, pp.76-87.
Owens, Joseph (1974), 'Aquinas as Aristotelian commentator', in *St. Thomas Aquinas 1274–1974. Commemorative Studies*, Vol. 1, Toronto, ON: Pontifical Institute of Mediaeval Studies, pp.213–38.
Patzer, A. (1986), *Der Sophist Hippias als Philosophiehistoriker*, Munich: Verlag Karl Alber.
Penner, T. (1971), 'Thought and desire in Plato', in G. Vlastos, G. (ed.), *Plato II: A Collection of Critical Essays*, Notre Dame, IN: University of Notre Dame Press, pp.96–118.
Pepe, L. (1996), *La misura e l'equivalenza. La fisica di Anassagora*, Naples: Loffredo.
Piché, David (1999), *La condamnation parisienne de 1277. Texte Latin, traduction, introduction et commentaire*, Paris: J. Vrin.
Plaskow, Judith (1994), 'Jewish theology in feminist perspective', in L. Davidman and S. Tenenbaum (eds), *Feminist Perspectives on Jewish Studies*, New Haven, CT: Yale University Press, pp.62–84.
Prichard, H.A. (1912), 'Does moral philosophy rest on a mistake?', *Mind*, 21, 21–7.
Ptolemy (1984), *Almagest*, trans. and annotated by G.T. Toomer, London: Duckworth.
Ravitsky, Aviezer (1996), *History and Faith: Studies in Jewish Philosophy*, Amsterdam: J.C. Gieben.
Reilly, James (1988), 'The *alia littera* in Thomas Aquinas' *Sententia libri Metaphysicae*', *Mediaeval Studies*, 50, 559–83.
Ricoeur, Paul (1978), 'Creativity in language: Word, polysemy, metaphor', in Charles E. Reagan and David Stewart (eds), *The Philosophy of Paul Ricoeur: An Anthology of His Work*, Boston: Beacon Press, pp. 109–33.
Rist, J.M. (1994), *Augustine: Ancient Thought Baptized*, Cambridge: Cambridge University Press.
Robinson, T.M. (1975), 'Parmenides on the ascertainment of the real', *Canadian Journal of Philosophy*, 4, 623–33.
Robinson, T.M. (1979), 'Parmenides on the real in its totality', *The Monist*, 62, 54–60.
Robinson, T.M. (1989), 'Parmenides and Heraclitus on what can be known', *Revue de Philosophie Ancienne*, 7, 157–67.
Rossetti, L. (1975), 'Platone e la tradizione filosofica pre-platonica', *Atti dell'Accademia di Scienze Morali e Politiche* (Naples), 85, 180–97.
Rossetti, L. (1990), 'Sulla differenza fra il fenomenismo di Protagora e il fenomenismo scettico', in A.J. Voelke (ed.), *Le Scepticisme antique: perspectives historiques et systématiques, Cahiers de la Revue de Théologie et de Philosophie*, 15, 55–67.

Rossetti, L. (1995), *Platone, Eutifrone*, Rome: Armando.
Rossetti, L. (1996), 'Sulla struttura macro-retorica del *Filebo*', in P. Cosenza (ed.), *Il Filebo di Platone e la sua fortuna*, Naples: D'Auria, pp.321–52.
Rossetti, L. (2001), 'Le dialogue socratique *in statu nascendi*', *Philosophie Antique*, 1, 11–35.
Rossetti, L. (2001), 'La nascita di un nuovo genere letterario all'inizio del IV secolo a.C.: il *logos sokratikos*', *Classica Cracoviensia*, 6, 187–202.
Rossetti, L. (2001), 'Socrate e il dialogo "ad alta interattività"', *Humanitas* (Coimbra), 53, 171–81.
Rudavsky, T.M. (2000), *Time Matters: Time, Creation and Cosmology in Medieval Jewish Philosophy*, Albany, NY: State University of New York Press.
Sabra, A.I. (1984), 'The Andalusian revolt against Ptolemaic astronomy', in E. Mendelsohn (ed.), *Transformation and Tradition in the Sciences*, Cambridge: Cambridge University Press, pp.133–53.
Sachs, O. (1995), *An Anthropologist on Mars*, New York: Alfred A. Knopf.
Sallis, J. (ed.) (1988), *The Collegium Phaenomenologicum*, Dordrecht: Kluwer.
Scott, C. (1988), 'The middle voice in *Being and Time*', in John Sallis (ed.), *The Collegium Phaenomenologicum*, Dordrecht: Kluwer, pp.159–73.
Scott, C. (1998), 'The middle voice of metaphysics', *Review of Metaphysics*, 42, 743–64.
Shapiro, Susan (1997), 'A matter of discipline: reading for gender in Jewish philosophy', in Miriam Peskowitz and Laura Levitt (eds), *Judaism since Gender*, New York: Routledge Publishers, pp.158–73.
Shorey, Paul (1924), 'The origin of the syllogism', *Classical Philology*, 19, 1–19.
Silvestre, M.L. (1992), 'L'eredità democritea nei dialoghi di Platone', *Atti dell'Accademia Pontaniana* (Naples), 41, 25–44.
Snell, B. (1944), 'Die Nachrichten über die Lehren des Thales und die Anfänge der griechischen Philosophie- und Literaturgeschichte', *Philologus*, 96, 170–82.
Solmsen, F. (1960), *Aristotle's System of the Physical World*, Ithaca, NY: Cornell University Press.
Solmsen, F. (1971), 'The tradition about Zeno of Elea re-examined', *Phronesis*, 16, 116–41.
Sorabji, R. (1983), *Time, Creation and the Continuum*, Ithaca, NY: Cornell University Press.
Stern, R. (1994), 'MacIntyre and historicism', in J. Horton and Susan Mendus (eds), *After MacIntyre*, Notre Dame, IN: University of Notre Dame Press, pp.146–75.
Stevenson, C L. (1962), 'On the reasons that can be given for the interpretation of a poem', in Joseph Margolis (ed.), *Philosophy Looks at the Arts*, New York: Scribner, pp.121–39.
Stokes, Michael C. (1971), *One and Many in Greek Philosophy*, Washington, DC: Center for Hellenic Studies.
Stump, E. and N. Kretzmann (eds) (2001), *The Cambridge Companion to Augustine*, Cambridge: Cambridge University Press.
Taylor, C.C.W. (2003), 'Plato on rationality and happiness', in Jiyuan Yu and Jorge J.E. Gracia (eds), *Rationality and Happiness: From the Ancients to the Early Medievals*, Rochester, NY: Rochester University Press.
Torrell, Jean-Pierre (1996), *Saint Thomas Aquinas. Vol. I: The Person and His Work*, Washington, DC: The Catholic University of America Press.
Van Steenberghen, Fernand (1977), *Maître Siger de Brabant*, Louvain-Paris: Éditions de l'Institut Supérieur de Philosophie.
Van Steenberghen, Fernand (1980), *Le problème de l'existence de Dieu dans les écrits de s. Thomas d'Aquin*, Louvain-la-Neuve: Éditions de l'Institut Supérieur de Philosophie.

Vlastos, G. (1953), 'Review of J. Zafiropoulo, *L'Ecole éléate* (Paris, 1950)', *Gnomon*, 25, 166–9.
Vlastos, G. (1969), 'Reasons and causes in the *Phaedo*', *Philosophical Review*, 78, 291–325.
Vlastos, G. (1975), 'Plato's testimony concerning Zeno of Elea', *Journal of Hellenic Studies*, 95, 136–62.
von Fritz, K. (1943), '*Noos* and *noein* in the Homeric poems', *Classical Philology*, 38, 79–93.
von Fritz, K. (1945/6), '*Noos, noein* and their derivatives in presocratic philosophy (excluding Anaxagoras)', *Classical Philology*, 40, 224–42 and 12–34.
Weisheipl, James, A. (1983), *Friar Thomas d'Aquino, His Life, Thought and Works*, 2nd edn, Washington, DC: The Catholic University of America Press.
Weitz, Morris (1964), *Hamlet and the Philosophy of Literary Criticism*, Chicago: University of Chicago Press.
Whitehead, A. (1929), *Process and Reality*, New York: Macmillan.
Williams, B. (1985), *Ethics and the Limits of Philosophy*, Cambridge, MA: Harvard University Press.
Wippel, John F. (1977), 'The Condemnations of 1270 and 1277 at Paris', *The Journal of Medieval and Renaissance Studies*, 7, 169–201.
Wippel, John F. (1984), *Metaphysical Themes in Thomas Aquinas*, Washington, DC: The Catholic University of America Press.
Wippel, John F. (1990), 'The Latin Avicenna as a source for Thomas Aquinas's metaphysics', *Freiburger Zeitschrift für Philosophie und Theologie*, 37, 51–90.
Wippel, John F. (1995), 'Thomas Aquinas and the Condemnation of 1277', *The Modern Schoolman*, 72, 233–7.
Wippel, John F. (2000), *The Metaphysical Thought of Thomas Aquinas: From Finite Being to Uncreated Being*, Washington, DC: The Catholic University of America Press.
Wolfson, H.A. (1963), 'Plan for the publication of a corpus commentariorum Averrois in Aristotelem', *Speculum*, 38, 88–104; republished in H.A. Wolfson (1973), *Studies in the History of Philosophy and Religion*, ed. I. Twersky and G.H. Williams, Cambridge, MA: Harvard University Press, pp.430–54.
Wolin, R. (2001), *Heidegger's Children: Hannah Arendt, Karl Löwith, Hans Jonas, and Herbert Marcuse*, Princeton, NJ: Princeton University Press.
Woltjer, R.H. (1904), *De Platone Prae-Socraticorum Philosophorum Existimatore et Judice*, Leiden: Brill.
Yu, J. (2001), 'Aristotle on *Eudaimonia*: After Plato's *Republic*', *History of Philosophy Quarterly*, 18, 115–38.
Zeller, E. (1892), 'Platos Mittheilungen über frühere und gleichzeitigen Philosophen', *Archiv für Geschichte der Philosophie*, 5, 165–84.
Zimmermann, Albert (1998), *Ontologie oder Metaphysik? Die Diskussion über den Geganstand der Metaphysik im 13. und 14. Jahrhundert.* Louvain: Peeters.

Name Index

Aaron (Moses' brother) 116–18
Abraham (prophet) 116
Abû Bakr 114
Abû Ya' qûb Yûsuf 125, 133n
Ackrill, J.L. 173, 180n
Acusilaos 18, 19
Adimantus 66
Adomenas, M. 31n
Aeschines of Athens 34n
Aeschines of Spettus 25
Aeschylus 49
Alexamenos of Teos 25
Alexander of Aphrodisias 111, 125, 127, 134n
Alfarabi 125, 137
Al-Ghazalî 126, 127, 134n
Alighieri, Dante *see* Dante Alighieri
Altman, Alexander 111, 121n
Amyclas of Heracleias 73n
Anaxagoras 11, 12, 15, 17, 22, 32n, 33n, 42, 47, 55, 64
Anaximander 47, 49, 50, 52
Anaximenes 17, 47, 49, 50, 52
Anscombe, Elizabeth 165, 166, 179n
Antisthenes 24, 25, 61
Apostle, H.G. 46n
Aquinas *see* Thomas Aquinas
Archytas of Tarentum 24
Aristippus 24, 25
Aristophanes 23
Aristotle 2–4, 8, 13, 27, 30, 34n, 37, 40–3, 45, 48, 49, 50, 51, 57, 61–73, 94, 99, 108n, 109–15, 118, 119, 121n, 125–30, 132, 133n, 134n, 137–40, 142–57, 158n–63n, 165–78, 178n–81n
Ashley, Benedict 160n
Athenaeus of Cyzicus 73n
Augustine, Saint 75–87, 87n, 88n
Austin, J.L. 2
Avempace (*Ibn Bájjah*) 125, 127

Avencebrol or Avicebron (*Ibn Gabirol*) 118, 123n
Averroës (*Ibn Rushd*) 8, 111, 125–33, 133n, 134n, 138, 140, 147, 148, 150, 162n
Avicenna (*Ibn Sina*) 125, 127, 131, 133n, 134n, 140, 148, 150, 162n, 163n
Axiothea of Phlius 73n,
Ayache, L. 32n

Bakr, Abû *see* Abû Bakr
Barbour, Ian 109, 120n
Barlow, John 105n
Bazán, Bernard C.
Beck, L.W. 107n
Berkeley, George 106n, 107n
Bias 12, 13
Boethius of Dacia 138
Braslavy, Sara-Klein 122n
Brentano, Franz 107n
Brodie, Sarah 181n
Brower, Jeffrey 87n
Burkett, W. 32n
Butterworth, Ch. 133n

Callippus of Athens 73n
Calvino, Italo 1, 9n
Cantor, Geoffrey 109, 119, 120n, 123n
Cassirer, Ernest 107n
Cézanne, Paul 98, 104
Charondas 18
Cherniss, H. 37, 45n, 62, 74n
Chevenal, Francis 164n
Cho, K.K. 108n
Collingwood, R.G. 168
Confucius 167
Cooper, J.M. 88n
Copernicus, Nicolaus 109
Cordero, N.L. 31n, 33n
Coriscus of Scepsis 73n
Cornford, F.M. 31n, 39

Cratylus 34n
Crito 24
Curd, Patricia 43, 46n

Damon 33n
Dante Alighieri 125
Davidson, Herbert 122n, 129, 134n, 135n
de Couesnongle, V. 164n
Demetrius of Amphipolis 73n
Democritus 11, 24, 32n, 33n, 40, 42, 47
Derrida, Jacques 3
Derveny Papyrus 24
Descartes, René 2, 48
Diderot, Denis 106n
Diels-Kranz 15, 32n, 47
Dilthey, W. 97
Dinostratus 73n
Diogenes Laertius 33n, 34n, 73n
Diogenes of Apollonia 42
Diogenes the Cynic 27
Dixsaut, M. 31n
Dobbs-Weinstein, Idit 117, 122n
Doig, James 140, 146, 158n, 160n, 162n, 163n
Druart, Th.-A. 133n
Düring, I. 74n

Elders, Leo 164n
Empedocles 11, 14, 17, 18, 20, 42, 47
Endress, G. 133n
Epicharmos 18
Erastus of Scepsis 73n
Eryximachus 19
Euchen, C. 73n
Euclides of Megara 25
Eudoxus of Cnidus 73n
Evaeon of Lampsacus 73n

Fakhry, M. 133n
Fisch, Menachen 119, 123n
Fishbane, Michael 117, 122n
Fotinis, A.P. 134n
Foucault, Michael, 8
Frede, Michael 34n
Frère, J. 31n
Fritz, K. von 38, 46n
Fronterotta, F. 31n

Gadamer, H.G. 107n, 108n

Galen (Claudius Galenus) 125
Gallop, David 39
Galuzzo, Gabrielle 163
Gauthier, R.-A. 137, 138, 158n
Gerson, Lloyd P. 46n
Gersonides (*RaLBaG*) 113
Giacometti, Alberto 48
Gilson, Étienne 139, 159n, 160n
Glaucon 24, 25, 66, 89
Goethe, Johann Wolfgang von 58
Gómez-Nogales, S. 134n
González, F.J. 34n
Gorgias 12, 14, 20, 22, 24, 29, 32n, 34n
Gracia, Jorge J.E. 9n, 10n, 179n, 181n
Graham, Daniel W. 74n
Grant, Edward 122n
Guthrie, W.K.C. 31n, 38, 46n

Hare, Peter H. 10n
Harvey, Steven 111, 121n
Harvey, Warren Zev 122n
Hegel, G. 168
Heidegger, Martin 89–105, 105n, 108n, 167
Heitsch, E. 38, 46n
Heraclides of Aenus 73n
Heraclides of Pontus 73n
Heraclitus 11, 15, 18–22, 30, 31n, 37, 38, 45, 47, 94, 99
Hershbell, J.P. 31n
Hesiod 12, 17–19
Hestiaeus of Perinthus 73n
Hett, W.S. 134n
Hicks, R.D. 40, 46n
Hippias of Elis 11–15, 19–21, 30, 32n, 33n, 73n
Hippocrates 11
Hippothales of Athens 73n,
Homer, 12, 16, 17–19, 28, 29, 49
Horton, John 180n
Hourani, G. 133n
Husserl, Edmund 96
Hyman, Arthur 122n

Ibn Gabirol see Avencebrol
Ibn Rushd see Averroës
Ibn Sina see Avicenna
Imbach, Ruedi 164n
Ion of Chios 18, 20
Irwin, T.H. 88n

Isaac 116
Isaac, R. Ioannes 160n
Isocrates 19, 24, 27, 61, 74n
Ivry, Alfred 8, 122n, 133n, 134n, 135n

Jacob 116
Jaeger, Werner 74n
James of Venice 146, 161n, 162n
Jenkins, John 158n, 180n
John Philoponus 40
Johnson, Mark 163n
Jordan, Mark 158n
Jouanna, J. 32n

Kahn, C.H. 44, 46n
Kant, Immanuel 51, 57, 69, 92, 93, 96, 97, 107n, 108n
Kaplan, Lawrence 122n
Kebes 24, 25
Kellner, Menachem 123n
Kenny, Anthony 173, 180n
Kenny, Chris 109, 120n, 123n
Kerferd, G.B. 32n
Ketchum, R.J. 32n
Kirk, G.S. 38, 46n
Kraemer, Joel L. 110, 121n, 122n
Kranz, W. *see* Diels-Kranz

Laks, A. 35n
Langermann, Y. Tzvi 118, 122n, 123n
Lastheneia of Mantinea 73n
Leodamus 73n
Lesher, J.H. 46n
Leucippus 32n, 42, 47
Libanius 33n
Lloyd, G.E.R. 30, 35n
Locke, John 106n
Longrigg, J. 32n
Lu, Hsiang-Shan 167, 179n
Lycurgus 18

MacDonald, S. 87n,
MacIntyre, A. 165–78, 179n–81n
Mahomet *see* Muhammad
Maimonides, Moses (*ben Maimon*) 110–20, 121n–23n
Mann, Wolfgang-Reiner 74n
Mansfelf, J. 32n
Mansion, Augustin 163n, 164n

Marcus Aurelius 2
Marius Victorinus 78
Marx, Alexander 121n
Matthews, Gareth B. 8, 9, 60n
Maurer, Armand 150, 151, 163n
McCabe, Mary Margaret 74n
McMullin, Ernan 121n
Meiland, J.W. 9n
Melissus 32n, 43, 44
Menaechmus 73n
Mencius 105n
Mendus, Susan 180n
Menn, S. 87n
Melamed, Abraham 123n
Merleau-Ponty, Maurice 98, 108n
Migliori, M. 31n
Miriam (Moses' sister) 116–18, 120
Mohammed *see* Muhammad
Molyneux, William 106n, 107n
Moses 116–18
Mouraviev, S. 31n, 32n
Mourelatos, A.P.D. 46n
Muhammad 129

Neusner, Jacob 119, 123n
Newton, Isaac 93
Nietzsche, Friedrich 8, 9, 47–59, 60n, 179n

O'Meara, D.J. 9n
Ocean (Greek god) 13, 33n
Orpheus 12, 18, 19
Owens, Joseph 137, 158n, 162n

Parmenides 11, 17–21, 29, 31n, 32n, 34n, 37–45, 47, 55–9, 94, 98, 99, 103
Patzer, A. 13, 32n
Paul, Saint (apostle) 79, 80
Penner, T. 88n
Pepe, L. 31n, 32n
Petruzella, Gerol 181n
Phaedo 25
Phaedrus 18, 19,
Pherecydes 18, 20
Philip of Mende 73n
Philip of Opus 73n
Philoponus *see* John Philoponus
Picasso, Pablo 48
Piché, David 159n

Pindar 17
Pines, Shlomo 121n
Pittacus 12,
Plaskow, Judith 123n
Plato 4, 8, 11–31, 31n–4n, 37, 42, 47–51, 54, 58, 61–73, 73n, 74n, 81, 82, 88n, 89, 91–7, 99–105, 105n–7n, 108n, 109, 111, 114, 125, 129, 150, 157
Plotinus 75
Polycrates the sophist 33n, 61, 74n
Porphyry 75, 125
Prichard, H.A. 165, 166, 178n
Proclus 137, 158n
Prodicus 11, 12, 14, 18
Protagoras 11, 12, 14, 18–22, 29, 31n–4n
Ptolemy (*Claudius Ptolemaeus*) 109, 111, 114, 115, 126
Puig, J. 133n
Pythagoras 11, 18, 47
Pythagoreans 18, 22, 27, 34n, 45
Python of Aenus 73n

Quine, N.V.O. 3

Raven, J.E. 46n
Reilly, James Jr. 161n, 162n
Ricoeur, Paul 9n
Rosetti, Livio 31n–3n
Ross, W.D. 135n, 162n, 178n
Rubin, William 48
Rudavsky, T.M. 122n

Sabra, A.I. 133n
Sachs, Oliver 106n
Schelling, Friedrich 108n
Schofield, M. 46n
Scott, C. 108n
Senden, Marius von 106n
Seneca 2
Shapiro, Susan 122n, 123n
Shorey, Paul 74n
Siger of Brabant 138, 159n
Silvestre, M.L. 32n
Simias 24, 25, 63
Simon 24, 25
Simonides 16
Smith, J.A. 45n, 134n
Snell, B. 13, 32n
Socrates 4, 7, 14, 16, 22, 23, 25, 27, 28, 33n, 34n, 37, 47, 48, 53–6, 58–61, 99,
Plato's *Socrates* 12–19, 21, 29, 63, 64, 65, 75, 76, 81, 82, 89, 90, 107n
Solomon (king) 117
Solon 18, 49, 50
Solsem, F. 31n, 74n
Sorabji, R. 121n
Speusippus 73n
Stern, R. 180n
Stevenson, C.L. 9n
Stokes, M.C. 45n

Tempier, Stephen (Bishop of Paris) 138
Thales 12, 13, 14, 18, 25, 29, 30, 33n, 47, 48, 49, 50, 51, 52, 55
Theatetus 73n
Themistius 111, 125
Thetys (Greek goddess) 13, 33n
Theudias of Magnesia 73n,
Thomas Aquinas, Saint 2, 3, 137, 138–57, 158n–64n, 175, 179n,
Thrasymachus 65, 66
Timolaus of Cyzicus 73n
Torrell, Jean-Pierre 138, 138, 139, 158n, 159n

Urmson, J.O. 135n, 178n

Valvo, Alberto 106n
Van Steenberghen, Fernan 149, 159n, 163n, 164n
Vico, Giovanni Battista 168
von Fritz, K. *see* Fritz, K. von
Vlastos, G. 31n, 38, 46n, 74n

Weisheipl, James A. 138, 158n, 159n
Weitz, Morris 9n
Whitehead, A. 108n
William of Moerbeke 147, 149, 153, 161n, 162n
Williams, Bernard 179n
Williams, Donald 48
Wippel, John F. 160n
Wolff, Christian 1
Wolfson, H.A. 133n
Wolin, R. 108n

Xeniades 32n
Xenocrates of Chalcedon 73n,

Xenophanes 18, 20, 30, 37, 39, 42, 47, 49, 56
Xenophon 24, 25, 33n, 34n

Yu, J. 181n

Zarathustra (Nietzsche's) 58
Zeller, E. 26, 33n, 34n
Zeno of Elea 11, 12, 32n, 33n, 43–5, 47

Subject Index

Akrasia 75–77, 79, 81–3, 86
Aletheia (Hermeneutic) 90–105
   essence of truth 90, 91, 94, 96,
   hideness of truth 94, 95, 100
Alexandrian philosophy (thought, tradition) 128
Anthropology (Aristotelian) 65–7, 116, 117, 127–29, 132, 169, 171–74, 176–78, 179n–81n
Aristotelian philosophy 52, 53, 111, 113–18, 120, 125–27, 130–32, 133n, 137–39
Astronomy *see* Science, Natural science
Augustinian philosophy 75–87, 87n, 88n, 101, 175, 179n

Berkelian idealism 38, 45

Cartesianism 98
Categories *see* Language
Christian tradition 109, 110, 113, 114, 137–39, 151, 157
Commentaries (as interpretation) 125, 126, 137, 138, 145,146, 155–57, 168, 178
Confucianism 105n,
Cosmogony *see* Science, Natural science, Christian tradition, Jewish tradition
Cosmology *see* Science, Natural science
Cosmos, Greek cosmology (*see also* Greek naturalistic philosophy) 39, 40, 42, 43

Definition (*species*) 149–51
Dialectic (Platonic) 53, 55, 73
Doxa 39, 44

Education *see Paideia*
Eleatics, Eleaticism 63
Enlightenment 166, 179n
Empiricism 106n
Esse-essence 146–48, 151
Existentialism 93

First philosophy *see* Science
Forms (Platonic) 63, 68, 70–1, 90, 94, 101–105, 108n, 129, 150, 157

God proofs *see* Natural theology
God's mind, God's understanding *see* Intellect, Natural theology
Greek classics 1–3, 6–9, 47
Greek 'naturalistic' Philosophy (Presocratic) 14, 20, 23, 27, 28, 33n, 99
Phisiologoi, 12, 14, 27, 108n
Greek philosophy, Greek tradition 2, 9, 11–16, 18, 21, 22, 24, 25, 27–30, 47, 50–3, 59, 61, 97, 98, 100, 108n, 129
   first Greek philosophers, 12–15, 17, 19–21, 23, 34n, 99

Heraclitean philosophy 103
Historicism *see* Moral relativism
Husserlian philosophy 97
Hylomorphism 64, 115, 118, 120, 128, 129, 131, 147,150, 151

Ideas (Plato's) *see* Forms
Intellect 67, 111, 115, 116, 118, 119, 127–32, 134n, 141, 150, 152–56, 177
Interpretation 1–7, 167, 176, 178, 179n
   aims of 6, 8, 9, 165–67
   as meaning 3, 4
   cultural 5
   Freudian 6
   hermeneutical 6, 8, 89, 92, 94, 96–8
   historical 5, 7, 12, 54, 55, 92, 93, 100, 104, 167, 168
   linguistic 4
   logical 5
   phenomenological 96, 97
   psychological 54, 55
   use and/or abuse of 8,133, 168

Subject Index

Jewish tradition 109, 110, 113–20, 122n, 123n

Kantian philosophy 178n
Knowledge (phenomenology) 90, 93, 96, 98, 99
Knowledge (*scio, episteme*) *see* Science

Language (Aristotelian philosophy of, Logic) 69–72
Liberal individualism 177, 179n

Manicheism 79, 83, 84
Metaphysical biology (Aristotle) *see* Anthropology
Milesian School 16, 49, 52
Modernity 168, 169, 176, 179n
Moral conflicts (*see also* Will) 78, 81, 82, 86, 87
Moral duty (*see also* Virtue ethics) 166, 168
Moral relativism 174, 175, 178, 180
Moslem tradition 113, 132, 133

Natural science 62–7, 111, 113–15, 128, 129, 142, 144, 145, 149, 152–55
Natural theology 111–13, 115, 120, 121n, 129, 132, 140–46, 149, 151–57, 177
Neoaristotelism 167, 175
Neoconfucianism 167
Neokantianism 96, 107n
Neoplatonism 116, 117, 127, 131, 137
Nous 37, 38, 41–2, 46
   as come to know, to be aware, to know 38–40, 42, 44

Occasionalism (medieval) 127
Ontological truth *see Aletheia*

Paideia 89–96, 100–104, 105n, 106n, 108n
Parmenidean philosophy 41
Perception (sight) 91, 95, 96, 106–107n
Phenomenological truth *see Aletheia*
Philosophical classics 1, 2
Platonists, Platonism 25, 64, 75, 82, 83, 85–7, 88n, 96, 101, 150, 153
Poets, old-epic poetry 13, 20, 23, 28, 30, 38, 50, 51
Political nature *see* tradition (moral-social)
Preplatonic philosophy (*see also* Socratics) 48, 51–6, 58, 59

Pre-Socratics, presocratic philosophy 8, 9, 11, 12, 16–18, 20–5, 28–30, 33n, 35n, 37, 38, 41, 42, 47–9, 51, 63, 64

Quiddity 149–51

Rationalism 106n
Representation (phenomenology) 98, 99, 102, 104
Roman Catholic 6

Science, Aristotelian and medieval, (*see also* Natural science) 62–4, 70–2, 109–12, 120, 127–30, 140–46, 149, 151
   Demonstrative syllogisms 65, 112, 119
   Knowledge (*scio, episteme*) 68, 69, 73, 112, 115, 129, 132, 134n, 141, 142, 151, 152
Seven wise men 13, 15, 50, 51
Socratics, Socratic Philosophy 16, 23–8, 30, 54, 55, 64, 61
Sophia, sophoi (*see also* Seven wise men) 13, 14, 17, 19, 21, 29
   Philosophia, philosophoi (as wisdom) 13, 14, 32n
Sophists, sophistry 12–30, 47, 61, 69
   Pre-Sophists 16, 18
Soul (rational and non-rational, divided) 80, 81, 83, 84, 85, 86, 95, 105n, 106n, 115–17, 120, 127, 129–32, 134n
Species 149–51
Substance/accidents 64, 116, 147, 150, 151

Teleology 168, 169, 171–74, 176, 180n
Theogonies 50
Theory of virtue *see* Virtue ethics
Thomism 175, 179n
Tradition (moral-social) 170–72, 174, 175, 177, 179n, 180n
Tragedian writers 17
Truth (phenomenology) *see Aletheia*

Understanding (as interpretation) 3, 4, 107n
Unmoved mover *see* Natural theology

Western philosophy, tradition 26, 37, 47–51, 53, 55, 59, 62, 75, 92, 97–9, 103, 126, 165, 167
Will (weak, compulsion) *see Akrasia*
Will conflict 76–83, 85, 86